Cosmic Prayer and Guided Transformation

Cosmic Prayer and Guided Transformation

Key Elements of the Emergent Christian Cosmology

ROBERT GOVAERTS

Foreword by
DAVID JASPER

☙PICKWICK *Publications* · Eugene, Oregon

COSMIC PRAYER AND GUIDED TRANSFORMATION
Key Elements of the Emergent Christian Cosmology

Copyright © 2012 Robert Govaerts. All rights reserved. Except for brief quotations in critical publications or reviews, no part of this book may be reproduced in any manner without prior written permission from the publisher. Write: Permissions, Wipf and Stock Publishers, 199 W. 8th Ave., Suite 3, Eugene, OR 97401.

Pickwick Publications
An Imprint of Wipf and Stock Publishers
199 W. 8th Ave., Suite 3
Eugene, OR 97401

www.wipfandstock.com

Unless indicated otherwise, all Scripture quotations in this book are taken from *The Holy Bible*, Revised Standard Version. Copyright © 1973 by Division of Christian Education of the National Council of the Churches of Christ in the United States of America. Used by permission

ISBN 13: 978-1-61097-860-6

Cataloging-in-Publication data:

Govaerts, Robert.

Cosmic prayer and guided transformation : key elements of the emergent Christian cosmology / Robert Govaerts, with a foreword by David Jasper.

xvi + 226 p. ; 23 cm. Includes bibliographical references and index.

ISBN 13: 978-1-61097-860-6

1. Trinity. 2. Nature—Religious aspects—Christianity. 3. Religion and science. 4. Ecotheology. 5. Maximus, Confessor, Saint, ca. 580–662. 6. Creation. I. Jasper, David. II. Title.

BT695.5 G72 2012

Manufactured in the U.S.A.

For all those who are praying for fullness of life in God,

for the well-being of God's creatures,

and for the greater glory of God

Contents

Foreword by David Jasper | ix
Preface | xi
Abbreviations | xiv

1 Introduction | 1
2 God's Spirit and Creative Word | 19
3 Cosmos | 50
4 Person | 85
5 Prayer | 108
6 Cosmic Prayer | 122
7 Guided Transformation | 148
8 Personal Existence in Christ and in the Spirit | 165
9 Conclusion | 182

Bibliography | 193
General Index | 215

Foreword

LEARNING THAT IS GENUINE and profound is worn lightly and offered in service. This is certainly the case in this remarkable book, from its quiet beginnings on the cliffs of Quarr Abbey in the Isle of Wight, through its narratives of theology, science, poetry, and the Bible in its complex articulation of a Christian cosmology that ends in a prayerful image of a world that is on the brink of destruction by human hands and yet held within the love of God.

This is a book that is written out of faith but still speaks in a universal voice. It seeks a recovery of a cosmological sense of wholeness in our post-Enlightenment, mechanistic culture through its meditative insistence on *perichoresis*—that sense of participation with the divine in the creative task, a theology that is not top-down, but recognizes that true love works both ways, from the divine to the human and the human to the divine, in a dance that celebrates the music and poetry of creation and calls us to play our part in full. At the book's center is the deep heart and mind of the seventh-century Christian theologian Maximus Confessor who taught as perhaps no-one else has taught so profoundly a kenotic theology of Christ who is both human and divine. Govaerts's learning, however, moves easily as well through biblical literature from the Genesis creation stories and Psalm 104, a song of God the creator and sustainer, to the Fourth Gospel, into the theology of the church fathers and modern theological thought, from Teilhard de Chardin and Process Thought to Moltmann, Balthasar, and contemporary feminist theology.

This alone would be remarkable, but then are added scientific reflections, ancient and modern, classical Greek philosophy, and a discourse on ancient cave paintings—all breathing the spirit of the cosmos sustained by love, yet fragile and endangered. But in the end, the spirit of this book is not simply academic in any narrow sense, for its learning is quietly

Foreword

passionate in its explorations of "guided transformation," a work written in faith whose heart is prayer and the liturgy. In its sense of the person known and realized within the purposeful unity of all creation there is a poetry and a music that is gloriously expressed in a poem referred to, Henry Vaughan's "The Morning-watch":

> . . . In what Rings,
> And *Hymning Circulations* the quick world
>   Awakes, and sings . . . .
>
> . . . , the great *chime*
> And *symphony* of nature. Prayer is
>   The world in tune, . . .

And so, finally, in all its interdisciplinary harmony of different voices, this book is liturgical and a call to be liturgical in prayer and praise as God's people in a task that cannot be an option, seeing salvation as a transformation in the divine presence not in any world to come so much as in the very creation of which we are all a part. This is a deeply Christian meditation which speaks to the world. It needs to be heard and reflected upon.

David Jasper
Professor of Literature and Theology, University of Glasgow

Preface

THIS BOOK IS THE result of a searching that begun in earnest in 2001 as I walked and stood in the little ancient seaside wood of Quarr Abbey on the Isle of Wight. Below the clay cliffs were lying several trees beside one another in the tidal zone. The wood and the entire abbey's coastline were drastically being altered by rapidly progressing erosion, whereby centuries-old oaks fell into the sea one after the other and the nearby farmland and ruins of the medieval abbey were being washed away. Wood paths that in previous years allowed one to make a circle were now ending at the muddy cliffs. The red squirrels that lived among the trees saw their world gradually become smaller. During these years at Quarr I wrote letters trying to obtain coastal defenses; meetings were organized with the council's responsible, with the engineering company contracted by the council, with the ferry company, with the Solent protection group, with neighbors whose properties were also affected, and with the Council for the Protection of Rural England (CPRE). A contributing factor for the erosion is that in the aftermath of the last glacial era—that is, from when ice started to retreat to the far northern areas around ten thousand years ago—Scotland continues to rise after the weight of ice has been lifted and as a consequence the South-East of England is sinking (about one to two millimeters a year). In addition, the erosion may to some extent be ascribed to the natural interaction between sea and land, as the Solent has been widening and deepening over thousands of years from a river valley to a veritable strait that takes nearly an hour to cross by ferry. In Roman times it was apparently still possible to wade through the water from the mainland to the island. The rate of erosion in recent years (about two meters a year) may well have increased because of the human caused aggravation in worldwide climate change and corresponding sea level rise. Still another contributing factor to the erosion may be the high waves

Preface

created by the ever larger containerships that pass through the Solent, as well as the dredging activities that create a large deep gully in the seafloor just offshore as a canal for the ever larger ferries that land nearby at Fishbourne, as they provide the regular connection with Portsmouth.

In the meantime monks prayed the liturgical offices in the abbey church. The psalms and hymns that were being sung and are still sung include celebrating God as the Creator of heaven and earth. Yet, these prayers seemed so unrelated to the web of life as it is. The patristic literature and the liturgy that are central to the monks' daily lives have been overtly concerned with the transcending realm and the salvation of the human soul into an eternal realm, but have been failing to instill a concern for the planet and its delicately balanced biosphere wherein the human is born. A contemplative lifestyle is intended to root the monk in the present, to foster collection of mind instead of division among a multiplicity of things, yet despite all this, the monk, even the monk, is, arguably, insufficiently being educated for a life rooted amidst the created reality wherein he is situated. There is insufficient realization that the monastic person and every human being is called to be a center of transformation not merely for the self, or for the monastic community or for the human community, but for all that exists. True, monastic life is often established in a particular place for centuries and the estates of abbeys and religious houses are often valuable assets; they are sizeable properties that provide separation from other people, occasion for tranquil walks, perhaps for growing things. But something is missing. Humanity, Christianity, and even monasticism, have lost their roots within the natural world and are ignorant of the human purpose and meaning as regards the universal reality. It has been insufficiently appreciated that when the air will have become so polluted as to be unbreathable, or water undrinkable, or when there is no place to live (as is the case for many in our times) then healthy children will no longer be around, humanity will perish and the entry into eternal glory will disappear. It is a very odd predicament for a religion that seeks to promote respect for human life and life as a gift of God. The fact is that the human-God and the inter-human relationship do not exist in a vacuum, but only in dependence upon the wider creation. When talking about the wider creation, the emphasis in magisterial documents has been and still is on the need for an equitable division of resources among people. This is a valid concern. But talking in terms of "the goods of the earth for the use of man" (e.g., Vatican II, *Gaudium et spes* 12 and 69) reduces the natural world to a collection of

Preface

objects to be used. It is stripped of its sacred dimension and made accessible for exploitation.

As I stood and prayed in that doomed ancient wood, I wondered about the meaning of it all. Is human consciousness a freak event in a desolate world that itself is devoid of intrinsic meaning? Are the living and dying of these trees, and the associated communities of squirrels, rodents, birds, and insects, a mere brute fact? Was I at that moment standing there alone in my sensitivity? Was God present among these trees, and at the beach? Or was this scene just a minor detail of a grand divine plan that is being enacted in minute detail? Or was perhaps the drama of suffering and death, even the unjust suffering on the cross, present even here among the falling trees? Is human consciousness perhaps embedded in a subjectivity that is being shared in by all existence, so that the wider created reality and the processes therein, have a subjectivity of their own in God's presence? Is there perhaps a destiny within God wherein humanity and the wider created reality share? Is the purpose and significance of the universally created order, as well as of each and every created being, to contribute to a relationship with God that becomes increasingly one of an intimate personal quality, that is, a relationship of love? Can we perceive human prayer and life within a contemporary cosmology as situated within such an all-embracing relationship and as expressive thereof?

Some months later, instead of making a life-commitment at the abbey, I left with the intention to pursue the matter, for it was at that time unfortunately impossible to do so at Quarr. Ten years have passed since. In this book I wish to share my reflection on what I consider key elements of an emergent Christian cosmology.

My thanks are due to those who have supported me during these past years, whereby I wish to make special mention of the following: Mr. Barry Swan who has most kindly and generously helped me improve the spelling and grammar of a first draft; Revd. Professor David Jasper for his kind advice and for providing the foreword; and my wife Karen A. Govaerts who has suggested several improvements and has been most supportive. I also thank my editor, Dr. Robin Parry, for his helpful comments and for implementing various alterations for the better.

Abbreviations

Amb.	Maximus *Ambiguorum liber* (or *Book on Difficulties*, it is commonly called *Ambigua*)
ANCL	Ante-Nicene Christian Library. 24 vols. Edited by Alexander Roberts and James Donaldson. Edinburgh: T. & T. Clark, 1857–72
ANF	Ante-Nicene Fathers. 10 vols. Edited by Alexander Roberts, James Donaldson, and A. Cleveland Coxe. Buffalo, NY: Christian Literature, 1885
CCC	*Catechism of the Catholic Church.* Translated from Latin. London: Chapman, 1994
CCSG	Corpus Christianorum Series Graeca. Turnhout, Belgium: Brepols, 1977–
CCSL	Corpus Christianorum Series Latina. Turnhout, Belgium: Brepols, 1953–
Char.	Maximus *Capita de charitate* (Four centuries or four hundred chapters on love)
Ep.	*Epistula* (Letter)
Exp. or. dom.	Maximus *Expositio orationis dominicae* (Commentary on the Our Father)
LCC	Library of Christian Classics. 26 vols. London: SCM, 1953–69
LCL	Loeb Classical Library. Cambridge: Harvard University Press, 1912–
Myst.	Maximus *Mystagogia* (*The Church's Mystagogy*)

Abbreviations

NCE	*New Catholic Encyclopedia*. 2nd ed. 15 vols. Detroit: Thomson & Gale in association with The Catholic University of America, Washington DC, 2003
NPNF	Nicene and Post-Nicene Fathers. 1st series. 14 vols. Edited by Philip Schaff; 2nd series. 14 vols. Edited by Philip Schaff and Henry Wace. 1886–1900. Reprint. Grand Rapids: Eerdmans, 1952–71
Op. th. pol.	Maximus *Opuscula theologica et polemica* (*Opuscules on Theology and Controversies*)
PG	Patrologia Graeca. 161 vols. Edited by J.-P. Migne. Paris: Imprimerie Catholique, 1857–66
PL	Patrologia Latina. 221 vols. Edited by J.-P. Migne. Paris: Imprimerie Catholique, 1841–61
SC	Sources Chrétiennes. Paris: Cerf, 1941–
Thal.	Maximus *Quaestiones ad Thalassium* (*Questions dedicated to Thalassius*)
The Philokalia	*The Philokalia: The Complete Text Compiled by St. Nikodimos of the Holy Mountain and St. Makarios of Corinth*. Edited and translated by G. E. H. Palmer, Philip Sherrard, and Kallistos Ware. Designed to appear in 5 vols. London and Boston: Faber & Faber, 1979–

1

Introduction

CHRISTIAN COSMOLOGICAL THOUGHT AND CONTEMPORARY SCIENCE

IN THE WEST SINCE the Enlightenment and until the beginning of the 1980s there had prevailed a notion of the universe that reduced it to a collection of material objects and that prevented the idea of a cosmos; that is, an ordered and harmonious whole. However, the possibility of cosmology has opened up in more recent decades with the emergence (in the first decades of the twentieth century) of more advanced theories of the physical universe: that is, special and general relativity, and quantum theory. Hence, the statement regarding the astrophysicist Arthur S. Eddington (1882–1944) as expressed by Rémi Brague in *The Wisdom of the World.* "We again see the beginnings of a cosmology with Eddington, starting with whom we have a unified, henceforth dynamic, model of the unity of the cosmos."[1]

The other highly important theory of the natural world, which contemporary Christian cosmological thought cannot silently bypass, and which has opened up new related insights, is the theory of natural evolution in the astronomical, geological, biological, and human spheres (anatomical, social, cultural). Ancient Christian writers such as Gregory

1. Brague, *Wisdom of the World*, 189.

Cosmic Prayer and Guided Transformation

of Nyssa, Nemesius of Emesa, and Augustine had a notion of evolution whereby God was believed to create each emergent entity at a proper and appropriate locus in space and time from principles, causes, and natural powers that he created in the beginning in accordance with his will, so that there was seen to be a seamless advance from the primitive to the complex and to human beings.[2] The modern evolutionary theory, however, invites us to consider that God ordained that the creative process takes place in the mutual and real cooperation of both creature and Creator; that it is not only "top-down," but also "bottom-up." Augustine and Thomas Aquinas, who both have been tremendously influential for the development and content of Christian doctrine, had each their notion of secondary causes that were instrumental to the divine primary cause, but which left very little scope for a real dialectical Creator-creature relationship. This is a major defect of their vision.[3] Pierre Teilhard de Chardin (1881–1955) made the first laudable attempt to integrate Christian theology and modern evolutionary theory, but not without a number of deficiencies. A reservation towards Teilhard is that his writings suggest at places that the order of divine grace is in the continuation of the order of created nature.[4] Since Teilhard, however, there have been numerous theologians who have positively reflected upon a traditional Christian

---

2. Nyssa *De hominis opificio* 29; PG 44:233D–36B; *In Hexaemeron*; PG 44:72B; Nemesius *De natura hominis* 3; PG 40:592–608; Augustine *De Genesi ad litteram* 5:5 (§13), 23 (§§44–45); PL 34:326, 337–38; Gore, *Belief*, 10.

3. For Augustine God's relation to creatures is within a sphere of an immutable order: e.g., *De libero arbitrio* 2:12; PL 32:1259; *Confessiones* 11:13, 14, 31; 13:16; PL 32:815–16, 826. He thus holds on to a stringent notion of divine providence: e.g., *De civitate dei* 12:22, 25; PL 41:373–75. Henry Chadwick quotes at "Augustine," 335 Augustine's frequent dictum: "In crowning our merits, God rewards only his own gifts." Gerald Bonner provides, as references for this saying, *Epistula* 194:5:19 and *De gratia et libero arbitrio* 6:15 (Bonner, "Predestination," 18). As illustrative of an even more stringent notion of divine providence, with reference to Augustine: Aquinas *Summa theologiae* 1a, q.103, art.7; q.116, art.1; *Compendium theologiae* 1:130.

4. As regards Teilhard de Chardin's idea that increased human communication and hence technology would bring us closer to God: Chardin, "Place of Technology," 155–63; Chardin, "Postscript," 308 note 1; Chardin, "Transformation," 299–309. As regards Teilhard's searching suggestion that God himself is being completed with the evolving universe: Chardin, "Christic," 96. As regards his idea that the universe is in concentration upon itself: Chardin, "Convergence," 291; Chardin, "Christic," 99. The combination of these latter two suggestions unfortunately renders his teaching too susceptible to an interpretation that obliterates the abyss that separates the creature from the Creator. Note also the warning pronounced in Apostolic Delegation, London, *Pierre Teilhard de Chardin: A Warning*.

outlook upon reality that could integrate the modern theories, including a theistic notion of natural evolution.

The perception that there is a two-way dynamic taking place in the creative process has been central in process thought, which was initiated by Teilhard's contemporary, the mathematician and philosopher Alfred North Whitehead (1861–1947), and taken up by the theologians Charles Hartshorne (1897–2000), John B. Cobb, and others, including several Jewish theologians. (Teilhard's works remained unpublished until the late 1950s so that there is no interdependence between Teilhard and Whitehead's process thought.) Process thought envisages that there is a mutual influence between God and world. It argues that God is not only affected, but in process of actualization as the world is being created out of a state of chaos. Hence, it does not subscribe to the traditional Christian doctrine of creation *ex nihilo*. Though attempts at revision have been made, process thought as initiated by Whitehead failed to maintain the orthodox Christian perception of a personal and trinitarian divinity, a truly dialectical Creator-creature relationship, and continuity with Scripture, Christian revelation, and the patristic reflection thereupon.[5] For situating the ideas proposed in this book it may be useful to note just one recent process theologian, namely the American Roman Catholic theologian John F. Haught, who proposes in *God After Darwin* (2000) a theology of evolution that combines ideas of Teilhard, Whitehead, and others. The theology that is going to be presented in this book is at variance with his, but what is interesting is that, following Whitehead, he holds that "the cosmos is a restless aim towards ever more intense configurations of beauty." According to Haught, "Whatever occurs in the evolving universe can contribute—at least in the long run—to the beauty that takes shape in the compassionate embrace of God." He thus believes that eventually the universe "comes to rest in the empathy of God."[6] I disagree with Haught's all-inclusive "whatever," according to which occurrences that "appear to us as absurdity and contradiction" would, from God's higher vantage point, contribute to "a harmony of contrasts, endowing even tragedy with redemptive significance."[7] I consider that there are ugly and despicable occurrences that have no share in a greater beauty, from whatever perspective. What is significant, however, is the notion that throughout the

---

5. Moltmann, *God in Creation*, 78–79; Fiddes, *Creative Suffering*, 40–45, 51, 93–98, 129–35.

6. Haught, *God After Darwin*, 128–30.

7. Ibid., 127.

evolutionary process there occurs a restless aiming and this for a participation in God. Haught considers, furthermore, that if the physical reality was essentially mindless, as is commonly presumed, it would be inherently unresponsive to any supposed divine power of attraction. Whereupon he compares Whitehead's idea of extending "subjectivity" to all that exists (to each atomic constituent of reality)—with which Whitehead radically distanced himself from the prevalent materialist metaphysical assumption that ultimately denies subjectivity an ontological status altogether—with Teilhard's, Michael Polanyi's, and the Jewish philosopher Hans Jonas's more restraint proposals.[8]

Throughout the following pages I invite further reflection upon the alleged subjectivity of various created entities and upon the notion of a restless aiming for participation in God. It is perhaps worth mentioning in advance that the corresponding idea of an interactive engagement between the Creator and those that are being created, as considered in this book, does not necessitate subscription to the notion that God is being actualized together with the universe and that He therefore evolves as time progresses. The suggested mutual engagement with the goal of a creaturely participation in God implies, however, a differentiating dynamic in God, albeit, as is upheld in this book, beyond the ambit of space and time that encompasses the created order and that co-emerges with it.

The attempt to reflect upon Christian faith with openness for contemporary thought informed by the natural sciences has been engaged upon by theologians that subscribe to *la nouvelle théologie* or its continuation, "the new theology."

LA NOUVELLE THÉOLOGIE

From the early mid twentieth century certain French theologians, among whom foremost was Henri de Lubac (1896–1991), as well as Marie-Dominique Chenu (1895–1990), Yves Congar (1904–95), Étienne Gilson (1884–1978), and Louis Bouyer (1913–2004), and German theologians, including Karl Rahner (1904–84), Hans Urs von Balthasar (1905–88), Hans Küng, and Joseph Ratzinger (Benedict XVI), wanted to encourage a constructive approach for a better understanding of the relation between nature[9] and grace, or between faith and reason. This movement

---

8. Ibid., 165–84.

9. "Nature" refers here not to the natural environment, as the word is nowadays

that came to be known as *la nouvelle théologie* wanted to reach beyond the scholastics' and Thomists' narrow reading of Augustine and Thomas Aquinas and bring current Christian thought into touch with its own roots in Scripture and the fathers (*ressourcement*), and into a dialogue with modernity and other religious faiths.[10] De Lubac, who himself came under severe attack from conservative scholastics and was made a figure of suspicion by them, was a fellow Jesuit and friend of Teilhard and wrote several biographical works in his defense, which saved Teilhard from condemnation. As von Balthasar, one of de Lubac's disciples, assesses, by reflecting upon Teilhard's work, de Lubac was brought to focus once more upon the idea of "nature as essentially a longing and transcendence, by virtue of the ordination to a transcendent, uniquely fulfilling principle."[11] For the objective of *ressourcement*, de Lubac and Jean Daniélou (1905–74) had themselves accomplished, since 1941, in the series *Sources Chrétiennes*, much editing and translating of large numbers of patristic works. The movement had a considerable influence on the reforms adopted at the Second Vatican Council. Moreover, their contribution has since facilitated the retracing of Christian cosmological reflection beyond the abandoned medieval cosmos: not so as to return to a pre-medieval perception, or to become a specialist area of modernism, but so as to transcend these in a critically and phenomenologically informed faith that is focused upon the relationship with Jesus Christ and God.

I cite as an early prime example of recovered insights from the worldview of the patristic era the study of St Maximus the Confessor (580–662) by von Balthasar, namely *Kosmische Liturgie* (1941, 1961), which followed his study of Origen, and which informed his later systematic works. De Lubac himself in his influential work *Catholicism* (1947) also employed insights of Maximus[12] and in the series *Sources Chrétiennes*, volume nine is dedicated to Maximus' *Four Centuries on Love*, translated by J. Pégon.

In the following chapters various insights of this great Byzantine theologian are being integrated: in particular, aspects of his developed Logos Christology, the concept *perichoresis*, which conveys the notion of a mutual permeation, his perception of the cosmic dynamic of

---

often employed, but to what is intrinsic to created existence; that is, the sum total of what naturally belongs to it.

10. Lubac, *Catholicism*, 293–302, 319–25; Ratzinger, "Foreword," 11–12.

11. Balthasar, *Theology of Henri de Lubac*, 88.

12. Lubac, *Catholicism*, 33–39, 382–83.

Cosmic Prayer and Guided Transformation

transformation towards God, and the notion of union with the divine nature that does not annihilate or annul the created natures. In accordance with the spirit of *la nouvelle théologie*, this reflection will bring Scripture and early writers, including Maximus, in dialogue with a contemporary phenomenological perception informed by the natural sciences.

THE NEW THEOLOGY

For gaining insight into the divine-creature relationship, which is in accord with the basic tenets of Christian revelation and patristic reflection, and with perceptible reality, it is valuable to discern the approach that can be distilled from works by Jürgen Moltmann, Thomas F. Torrance (1913–2007), Arthur R. Peacocke (1924–2006), Colin E. Gunton (1941–2003), Paul S. Fiddes, Denis Edwards, and Christopher Southgate. For these, most or all of the following aspects within their theological approach seem to cohere: the attempt to take on board contemporary scientific insights and to envisage a truly dialectical Creator-creature relationship; emphasis on the divine existence as personal and as a trinitarian communion of persons; emphasis on the self-giving in love of each person in the intra-divine communion; a divine creative initiative that aims at the participation of creation in the divine communion and that involves a divine kenosis and a mode of suffering; the notion of *perichoresis* as applicable to both the intra-trinitarian communion and to the creaturely participation therein; participation of the entire creaturely realm in an active dynamic, in "prayer," that is focused upon God and participation in God.

All these aspects are encountered in Moltmann. The notion of God's suffering is present throughout several of Moltmann's works following his *The Crucified God* (1973). In *The Trinity and the Kingdom of God* (1980) he discusses the return to trinitarian theology; also the idea of the eternal *perichoresis* within the immanent Trinity, which he obtains from John Damascene (675–749).[13] In *God in Creation* (1985) he expands the application of the concept of *perichoresis*. "Our starting point here is that all relationships which are analogous to God reflect the primal, reciprocal indwelling and mutual interpenetration of the trinitarian perichoresis: God *in* the world and the world *in* God."[14] Further, he envisages

---

13. Moltmann, *Trinity and Kingdom*, 174–76.
14. Moltmann, *God in Creation*, 17 (Moltmann's emphasis).

that besides human beings the wider creation also offers praise to God.[15] Moreover, later in the work he speaks of "'the accompanying activity of God' (*concursus Dei generalis et specialis*) in the history of the world and the life history of each individual creature in it" (compare the notion of guided transformation introduced in this book).[16] In *The Way of Jesus Christ* (1989) he envisages that God by his continuing pronouncement of the Word "is the foundation and continuance of all things . . . is the innermost life of the world" and that his purpose for creation is "that all created beings may find their happiness in his infinite abundance."[17] He speaks about God's "longsuffering" in creating and about the "compassion" of God in the passion of Christ, whereby he considers that "the whole Trinity is caught up in the movement towards self-surrender."[18] Moltmann gives particular attention to the cosmic significance of the passion of Christ.[19] Finally, in *The Spirit of Life* (1991) he elaborates on the insight that in the Spirit God is present within the entire creation. In the context of the charismatic experience of life he speaks also here of *perichoresis* and reciprocal participation.[20]

Torrance, in his turn, analyzed in his *Divine and Contingent Order* (1981) the significance of relativity and quantum theory for a perception of the created order as contingent—that is, as displaying both an integrity of its own and an intrinsic freedom, but as having no self-subsistence or ultimate stability of its own, and as being dependent on God's eternal rationality and reliability, this in a dynamic manner, without being determined by this relationship with any arbitrary and static necessity. Torrance criticizes, and in my assessment validly so, the Augustinio-Thomistic approach for its "absence of any real notion of contingent order" and its "inadequate appreciation of the gravity of evil."[21] In this same work he mentions Paul's notion of a creation in the agony of travail (Rom 8:22) and envisages its praise of God "under the creative impact of the incarnate Word of God."[22] In his discussion of divine providence in *The*

---

15. Ibid., 71.
16. Ibid., 211.
17. Moltmann, *Jesus Christ*, 290.
18. Ibid., 178–79, 290.
19. Ibid., 252–56.
20. Moltmann, *Spirit*, 195–96.
21. Torrance, *Divine and Contingent Order*, 117.
22. Ibid., 134, 141.

Christian Doctrine of God (1996) Torrance reflects further on the contingent coexistence of the world with God, whereby he speaks of God's "unlimited freedom" and "infinite flexibility"; of creation's "covenanted" coexistence with God; of evil as a power that is "not just privative but directly negative in its character"; and of the role of angels.[23] Torrance's perception of the covenanted relation to God of the created universe, which is of an essentially contingent nature, can thus be seen to be that of a truly dialectical Creator-creature relationship. Prayer can then truly exist, and this not only as a human occupation. In addition, Torrance has written extensively about God as trinitarian, as a *perichoretic* community of persons.[24] Following Karl Barth, he criticizes also here, and again in my assessment validly so, Aquinas's approach. He criticizes the latter for his rational approach to the doctrine of God separate from the revealed doctrine of the Triune God, and for his assignment of particular characteristics to each of the divine persons held in distinction from the others (the so-called law of appropriations introduced by Latin theology).[25] From his study of Greek patristic authors he obtained the idea that the divine persons exist in their relationships; that these are intrinsic to them. With Moltmann, he discerns, moreover, that God is not utterly unchangeable and impassible, but instead that Father, Son, and Spirit are *perichoretically* united in suffering and in every activity.[26] I do not, however, find in Torrance the idea of extending the concept of *perichoresis* to include the entire created reality in the dynamic divine communion.

The work of Peacocke, the late biochemist turned Anglican priest, among which his *Theology for a Scientific Age* (1990, 1993), is also still relevant for our discussion. In his theology, God is believed in as truly involved and concerned with his creatures and hence, following especially Moltmann, is a suffering God. Central to this theology is, therefore, that God is not emphatically perceived in mere philosophical terms, such as ground of being, one, and omnipresent, but foremost as the ultimate personal, and that he gives created entities the goal to partake in the intra-divine personal existence, by means of the evolutionary process and human transformation, by his kenosis, or self-emptying, and by his

---

23. Torrance, *Christian Doctrine*, 221–34.

24. Torrance, *Trinitarian Perspectives*, 92, 98–99, 120–21, 133–35; Torrance, *Christian Doctrine*, 168–202.

25. Torrance, *Christian Doctrine*, 10, 200.

26. Ibid., 246–54.

Introduction

self-giving as shown in the Incarnation.[27] However, Peacocke does not discuss *perichoresis* or the cosmicality of prayer. For whereas he perceives natural evolution to be active in the emergence of humanity and in its continued development, he considers that a distinctive feature of human beings is the manifestation of "a sense of purpose and intentionality" and "the propensity to worship and prayer to another order of Being conceived as the source of all other lesser being," and that this represents a genuine discontinuity in the evolutionary process, a new order of existence.[28] In this book, however, I argue that this human propensity is situated, in a continuous manner, exactly along the central axis of the evolutionary process and the universal transformation towards personalization and participation in the intra-divine communion.

As the other here mentioned authors, the late Gunton devoted himself to developing a trinitarian theology and this with realization of its ecological significance. Though the theme of divine suffering is not so prominent in Gunton, in *Christ and Creation* (1992) he acknowledges suffering of the whole Godhead as the outcome of God's relation with the created reality that is being perceived as free and fallen.[29] According to Gunton, "God's power, . . . a concept frequently used of the action of the Spirit, consists in enabling, in directing the creation to perfectedness in freedom" (compare again the notion of guided transformation introduced later in this book).[30] For Gunton, the goal of creation is "that all things may through being perfected praise the one who made them."[31] He further considers that because of the self-inflicted loss of freedom (in the fall), "what is needed is not simply enabling but redemption."[32] However, he holds thereby that had there not been a fall into sin, it would still have been the Father's intention to enter into a personal relationship with the created order through the Incarnation of his Son (which is the Scotist view of the Incarnation), which conceivably would have taken a different form than it did. He criticizes Aquinas for holding the view that the Incarnation occurred only because of sin and, similar to Torrance's criticism, for reading everything back into God's eternal principles. He

27. Peacocke, *Theology*, 106–13, 303–11, etc.
28. Ibid., 75–76.
29. Gunton, *Christ and Creation*, 87–88.
30. Ibid., 91.
31. Ibid., 96, 124.
32. Ibid., 91.

criticizes also Barth for holding the implicit view that everything is "the playing out of that which has already been decided in advance" and for the relative neglect of creation as a whole.[33] Gunton notes the Orthodox theologian John D. Zizioulas (Metropolitan John of Pergamon)'s criticism of Torrance for perceiving humanity's relation to creation too much in terms of rationality. Zizioulas alternatively promotes the idea of human priesthood for all creation. But Zizioulas's view is, according to Gunton, on its turn to be criticized for "over-stressing human activity towards the world, while under-rating a listening to and response to the God-given structures of createdness."[34] Worth observing also is that in *The One, the Three and the Many* (1993) Gunton reflects upon all existence in light of the concepts *perichoresis*, substantiality, and relationality.[35]

The same theological insights that we have listed are lighted upon by Fiddes in his works *The Creative Suffering of God* (1988) and *Participating in God* (2000). In his later book, which is "a path from experience to doctrine,"[36] significant attention is given to engagement in prayer. He describes how as we pray "we enter the community of prayer," and that "in intercession we meet others in the perichoresis, the divine dance of Father, Son, and Spirit."[37] Fiddes also discusses "prayer and the natural world."[38] In this context, he speaks about God's activity within the entire natural order as "guiding it patiently, offering innovation through the influence of the Holy Spirit and calling out response from it" (compare once more the idea of guided transformation worked out in this book).[39]

Noteworthy also is Edwards's *The God of Evolution* (1999). This author, a Roman Catholic priest of the diocese of Adelaide, develops the idea of "a God of mutual relations, a God who is communion in love."[40] Again, the idea of *perichoresis* features, with reference to John Damascene.[41] Edwards subsequently argues that "the universe can be understood as unfolding 'within' the trinitarian relations of mutual love."[42] He

33. Ibid., 93–95.
34. Ibid., 120.
35. Gunton, *One, Three and Many*, 164–73, 203–4, 214, 229–31.
36. Fiddes, *Participating in God*, 8.
37. Ibid., 123.
38. Ibid., 144–48.
39. Ibid., 144.
40. Edwards, *God of Evolution*, 15.
41. Ibid., 21.
42. Ibid., 30.

finds inspiration for this in Richard of St Victor (d.1173) and in Bonaventure (1221–74).[43] He also finds inspiration for this view in von Balthasar's *Theo-Drama* and in Moltmann, who both, in addition, lead him to the concept of divine kenosis, "of creating space for the other."[44] With reference to Mary Catherine Hilkert, Edwards perceives from this notion of God "a worldview and a praxis in which relations are primary,"[45] an idea which we find to have been developed at length by Fiddes and this in continuation of Barth.[46] With reference to Peacocke and Keith Ward, Edwards thereupon reflects upon a dynamic and reciprocal creative process.[47] Undoubtedly by inspiration obtained through Moltmann, Edwards further expands a notion of *perichoresis* whereby the Spirit's action draws each creature into the trinitarian *perichoresis*.[48]

Finally, as participant in these authors' theological approach, it fits to mention Southgate's recent work *The Groaning of Creation* (2008). Southgate aims to contribute developing a theology of evolutionary creation by means of, among others, Edwards's reflection on the Spirit's action in creation (as regards the Spirit's association with both particularity and self-transcendence) and Maximus' doctrine of the *logoi*.[49]

These authors' approach is not immanentist (that is, it does not exclude transcendence, but recognizes both immanence and transcendence as valuable and complementary concepts in the doctrine of God) and, as is indicated by Fiddes, they do not make opposite, nor conflagrate, our experience as a mode of access to God and God's self-disclosure.[50] Moreover, neither would these authors hold that there is anything independent from God, but rather these authors reflect that everything that is becoming comes to be a manifestation of the life of God and this within him, while God, however, remains essentially transcendent.

It may be interesting to observe that significant contributions that can complement the overall theological approach found in these authors have been made by the late Roman Catholic feminist theologian

---

43. Ibid., 21–23, 31–32; Edwards, "Discovery," 158–63.
44. Edwards, *God of Evolution*, 31–32.
45. Ibid., 33, 133 n. 28.
46. Fiddes, *Creative Suffering*, 139–42; Fiddes, *Participating in God*, 81, 89.
47. Edwards, *God of Evolution*, 51–55.
48. Ibid., 94–96.
49. Southgate, *Groaning of Creation*, 60–62.
50. Fiddes, *Participating in God*, 8.

Cosmic Prayer and Guided Transformation

Catherine Mowry LaCugna (1952–97) and by ecofeminist theologians, including Rosemary Radford Ruether and Sallie McFague, even though their theology is, overall, at variance with certain key aspects of this group and to various extents with faith in a trinitarian personal community that is both transcendent and immanent.

LaCugna's project in *God for Us* (1991) is to show the significance of trinitarian theology for practical life. In a balanced critical historical analysis she explains that following Augustine's preoccupation with intradivine processions and especially following Thomas Aquinas, a trend solidified in theology for separating the theology of God from the economy of salvation. This trend she considers as having already emerged with the Cappadocians.[51] As Fiddes, she describes persons in terms of relation grounded in the trinitarian communion.[52] She discusses the *perichoresis* of the three divine persons and speaks of the "divine dance."[53] A key thought of LaCugna involves disavowal of differentiation between the intrinsic and economic Trinity. As such, for LaCugna, "there are not two sets of communion—one among the divine persons, the other among human beings," there is "the one *perichōrēsis*, the one mystery of communion [which] includes God and humanity, as beloved partners in the dance."[54] She puts it also succinctly as follows: "God for Us is who God is as God."[55] She is thereby convinced that "the reign of God cannot definitively be established until *every* creature is incorporated into the new order of things, the new heaven, the new earth."[56] What can be noted as absent in her work is a sustained discussion of a Creator-creature dialectic (even though she devotes a chapter around the question as to whom Christian prayer is addressed). While LaCugna's contribution deserves admiration, we can appreciate Aristotle Papanikolaou's reservation as he considers her theology to lean towards a pantheistic tendency, (which is a common feature among feminist theologians).[57]

Rosemary Radford Ruether's *Gaia and God* (1992) aims to expose the various influences of dominion that have influenced Christianity,

---

51. LaCugna, *God for Us*, 10, 70–73.
52. Ibid., 14.
53. Ibid., 270–78.
54. Ibid., 274.
55. Ibid., 305.
56. Ibid., 399 (LaCugna's emphasis).
57. Papanikolaou, Review of *God for Us*, 437–38.

such as patriarchy, anti-material dualism, and the human over the non-human, while she wants to uphold the positive insights of ancient Hebraism and Christianity as found in the covenantal and sacramental traditions. She assumes thereby that "earth forms a living system, of which humans are an inextricable part."[58] Associating herself to some extent with process theologians she speaks of God as "the great Thou, the personal center of the universal process," who is open to dialogue with the smaller created centers that eventually enter into a participatory union.[59] Absent in Ruether, however, is a trinitarian communion of persons and the valuable concept of *perichoresis*. This does not prevent her from suggesting that, "as She bodies forth in us, all the beings respond in the bodying forth of their diverse creative work that makes the world."[60] Interestingly, she reads Col 1:15–20 as if to speak of the church itself as cosmological, as not simply a group of human believers.[61]

Again, Sallie McFague's *The Body of God* (1993) does not consider a trinitarian communion of persons, even though certain alternative trinitarian considerations are not entirely absent, and hence neither creaturely participation in the divine communion.[62] However, her approach highlights that the revelation in and by Jesus allows us to interpret the direction of creation that takes place through an evolutionary process as being toward all-inclusive love, especially for the oppressed and the vulnerable.[63] The vulnerable of our time period are, as she emphasizes, not only human but nature as a whole and various threatened species therein.[64] McFague's attention for the particular and for the interdependent web of life forms corroborates my critique of the Augustinio-Thomistic notion of the greater good within an all-inclusive divine provision, and she herself includes a critique of Augustine and Aquinas.[65] As she considers the universe and all bodies therein to be God's body, she also reflects upon the suffering of God with those who suffer.[66] Accordingly, she implicitly shares the insight that the creative process takes place as a two-way event

---

58. Ruether, *Gaia and God*, 5.
59. Ibid., 253.
60. Ibid.
61. Ibid., 233.
62. See the critique of McFague at Fiddes, *Participating in God*, 299–300.
63. McFague, *Body of God*, 160.
64. Ibid., 163–67.
65. Ibid., 32, 233 n. 21.
66. Ibid., 173, 176, 179, 190.

Cosmic Prayer and Guided Transformation

(not merely "top-down") wherein creatures, especially humanity, have an effective responsibility for all existence.[67]

The various aspects that I listed as characteristic of the new theology are crucial to my own investigation. They are aspects that encompass various key elements of the emergent Christian cosmology and that are explored in the following chapters.[68]

KEY ELEMENTS OF THE EMERGENT CHRISTIAN COSMOLOGY

The medieval cosmology that will be introduced later in the book can be found represented by a visual image, for example, in the works of Hildegard of Bingen, wherein the various beings are attributed their own assigned place along a number of rotating concentric spheres. In light of natural evolution theory and in light of a corresponding heightened sense of natural and human history, the new cosmology is probably less easily captured by a comparable static picture. Visual art may still capture a sense of the cosmos but it would need to express the dynamism involved. Cosmos and *cosmogenesis* have more than ever become inseparable. Cosmos, understood as an ordered and harmonious whole, is something that is not fully actualized upon the earth as it is; rather, it involves a perfection that is aimed for as a destiny for the entire created reality and those therein. Cosmology needs, therefore, provide us not merely with a visual image but with a narrative or story that provides an account concerning where everything comes from, where living beings and humanity are situated in the process of universal becoming and where everything is heading towards. It needs, moreover, to provide an account of the origin

---

67. Ibid., 173–76.

68. Perhaps some readers may wish to remind me that I have omitted introducing the movement promoted by John Milbank, Catherine Pickstock, and Graham Ward, as presented in their edited work *Radical Orthodoxy: A New Theology* (1999) and which is pursued in a series by various like-minded contributors. Although I have not informed myself any further of their most recent publications, on the basis of the mentioned work and of the early articles and volumes by Michael Hanby (*Augustine and Modernity*, 2003) and Simon Oliver (*Philosophy, God and Motion*, 2005), I have concluded that this movement is not a part of the new theology that I have introduced in the main text above. Their entire project is very much geared towards envisioning the creative process as exclusive "top-down." "Radical Orthodoxy" upholds, in the wake of Plato, Augustine, and Aquinas, the notion of an eternal law, but insufficiently the notion of divine intention of a creaturely participation in a real personal relationship.

of love and hatred, of good and evil, and account for the struggle between them. Such narrative is crucial for giving humanity a purpose and outlook. The need for such a story that situates humanity within the whole of reality has been clearly expressed by Thomas Berry (1914–2009) in his work *The Dream of the Earth* (1988) and in later publications. In his joint publication with Brian Swimme *The Universe Story* (1992) it is stated, "Cosmology aims at articulating the story of the universe so that humans can enter fruitfully into the web of relationships within the universe."[69] This is a useful perception, but it should, of course, not let us lose sight that from a Christian faith perspective there only is a universe because of God's prior existence, who is at the origin of all that is and without whom nothing would exist. A Christian cosmology articulates a story wherein the universe has its beginning and end in God. This basic axiom has led me to perceive the structure of this book in such manner that it is reflected thereby: the following chapter considers the universal creation's origin in God, and chapter 8 considers its destiny in God. This does not mean that the various chapters of this book follow the process of a natural history, for this is not another "universe story," but it is nevertheless appropriate that this discussion is framed as such. Moreover, it is hoped that the exploration undertaken in this book may enable the appropriation of a detailed universe story within the emergent Christian cosmology.

Absolutely crucial to a contemporary Christian and cosmic story is the idea of a true dialectical Creator-creature relationship wherein the creaturely pole of the relationship is not seen as represented by humanity only. The centrality of this idea is, as we saw, well attested by the theologians that validly represent the new theology. The theistic alternative to this is a notion of a unidirectional determining by God of all that occurs. This alternative can allow for secondary agencies that are instrumental for the actualization of an all-inclusive divine plan, but this in immediate dependence upon God himself, understood as the primary agent. The course of events within creation is then perceived as ordained by God, who is thereby highly implicated in the immense suffering and evil that occurs, while remaining himself aloft from these in his transcendence. Even the Incarnation in Jesus would accordingly be understood as mainly a downward event wherein God remains totally in control and wherein Jesus' humanity is of a mere instrumental nature. Admittedly, even in a dialectical relationship wherein both God and the various creatures are

---

69. Swimme and Berry, *Universe Story*, 23.

responsible for events, God remains implicated as the origin of all that is, but less directly. For by inscribing a degree of indeterminacy in the natural laws that is at the root of chance events in the universe's becoming and of freedom in the biosphere, there has emerged as accompanying this freedom a real delegated power and responsibility within the created order, so that not all that happens needs to be part of a divine plan. The freedom that ensues can be misused by the created entities, and for those creatures that are destined to be in God's image, namely humans, there is freedom that enables to love and to do much good, but also the possibility for great harm and evil. Creation's freedom comes for God with a cost, namely a divine kenosis and a mode of suffering in creating. As such, within a true dialectical Creator-creature relationship God does not remain aloft but, while preserving his transcendence, is truly involved and affected. The purpose for which God brings about universal creation in such an involved manner is that his creative initiatives would be directing each and every one towards a participation in him. If God is love, then this participation in him is a participation in love (1 John 4:8). Love, however, can only take place in freedom. There is therefore a divine informing but not rigid determining. Hence, a key element within such a theological and cosmological perception is the idea of a guided transformation. A chapter will be dedicated to this idea.

Christian faith professes God to be personal and the transformation towards participation in him is therefore a transformation towards the personal. Hence, a chapter of this book will be dedicated to reflecting what is understood by the personal and by "person." What can already be said is that personal existence does not take place in isolation, but involves both an individual or unshared aspect and a communal or shared aspect. A personal God is therefore not an isolated monad, but a community of persons. Indeed, central to a contemporary Christian cosmology that is true to its scriptural and patristic tradition is the idea of God as a Trinity; that is, a community of three divine persons. God is not an abstraction that is indicated by a number of superlatives, but personal. If God would be less than personal then he would be less and not more than his creatures. God has made himself known as personal and as entering into a personal dialogue with the Hebrew patriarchs and prophets. Whereas with Jesus, God is believed to have entered not only into a personal dialogue with humanity, but to have entered as the Incarnate Son in our midst, so as to make himself known, so as to make known what it is to be a human being, and so as to exemplify the divine-creaturely union into which all are called.

The creaturely participation in God is a participation in the divine community. It can take place because of God's creative outreach that brings about universal creation and because of the latter's outreach towards its Creator. Created reality is called to enter into a reciprocal permeation or a mutual turning around with God, which brings about the unity whereby the created reality is adopted into the divine communion, while both the Creator and the created retain their own distinctiveness. This idea of a reciprocal permeation, that is, of *perichoresis*, will be discussed towards the end of the book in the chapter that deals with the created reality's destiny, which is a personal existence in Christ and in the Spirit.

I have mentioned the idea of a dialectical Creator-creature relationship that involves the various created entities, and I have spoken about a creaturely outreach towards God. For the human being this outreach takes place in prayer. For considering the outreach of the various beings, we can think in terms of a creaturely longing, or to make it plain that the longing is for God and not merely for some intra-mundane good, the concept "cosmic prayer" can be entertained. I consider that both human and cosmic prayer are highly significant concepts or ideas for a Christian cosmology that envisages that there is a spiritual dimension to the occurrence of natural evolution. Both concepts of prayer and cosmic prayer will be explored in separate chapters. The outreach in prayer and cosmic prayer is related to the mentioned participation in love, and both prayerful longing and loving will be discerned as belonging to an existence that strives for greater participation in the personal and in the communion of the divine persons.

In light of the suggested inclusiveness of the wider creation in the mentioned various ideas, it may be envisioned that the human outreach for God needs not be a reaching to be out of the wider creation. This is in agreement with the contemporary insight that entering into God's presence is not a going over from here to elsewhere, for God is not located at another place in space. Moreover, perhaps that the reflection here entertained allows us to appreciate as enlightened Paul's assertion that the wider creation itself has been gifted with a hope (Rom 8:20) to which corresponds a longing to be delivered from all that is evil and to be transformed towards participation into the divine realm (8:21). It is thereby

Cosmic Prayer and Guided Transformation

a transformation towards a harmonious whole, or cosmos, within the embrace of God.

Let us, in the following chapters, reflect upon all this in greater detail, beginning with the created order's origin in God.

2

God's Spirit and Creative Word

THE SPIRIT OVER THE DARK WATERS

For our reflection upon the created order's origin in God with which a Christian cosmological story begins, it is suited that we turn to the beginning of Genesis and see whether any inspiration can still be found there. A first general observation is that there are two creation stories: the Priestly (Gen 1:1—2:4a) and the Yahwistic story (2:4b–25). Both claim that the God of the Hebrews is God of heaven and earth and of all that exists. But there are some notable differences. The Yahwistic story begins with the fashioning of a male human being from the dust of the earth and by breathing into his nostrils the breath of life (2:7). The wider creation is subsequently fashioned around this first man, also out of the ground, whereas the female is fashioned from a rib of the male. As such, this mythological story traces the ancestry of the Hebrew people to a first couple and accounts for its strong patriarchal tradition as instituted by God. The Priestly creation story is more matter of fact. It again traces the ancestry of the Hebrew people back to a first human couple, which is believed as having been fashioned by God himself without any creaturely mediation (1:26), but the story goes back even further, to the very beginnings of the heavens and the earth. The human couple is created immediately together as male and female, as together constituting the human being, so that they are equal in dignity and each other's complement. They are created towards the end of God's creative initiatives and thus as its crown. God himself is presented differently. The Spirit or breath of God seems to take on a life by itself, as it is said to move over the waters; God makes a commanding pronouncement at every initiative; and he addresses himself in the plural (v. 26); even though he is the one God of the Hebrews and so the story quickly afterwards turns to the singular "I" (vv. 29–30). So, let us meditate further upon this first creation story, with which the Bible begins.

"In the beginning (*bereshit*) God created the heavens and the earth. The earth was without form and void" (1:1–2a). The words that open the Bible have been translated in various ways, but I retain here the traditional translation "in the beginning," as found in the Revised Standard Version translation. As the late German rabbi Benno Jacob (1862–1945) comments: "The characteristic biblical style begins a narrative with the word 'and.' Only the creation could not start in this manner. The Hebrew word for beginning signifies the first link in a chain; after it similar links follow."[1] All events that happen within the created order are subsequent to God's creative initiative. This traditional translation is favored by at least some modern commentators,[2] and it was also read in this manner by John the Evangelist, for he implicitly recalls the creation story by starting his gospel with the words "in the beginning (Ἐν ἀρχῇ)" (John 1:1). This opening of the Bible needs, however, not to be interpreted as a statement that wants to communicate the abstract notion of creation out of nothing. When God began his creative initiatives in the beginning, the earth was without form and void.[3] By his initiatives God is going to bring order and to make a world that can be lived in, in place of the desolation. Interesting as well in this first verse is, as Jacobs informs: "The Hebrew word for God is a grammatical plural, but it is always used in conjunction with singular verbs. The monotheistic conception of the Bible is thus clearly demonstrated."[4] It would take a new religion about five hundred years later, namely Christianity, to unfold this grammatical plural by its proclamation that God is Father, Son and Spirit. But already in Genesis 1 and in other Old Testament texts such as Ps 110:1; Isa 32:15; Zech 9:9–12;

---

1. Jacob, *Genesis*, 2.
2. E.g., Kessler and Deurloo, *Commentary on Genesis*, 16.
3. Fergusson, *Cosmos and Creator*, 12–13.
4. Jacob, *Genesis*, 2.

and Dan 7:13–14 that were all very meaningful for Jesus, there is a partial unveiling of the trinitarian mystery.

In comparison to this opening of the creation story, contemporary science has traced the beginning at which God would have begun to create much further back in time. For in truth, the beginning of created reality took place long before the earth existed. Recent estimates date the age of the universe as about 13.7 billion years old. The earth emerged after perhaps nine billion years of astronomical evolvement. It was molded from the dust of the first generations of stars that already had gone through their life cycle and had exploded. The expansiveness of the physical universe and the time periods involved are of a radically different order than that of the world that could be imagined by the Hebrews. In their tribal stories they added up the ages reached by their alleged successive ancestors and thus would have concluded that the first human couple was created by God about four thousand years before Christianity emerged, and they believed that this took place near the very beginning of the earth and the heavens themselves. But this does not imply that the Genesis story has become totally useless.

As understood nowadays, the early earth was a liquid sphere surrounded by a cold and dark expanse (compare Gen 1:2b). Over a period of a few hundred millions of years a thin crust was formed that was constantly being pierced by the eruptions of volcanoes that poured out hot magma from the liquid interior, into a gaseous vapor that was probably non-transparent. Rising water vapor permeated this fog. Some of this escaped into space, but as it came into contact with the freezing cold and because of the earth's gravitation field, much of it beat down as a heavy rain, covering the surface with oceans and seas. The murky atmosphere that was being formed started to retain the heat of the Sun near the surface. Meteorites constantly bombarded the young planet, for there was still much material around that was being caught by the Sun's and the various surrounding planets' gravitational fields. There prevailed storms and lightning. The earth was then indeed without form and void. There was no plant or animal life and the geological landscape still needed to take shape. Chaotic conditions prevailed at the surface of this globe of boiling magma. Yet, there was heat, there were various material components, there was water, and lightning as catalyst, so that there were the required conditions for complex chemical reactions to take place and for life to conquer the waters.

Cosmic Prayer and Guided Transformation

As Genesis narrates, "The Spirit of God was moving over the face of the waters" (1:2c). From a faith perspective it can still validly be believed that the Spirit of God was there over the chaotic beginnings of the earth, even though this took place in a much more distant time, and it can be believed that the Spirit was at the beginning of the universe itself. Accordingly, when God began to create at first by speaking his creative words, God's Spirit was there to accompany these declarations of creative initiative. God's Spirit was, as it were, preparing the ground, or the waters, for reception of God's *in-formative* word. It is an idea that is adopted within Christian tradition and promoted by Basil the Great (c.329–379), for whom the informative word is perceived as personified in Christ, the Son who came down (and continues to come down) to the created order. "Christ comes, the Spirit goes before. He is present in the flesh, and the Spirit is inseparable from Him."[5]

The first creative pronouncement of God, according to Genesis, is, "Let there be light" (1:3). This word and the succeeding ones, give rise to the successive days that are periods of light, in contrast to the night when darkness covers the earth. In the prologue to John's Gospel, the Word personified, or the Son, is identified with the light that enters into the world as Jesus Christ (vv. 1–14). Focusing on the idea of light, again from our contemporary perspective, it is inspiring to note that in the Genesis narrative the Spirit precedes the light that shone in the world and the universe and that the Spirit is present together with it, as in truth he is present with Christ the Incarnate Son. For the natural sciences invite us to think of the very first beginnings of the universe as a highly energized plasma, which expanded so rapidly that it is depicted as a colossal explosion, whereby light emerges. At the very first instants, this plasma was so dense that gravity was so colossal a force that no light waves were as yet able to escape and shine forth. The temperature would, moreover, have been so high that the accompanying radiation that managed to leak out at first would have been beyond frequencies that can be seen. If we project the Genesis account onto this distant earliest universe, we can hold that the Spirit was preceding the light that announced the emerging macroscopic order that we witness in the physical universe. For the Spirit was present even over the chaos of that fiery plasma that was to unfold as the universe, preparing for the creative word of God, which itself was preparing for the Spirit's presence in the macroscopic universe and in

---

5. Basil *Liber de Spiritu Sancto* 19:49; PG 32:157A; trans. Lossky, *Mystical Theology*, 157.

God's Spirit and Creative Word

those therein. For that fiery plasma was being so finely tuned that it could give rise to a macroscopic universe wherein order prevails, and wherein life and conscious awareness would take place.

It is, however, certainly not the case that the Spirit's presence, as representative of God's presence, was all-determining. The initial universe was of such minute dimensions that the physical effects characteristic of the microscopic order, that is, quantum effects, were involved. These include an intrinsic uncertainty of physical effects within the limits prescribed by the natural laws. Despite the Spirit's presence, and thanks to the Spirit, the conditions for chance and freedom, both within the physical and metaphysical realm, were already being created. This is not contradicted by the Genesis account. It narrates that God created the firmament and that he brought order on earth; but there is no claim that God's creative presence was all-determining. God allowed for an initial chaos as an opportunity for the emergence of creatures with identities distinctive from God, even though every feature and capacity stems from God.

This leads us to question whether there was anything before God created it and whether the contingent order has a ground of existence independent from God. Let us, therefore, meditate a little more upon these first verses of Genesis and upon the early universe as presented by the natural sciences. The authors of Genesis 1 envisaged that before God had made any creative pronouncement there was the earth, without form and void. Something that is without form and void is pretty close to being nothing at all and it hardly has any being. Yet, at the horizon of their most distant imaginary view there was still this earthly void covered with dark waters. From a contemporary perspective it can be held that God made indeed the earth itself from dust and clumps of stellar matter. Whereas at the horizon of our most distant imaginary view there is altogether no earth, but there is the initial plasma of the earliest universe covered in complete darkness. The natural sciences inform us that this plasma was minute. It was a void without form. It could be objected that it was so incredibly tiny that it can hardly be called a void. This is true from our perspective, but of course, the presence of God and God's Spirit is independent from our human perspective and not restricted by space and time, however small or large, or whatever the shortness or duration of existence. For God's Spirit it was conceivably as the dark waters of the early earth over which it hovered, and which it permeated with the glow of its presence, and enlivened. Nevertheless, even though the initial plasma, this tiniest void, can be imagined as dark waters, without the capacities bestowed on it by God, even more so than the early earth, it was *no thing* at all. So, with this most distant horizon in mind, creaturehood can be perceived as "not God," as at root a sheer nothingness that is informed by God's Spirit and Word so as to manifest itself as a manifoldness of created entities. Hence, in answer to the question posed at the beginning of this paragraph: apart from God, there appears to be nothing at all.

Long after God set the universe into motion from out of the initial void, there still persists a void that is without form and chaotic, and from out of which God continues to call things into being by the Spirit and Word. As such, for the ancient Hebrew there was then truly still the void and chaos of the early earth and the dark waters. The Hebrew held, moreover, that the dark void persisted within the oceans and seas. For, the chaotic world under the surface was looked upon as a mysterious realm of permanent darkness, inhabited by various weird entities. The seas were, moreover, so endlessly deep that if they tried to fathom them with the means available to them, they were found quasi-bottomless. This did not exclude that the Spirit could be believed in as moving over the waters and even, accompanied by God's Word, animate them and bring forth various living creatures from them. Besides this, chaos and the void still reigned for them in the darkness of the night. For the Hebrew the light shines into the darkness, but darkness is thereby not permanently overcome (e.g., Job 10:21–22). From our contemporary perspective informed by science, these realms of chaos that were part of the ancient worldview and from which God calls forth various entities, are still there. It applies even for what concerns the darkness of the night, if we consider the night sky that envelops the earth and that is filled by billions of mysterious galaxies. On top of all this, we are invited to believe in the existence of a quantum-vacuum that underlies the whole of physical reality. It too is a chaotic realm that is shrouded from our eyes by a kind of darkness, a nothingness in which a teeming activity takes place beyond the ambit of time and space, and out of which matter as well as the accompanying configuration made up of space and time permanently come forth. It too, as the ancient Hebrews' dark waters, is visited by God's Spirit and Word, so as to be, as it were, animated, and bring forth a multitude of elementary particles, yet, without being strictly determined by the Spirit and Word. Even within the macroscopic physical reality, chaos is still present as a recognized feature of reality. For even though physical laws govern all of physical reality,

God's Spirit and Creative Word

there is within this reality a fundamental unpredictability inscribed in function of the emergence of freedom, responsibility, and love.

I have to mention one more *locus* where the dark waters are found among us, both as it was perceived by the Hebrew as well as from our contemporary perspective. Perhaps the reader has already guessed it. It is the womb of the female. Comparison with the early earth that was void and without form is pertinent. From out of the earth a multiplicity of entities emerge, from non-being they enter into being, as the Spirit moves about and the Word informs. Similarly, from out of the womb new life emerges, from non-being it enters into being, through the Spirit who bestows life and through the Word who informs by means of the species' DNA as contained in the genetic material contributed by the parents.

The mysterious chaotic "deep" (*tohu wabohu*) that is discerned at the beginning of the universe, as well as at the beginning of the earth (Gen 1:2b), and that is still present among us, is generally considered as part of the physical world. In it there is a teeming activity that is being enabled by God, yet it is *no thing*. This quasi-physical realm shrouded in *Ur*-darkness is at the origin of all that is being created, and as such it is worth pondering upon. For, it is most curious that everything emerging from it owes every capacity and potentiality to God and yet remains distinct from him; the created reality always remains contingent and created, even though its destiny is a participation in the divine communion itself. A glimpse upon this mysterious realm of the "deep" is perhaps shed by noting that it requires, as it were, conquering by the light that shines upon and within it, even now. The light, which God brings forth at the beginning of his creative works, and which he separates from the darkness, is presented as a physical light, but with quasi-beyond-natural qualities; it is not dependent upon the later created heavenly bodies and it introduces the creation of various distinctive created entities. Light also allows discernment of these various entities and as such it has anticipated the emergence of conscious awareness, whereby it (the light) has taken on anew a metaphysical quality and enlightens the minds of a multitude of created entities. Correspondingly, it can be conjectured that the chaotic deep that is engulfed within the quasi-physical *Ur*-darkness is as an abyss that pulls the various created entities that are emerging back into nothingness. Arguably, it challenges continuation of the dynamic towards creaturely differentiation and realization. It is an aperture in nothingness, which by God's doing is at the origin of all that is being created, and yet, as aperture it threatens to draw the emergent entities back so as to be their end as well. As such, the *Ur*-darkness of the deep forebodes a darkness of a metaphysical or moral quality, when the created no longer adheres to God's creative power. But as John has written, "The light shines in the darkness, and the darkness has not overcome it" (John 1:5). By adhering to God's Word and by moving towards him, the created entities can attain a fullness of being within a network of relationships within him that permanently precludes annihilation. The multiplicity of created beings that attain it shall be permeated by the light of the glory of God and there shall be no night anymore (Isa 60:19–20; Rev 21:23–25; 22:5).

From the foregoing it can be appreciated that the celebrated expression that is adopted by orthodox Christianity, namely *creatio ex nihilo*, can be understood as creation out of nothing, so that *no thing* becomes *some thing*, while it has also validly come to be understood as a creation that leads from non-being to being.

The here presented reflection upon the dark waters that are at the beginning of creation is, of course, still rather unsatisfactory for perceiving how what is contingent and not God can come forth from God. The mystery remains. What we have so far not sufficiently dwelled upon, however, is that the entire Trinity is involved. God's creative outreach involves God entirely, including the cooperation of both Word and Spirit. For what concerns the Spirit: without him, a created order would probably not be possible at all. God's Spirit prepares for the effectiveness of God's creative words. It can be imagined that in case the Spirit would not move over the waters, that then the Word would sound in the abyss and either no reaction would follow, or there would return an echo devoid of life. But because the dark waters receive the glow of the Spirit's presence, the sound of the divine words can vibrate as it were within the "deep" that thereby becomes the *locus* of the communion of Word and Spirit. For what concerns God the Father: he is inseparable from Word and Spirit, for he is the unbegotten principle who begets the Son or Word and the proceeding Spirit; he authorizes the creative outreach; and by his activity (or creative energy) that is guided by Word and Spirit the created order is called forth. Hence, according to mainstream Christian doctrine, the contingent order is called forth within the communion of the economic Trinity. In its multiplicity of contingent entities, it is destined to be in the Spirit, in the Son and from the Father, as an authentic contribution to the Trinity's enduring glory and dynamic of love.

In this and the preceding pages we have discerned with the help of Genesis 1 that the created order emerges out of the dark void within the

God's Spirit and Creative Word

trinitarian communion. Interestingly, in the book of Proverbs it is narrated that there was a created reality prior to the beginning of the heavens and the earth. The mystery of the emergence of a contingent order that has an own subjectivity that is not God, receives a fresh insight with the idea that God created a primordial subjective being that is not the earth nor the heavens, and that assisted God in all his creative initiatives. It is a personified Wisdom who claims, "The Lord created me at the beginning of his work, the first of his acts of old. Ages ago I was set up, at the first, before the beginning of the earth" (Prov 8:23). She also claims, "When he established the heavens, I was there, when he drew a circle on the face of the deep . . . then I was beside him, like a master workman" (8:27–30). This Lady Wisdom is created and thus distinct from God's Spirit. It is not her whom God breathes as the breath of life (Gen 2:7). Yet, she is there right at the beginning with the Spirit. Wisdom is from and with God. Since God makes the world by His wisdom (Jer 10:12), she is bestowed upon the created order and is immanent in it (Gen 2:6; Sir 24:3).[6] As such, she represents a metaphysical brightness and a cooperative responsiveness within creation that ultimately stem from God. In the next section and throughout this book I invite us to continue reflection upon this subjective quality of universal creation and those therein. It can further be observed that much later, in the Christian era, Irenaeus (c.130–c.200) upholds faith in the one God in his treatise *Against Heresies* by confessing that the Son is God's Word and that the Spirit is God's wisdom. Borrowing the language used by Theophilus of Antioch, Irenaeus calls them God's own hands by which he created all things. Comparison of Genesis 1 and Proverbs 8 has, of course, been suggestive for identifying the Spirit with wisdom, and Irenaeus quotes the above represented verses of Proverbs for this purpose.[7] Strictly, Irenaeus' equation of Spirit and wisdom may be possible, even while keeping to the line of thinking presented here, by distinguishing in contradistinction to Irenaeus, God's wisdom and Lady Wisdom, similar to the distinction that came to be made between Christ's divinity and humanity. The equation of God's Spirit and wisdom as envisaged by Irenaeus is, however, not desirable. Scriptural texts such as Acts 6:3 envisage the Spirit and wisdom to be found together, but do not equate them. We are summoned to take extra care not to overlook or deny the mystery of the created subjectivity. For as argued in this work,

---

6. Perdue, *Wisdom and Creation*, 89–91, 267–70, 326–27, 331–32.

7. Irenaeus *Adversus haereses* 4:20:1–3; PG 7:1032–34; trans. Roberts and Rambaut, "Irenaeus. Against Heresies," 439–40.

the creative order, as that which is not God, reaches for God and has a destiny in the personal communion within him that is not restricted to the human being.

Let us then consider the role played by the divine Word.

THE SPEECH OF GOD AND THE EMERGENCE OF EVERYTHING

As for the reflection upon the contribution of the Spirit in the divine act of creation, so also here I start with the beginning of the Bible for reflection upon the creative words of God.

A number of times we find in Genesis 1 the formula, "God said," followed by a wish, which is immediately actualized, so that the reply follows, "And it was so" (vv. 7, 9, 11, 15, 24, 30). This presentation of God's creative work implies that for the ancient Hebrew the created order does not emanate from God in a Proclean sense (that is, necessarily), but is the result of an act of will. God is prior—that is, of another order of existence—to created beings. It can thereby be observed that to create order out of chaos is a hallmark of intelligence. Hence, God is shown to be the ultimate intelligence, and this not as a mere mind, but as having a will. God is also pictured as displaying satisfaction and delight with the result of his creative initiatives. All this indicates that the Creator God is the supreme personal being. Concerning the speaking of God: it brings order in what was formless; it reaches into the abyss that surrounds God; what was chaos becomes an organized cosmos constituted by distinctive created entities; and that what did not exist in any way whatsoever comes to be. From this appears that the speaking activity is as an active and powerful extension of God's own being. God's speech can thus indeed be compared with a hand that skillfully works and creates, besides the Spirit as God's other hand. Even the entities that emerge as an enactment of the speech can be estimated to be willed extensions of God's own being to the extent that they come to share in being at all and are actualized. The participating realities remain thereby, however, distinct from God's essential being because they are created and contingent.

Not all the created entities that are mentioned in Genesis 1 are mere passive receptacles of the divine commands; they are not mere clumps of inert matter that receive an imprint. When, for example, God says, "Let the earth put forth vegetation" and gives some specifications mentioning

God's Spirit and Creative Word

plants and fruit trees (v. 11), this wish is no longer pronounced in a void, but is conceivably at least partly addressed as a command to the bare earth. The command summons the earth to become an instrument for further creation, and indeed, "the earth brought forth vegetation" as specified by God (v. 12). Arguably, for the authors of Genesis 1, the earth is, moreover, not merely slavishly executing the command, but is enabled to make an authentic contribution in the realization of the wish. Because, for sure, not every plant and fruit tree that emerges from the ground needed to be decreed by God. This thought can even be taken further. For would it really detract from God's glory if not even the various kinds of plants and trees were decreed in detail? The answer is "no." From our contemporary perspective such interpretation of the text is certainly the more appealing. For, contrary to the ordering that is found in the text, vegetation emerged according to the natural sciences much later than animate life in the waters and on the land. In David Attenborough's *Life on Earth* we find that before there was any vegetation, the seas contained various gigantic and highly intelligent squid and octopus, and on land there were centipedes, millipedes, scorpions, and spiders.[8] Therefore, prior to bringing forth vegetation, the earth was in reality not entirely bare. This would make it from our perspective the more reasonable to acknowledge regarding this command about vegetation that the earth had already been enabled to make an authentic contribution to the fulfillment of the divine wish that there should be greatly varied vegetation. It can be noted that further down in the text, besides the earth as a whole, also the various sea creatures and birds are called upon to offer their active participation in the creative work, as God blessed them, saying, "Be fruitful and multiply" (v. 22). When eventually followed the divine decision to make the human being in the image of God, a creature resulted that could consciously listen to the same command to be fruitful and to multiply, and to the further divine decree to have dominion over every living being and to have available for food all that is of vegetative origin (vv. 28–29). With the human being on the scene, God can enter into a dialogue with his handiwork and address the human creature directly. This aspect is worked out in the mythology of the following chapters of Genesis. In sum, the various mentioned created entities are not passive receptacles of the divine words; they are not mere objects, but are created

---

8. Attenborough, *Life on Earth*, 20–70, 131–49, 310–11.

as subjective beings that each in their own vocation contribute in the continuing creative process.

But by supposing that the earth, the waters, and the ecosystems therein can make an authentic contribution in the emergence of other life forms not entirely determined by God, have we not denied that every form of existence is created by a divine word? The entire subject will need discussing in greater detail in chapter 7, which is on guided transformation. A few observations can, however, already be made. I suggested that God's speaking is an extension of his own being and, as such, his speech or words are full of life. As being alive, the words are manifold in their effects. If what emerge from them would be merely exquisite forms of beauty, but devoid of selfhood, then the effectiveness of the divine words would be much reduced to what is proposed here. For the purpose of the divine words, as here envisaged in accordance with tradition, is to create a contingent reality that is opened up to a participation not only in the physical, but in the metaphysical realm as well. Indeed, the earth, though initially a deadly void and formless, was opened up to the metaphysical realm. Through the presence of the Spirit and the divine pronouncement of the various purposeful words, its surface area became a suited place for the emergence of various living forms. The earth became increasingly attuned to the divine creative powers and as various ecosystems developed, the earth became as a nurturing mother for a multiplicity of hosts. The earth itself became, as it were, alive; it contributed in the emergence of a relationship between the created order and the Creator God. As such, the divine words were effective in enabling the earth to become participant in providential care for those living upon her and to become participant in the creaturely reaching for relationship and communion with God. For what concerns the various living beings on the earth, in accordance with Genesis, they can be perceived to display the creative effectiveness of the divine words by the very fact that they are participant in the gift of life, that they are fruitful and able to multiply, and above all, as applies for many creatures, that they can be participant in a relationship with God in such manner that they give delight to God. From a contemporary faith perspective, it is realized more clearly that the gift of life is enabled by the divine words that are encoded within the genetic material and handed down the ages. This does, however, not imply that all variants within the genetic material are decreed, or even willed, by God.

The significance of the pronouncement of a word, or even of the word itself, is indicated by the Hebrew term that is used at Genesis 1 and at various places throughout the Hebrew Scriptures. The Hebrew verb that means "to speak" is *dibber*. Information on this term is found in *The Theological Dictionary of the Old Testament*, in which there is a substantial contribution by W. H. Schmidt on the Hebrew substantive *dābār*, which can mean either "a single word" or "speech," and on its various related forms.[9] Schmidt informs us that the root *dbr* occurs not only in Old Testament Hebrew, but also in Aramaic and Phoenician-Punic, and that as a verb it means "to speak," and as a substantive, "word" or "thing, matter." Both as a verb and as a substantive it can also be given by the context a more specific meaning than these general ones. What is interesting is that these ancient cultures could perceive something as insubstantial as a "word" and something as material as a "thing" as related in such manner that a single root was chosen to indicate them both. It indicates that the whole of reality was perceived as having at root a spiritual aspect without which it would not exist. This is very much illustrated in Genesis 1 where the created order emerges through the cooperation of Spirit and Word.

This creative power of the word spoken by God as explained in Genesis 1 is also chanted in Psalm 33: "By the word of the Lord the heavens were made, and all their host by the breath of his mouth" (v. 6); "He spoke, and it came to be; he commanded, and it stood forth" (v. 9). The act of universal creation is also chanted in the following beautiful verse in Judith, whereby both the divine speech and the Spirit, or divine breath, are recognized as closely cooperative:

> Let all thy creatures serve thee,
> for thou didst speak, and they were made.
> Thou didst send forth thy Spirit, and it formed them;
> there is none that can resist thy voice. (16:14)

The substantive *dābār* in its meaning of "word" is often found in the prophetic literature as well. We find here again testimony to the powerfulness of God's speech, as it is mediated by the prophet as a chosen spokesperson for God. The solemn character of the word spoken by a prophet in God's name and its inevitable actualization is emphasized at Deut 18:15–22. In the same tone, at Jer 23:29 God is heard to confirm to Jeremiah, "Is not my word like fire . . . and like a hammer which breaks the rock in pieces?" It is, moreover, the case that the word heard and passed on by the prophet not only predicts a certain course of events, it often has greater immediacy and itself initiates the events through the

---

9. Schmidt, "*dābhar*," 84–125.

prophet's symbolic enactment. An illustration of this is found at Ezek 12:1–28. While at Isa 55:11, God's word is said not to return to him empty, but to accomplish that for which it was sent.

As already shown in Genesis 1, God's word tends to find its fulfillment through the employment of various created entities, which may or may not be conscious of the role they are playing in its fulfillment. For example, at various instances God's word is said to be delivered by means of angels. In this belief Psalm 103 invites the faithful to sing:

> Bless the Lord, O you his angels,
> you mighty ones who do his word,
> hearkening to the voice of his word!
> Bless the Lord, all his hosts,
> his ministers that do his will!
> (vv. 20–21)

The prophets, of course, know themselves called to be instrumental to the fulfillment of God's word. Besides them, it is, for example, narrated that a flood was summoned to materialize God's punishment in the time of Noah, who received God's word of the impending disaster (Gen 7:4), and quails were summoned and fell, as announced by God to Moses, in the camp of the Israelites for food during the exodus from Egypt (Exod 16:13). Or again, the prophets announced at various moments in the Jewish history that God was going to punish by means of invading people, who were thus believed to be instrumental to God's purposes without them being aware of it. From our contemporary perspective considered, we tend to agree quite easily that when the prophets pleaded for justice, for care for the poor and for moral integrity, it was God's word they spoke or at least in accordance with God's will. But when they claimed that the movements of the peoples that were taking place and that the military campaigns of growing empires were being directed by God because the Israelites did not worship him as laid down in the law or abandoned justice, then we have some more doubts about this. We are rather inclined to think that in these cases the prophets were reading the signs of the times and had a foreboding of the imminent threat, than that they heard God speaking directly in their ear about what was going to happen. In sum, God's word may indeed realize its creative objective unmediated, by its immediate working within the "deep" shrouded in *Ur*-darkness, and within creation, but often it is mediated by earlier created entities or by entities created for the very purpose of fulfilling his words. For the human

God's Spirit and Creative Word

being, God's word may indeed reveal itself immediately, from person to person as it were, but often it requires interpretation what God's word is really saying in the given circumstances and it requires a considerable gift of discernment, for which a balanced belief and a share in wisdom are indispensable.

As for the powerfulness of God's speech, not so much what concerns its creative effectiveness in bringing about various beings, but what concerns its decisive judgment, we find it expressed in the New Testament at Heb 4:12. "The word of God [ὁ λόγος τοῦ θεοῦ] is living and active, sharper than any two-edged sword." Again, at John 11:49–53 we find an example of what is alleged to have been a prophetic pronouncement of God's word, whereby it attained a predictive value and decisive effectiveness.

So far, our discussion has recalled the creative and judgmental effectiveness of God's speech whereby created entities are often instrumental. The created subject, however, is also called to orient itself towards God in the awareness of belonging to him, and as such to address God with its own words, which he graciously takes up and makes his own. An example by excellence attributed to Jesus is displayed at John 12:27–28: "'Father, glorify thy name.' Then a voice came from heaven, 'I have glorified it, and I will glorify it again.'" Jesus taught by his miraculous signs and instruction that a word addressed to God in faith, a prayer, is heard and, if in accord with God's will, instantly fulfilled or materialized within the present earthly existence. Examples are Mark 11:24; Matt 7:7–11; John 11:41–44. One can note also the exchange between Jesus and the centurion at Capernaum as narrated at Matt 8:5–13, or at its parallel Luke 7:1–10, or the variant of the story at John 4:46–53.

But the purpose of the creature does not end even with this. After Jesus, the created order is destined to become participant in the mystery that exists in him. What this mystery in Jesus is, we find revealed in the New Testament. Mark presents Jesus as the beloved Son of God, to whom God admonishes that we need to listen (1:11; 9:7). Hence, Jesus is the ultimate prophet, who not only mediates and speaks God's word, but who is its very embodiment. Matthew presents us with Jesus' Sermon on the Mount wherein Jesus claims for his teaching an authority that surpasses the law and the prophets (5:21–22, 27–28, 31–34, 38–39, 43–44). Luke, in his turn, presents Jesus as the one in whom the Hebrew Scriptures find their fulfillment (4:21) and as being full of the Holy Spirit (4:1, 18), indeed, as having been conceived through the Spirit, so as to be the Son of God (1:32–35). Whereas at John 1:14 and 1 John 1:1 Jesus is identified with the Word of God. Jesus, the Jew who lived at Nazareth, has manifested indeed the power of God's Word. We are reminded of the mystery of the feeding of the multitudes where Jesus is said to have blessed a small amount of food, which thereupon by his intention became multiplied (Mark 6:35–44; 8:1–9 and parallel texts). Other examples wherein he displayed the power of God's word are the scenes of healing such as is narrated of the woman who had been bent over for eighteen years (Luke 13:10–13). The amazing thing is, moreover, that Jesus did not intend to preserve this power for himself, but he intended his disciples to become participants in it. Just as God sends his angels and prophets as his messengers, so also Jesus, the Incarnate Son or Word, sends out his disciples (Mark 6:7–13 and par.). He sends them as one who is equal to them in their humanity and who offers them to have part in his divine existence and glory. The Christian is called to be born again in Christ and in the Spirit. Even more encompassing, every human being and the wider creation can be perceived as being called to embody the divine Word by their existence, to be attuned to the power of the divine speech, to live in the Spirit. The created reality is thus graciously invited to make its own contribution within the communion of Father, Son, and Spirit. It is in God that the created finds its destiny and fullness of being. We will trace the journey towards this realization in greater detail throughout the following chapters.

A final observation that flows from this is that the divine Word not only brings into being, it also lift up to a transformed existence at a higher level with the cooperative receptivity of a created reality. Examples of this are the miracle at Cana (John 2:3–11), and supremely, the Eucharist (Mark 14:22–24; Matt 26:26–28; Luke 22:17–20; 1 Cor 10:16; 11:23–27). Further, as observed in the preceding paragraph, Mark presents Jesus as the ultimate prophet, and being this, Jesus' symbolic action during his last week initiated, arguably, not only some historically localized events, but the renewal of all created reality.[10] This creation renewed is in the fullness of light, it is purged of darkness and of all that is evil. It has attained fullness of being.

---

10. O'Mahony, *Praying St Mark's Gospel*, 81–87, 98–104, 133; Patella, *Lord of the Cosmos*, 32.

THE CREATIVE WORD AND ITS CONSTITUENT LOGOI

In the previous section we obtained an idea of the creative effectiveness of God's speech. We envisaged that God's speech in all its powerfulness is not a rigid determining that would stultify the possibility of a contingent freedom and participation in the personal and loving divine communion. The purpose of the present section is to obtain a more detailed notion of the divine speech. A number of ancient writers can help us thereby as they considered the divine Word or Logos to contain a multiplicity of *logoi*. The Greek word λόγος in the singular has a variety of meanings, including "principle," "reason," and "word." So as to retain this richness of meaning and so as to make it obvious that it is being employed as it were as a technical term, it is customary not to translate the singular *logos* or its plural *logoi*. Logos and its translation as "Word" are, however, both used to indicate the Son of God, who is being identified with God's speech.

The doctrine of the *logoi* has a prehistory that is twofold in origin. The first root-tradition we already found to lie in Hebrew Scripture and in the New Testament: we considered the words spoken by God as narrated at Genesis 1; the wisdom that has been created at first; the mediatory role of a multitude of spiritual beings and of the prophets; and the unique Incarnate Word, who came to speak God's words as a human being and as a divine person, and with whom the distinction between divine speech and mediation could no longer be made. The second root-tradition is constituted by the various ancient Hellenic philosophers. The contribution of the various philosophers involved and the coming together of both traditions in the works of Philo the Hellenic Jew from Alexandria and in the works of early Christian writers, leading up to the synthesis found in Maximus, have been explored by Assaad Elias Kattan in his work *Verleiblichung und Synergie* (2003), while a contributing analysis (focusing rather on the Platonic Ideas) in the English language is provided by Torstein Theodor Tollefsen in *The Christocentric Cosmology of St Maximus the Confessor* (2008). With their help and some complementary resources is succinctly surveyed here following the historic development of the doctrine so that it may help us to situate the thought of Maximus, of whose contribution I will give some more detail. It is hoped that having an idea of the latter's perception of the *logoi* that are constitutive of God's creative speech, will inspire our perception of God's creative activity.

The beginnings of the *logos* doctrine in the ancient Hellenic philosophers can be found in Heraclitus, who was active around 500 BC in

Ephesus and of whom only fragments of writings survived. Heraclitus used *logos* in the meaning of "word," or "reason," as well as of "proportion," or "relation." It appears that for him everything is destined to occur in accordance with it. It would thereby indicate the unity that underlies all things and would call for their conformity to this unity. Heraclitus admonishes that for human beings it is advisable to act in accordance with the *logos* that they are able to discern.[11]

In Plato (c.427–c.347 BC) the term *logos* indicates a word that has a connotation of truth. It features in the Dialogues wherein the main character Socrates confronts rhetorical speakers devoid of truth. The term *logos* is then also opposed to the term *mythos*, which indicates a fable or myth, whose truth content is at most questionable. In Plato's doctrine of the Ideas, which has a central significance in his overall philosophic inheritance, *logos* has no great part. It is, however, according to Kattan, clearly in the foreground of Plato's psychology as found in the fourth book of the *Republic*. It is, overall, understood as giving expression to the measure for appropriate behavior. As such, *logos* has a connotation that is not confined to the sphere of what is rational or true, but encompasses the ethical dimension of life as well.[12] This characteristic is noteworthy in light of the later association of *logos* with the personal Christian God and for its eventual identification with the Son of God. Since we are in this chapter interested in the origin of all that exists, a few words are called for about Plato's notion of the eternal Ideas that are central in his cosmology, which is foremost developed in *Timaeus*. At the origin of the world, Plato posits a Demiurge or Maker, who creates by bringing order in imperfect matter devoid of form. This personified ordering principle can model his work on the eternal Ideas that are external to him and that collectively form a perfect and eternal paradigm for his work. As such, for Plato the origin of the world is not single: there are the Ideas, the Demiurge, and the eternal unformed matter. In his posteriority, however, the concepts of *logos* and Ideas will not remain independently side-by-side, but will be integrated in a *logos* that is of cosmic significance, and in Christian monotheism it will be located within the Godhead.

Aristotle (c.384–c.322 BC) studied under Plato in Athens until the latter's death. He later applied himself especially to the study of the animal world. When he tried thereby to apply the principles he had learned

---

11. Kattan, *Verleiblichung und Synergie*, 3–6.
12. Ibid., 7–9.

from Plato, he found it impossible to account for his discoveries in terms of quasi-mathematical ideals: the various animals and their behavior could not be defined or explained in the abstract, and there were various degrees of perfection. He found rather that for understanding nature it was necessary to study in detail that what was under our eyes. He held that the primary task was taxonomy, namely the classification of various things, and that the second task was physiology, the study of the various stages along which an individual attains maturity. Aristotle posits, moreover, in his book *On the Animal Body Parts* (*De partibus animalium*), that rationality (*logos*) is not only attributable to the human mind, but is a principle that can be discerned throughout the natural order. Perhaps there can here be discerned a resonance with Heraclitus' perception of *logos*.[13]

After Aristotle's death two major schools developed, namely that of Epicurus and of the Stoics. It is the latter that is important for what concerns the *logos* doctrine. Stoicism began around 300 BC with Zeno of Citium (c.336–c.264 BC) and continued to develop over a period of five centuries. Two principles were discerned as at the root of all existence: unqualified or formless matter (ἡ ἄποιος ὕλη), which is the receptive or passive principle, and the active principle (ὁ λόγος), which gives form to matter and which calls forth the various forms of existence. The active principle they also called Spirit (πνεῦμα) or Creative Fire (πῦρ τεχνικόν). The Stoics were convinced that everything happened in accordance with this divine principle or *logos* and that it was at the root of every being, movement, and ordering within nature. Following Heraclitus, the Stoics thus believed in determinism. Kattan points out that the later Stoics came to perceive the *logos* or divine fire as the mind and soul of nature, and this not as above nature, but as being immanent within it. The Stoics called it a *logos spermatikos*, that is, as having seed-like capacities in that it is active within the passive matter and calls forth from it the various forms that make up a world imbued with rationality. So as to account for the multiplicity of entities that are called forth by the one *logos* or divinity, the Stoics introduced speaking of *logoi spermatikoi* in the plural, which were held to be contained within the single active divine principle. The Stoics agreed, moreover, that the universal soul or fire must itself have some material characteristics, as an ethereal substance that is spread out everywhere. For, they argued, an abstract and immaterial reality cannot

13. Toulmin and Goodfield, *Architecture of Matter*, 89–96; Kattan, *Verleiblichung und Synergie*, 10.

produce material effects. This fire, or ether, they held to be mixed with air, thereby becoming water and earth, depending upon the composition. The human soul, itself material, would after death return to the pure cosmic fire in the outer heavens.[14]

This brings us to the Intertestamental and New Testament periods, which is informed by both the Hebrew and the Hellenic philosophical traditions. Both traditions touched in the Hellenic Jew, Philo of Alexandria (c.15 BC–50 AD). Kattan considers that Philo represents a further step on the way towards a hypostasizing of the *logos*; that is, towards it being perceived as a concrete existent reality, albeit of a transcendental nature. In contradistinction to the Stoics, he did not hold that the *logos* is the highest ontological entity, but is subjected to God. Philo, faithful to his Jewish monotheistic background, identifies God as the Creator of all that receives existence. Besides this, he adopted continuity with the Platonic tradition. He thus perceived the *logos* as containing the Ideas and that, as such, the *logos* is both God's image and instrument for creating. As regards the Ideas, they are not, as for Plato, without beginning and independent of the Creator. Philo identifies them with the intelligible world (κόσμος νοητός), which the Jewish Scriptures presents as constituted by various spiritual beings. Philo's *On the Creation of the World* (*De opificio mundo*) thus depicts that this intelligible world contained in the *logos* serves God as a paradigm for the creation of the visible world (κόσμος αἰσθητός).[15] Further, as regards the *logos*, Tollefsen indicates that Philo describes it in the *Allegorical Interpretation* (*Legum allegoriae*) as the "shadow" of God; Tollefsen's impression is that it is "a kind of intermediary being, perhaps not a being with a complete hypostatic reality of its own."[16]

Next, we encounter the term *logos* in the New Testament as already described in the previous section. Thereupon, among the early Christian writers the *logos* doctrine developed by way of Justin Martyr and Origen. Justin Martyr (d.165) of Shechem in Palestine was a philosopher who after his conversion set up a school of Christian instruction in Rome. Justin embraced the concept of *logos* as a possible bridge between the Jewish Scriptures, the Christian apostolic writings and the thought-world

---

14. Toulmin and Goodfield, *Architecture of Matter*, 102–11; Strycker, *Beknopte Geschiedenis*, 161–66; Kattan, *Verleiblichung und Synergie*, 11–13; Tollefsen, *Christocentric Cosmology*, 26–27.

15. Kattan, *Verleiblichung und Synergie*, 14–18.

16. Tollefsen, *Christocentric Cosmology*, 35.

God's Spirit and Creative Word

of Greek philosophy that accompanied the Roman cult.[17] In continuity of John's Gospel, Justin used Logos to indicate the divine Son, whom John 1:14 proclaimed to have become flesh. Justin emphasized that it was justifiable to honor the historical person Jesus, who had been crucified, as to be the Son of God; for the Son or Logos was capable to obtain an earthly existence from the Virgin (compare Isa 7:14; Matt 1:23). Added to this, the originality of Justin's thought consisted in presenting the Incarnation as to be in continuity of earlier events whereby the Logos had already appeared on earth for the purpose of making known the will of the Father.[18] Justin linked this original idea at another place with the Stoic term σπερματικὸς Λόγος to indicate the Logos as the source of innate human knowledge concerning the divine truth. Justin, however, would have employed the concept without a particular allegiance to any Greek philosophy. He held that the divine Logos had been present in the words of the prophets, in the teachings of the philosophers, though in a limited way, and that it is present to all people by nature. This same Logos is Christ, and has manifested itself in its fullness in Jesus.[19] It can further be noted that Justin argues that although we can call this Son sometimes God, sometimes Lord and Logos, this does not contradict faith in the one God. Justin considered that the Logos is subordinate to the Father with the prophetic Spirit in third place.

Origin (c.185–253/4) pursued Justin's work of expounding Christian faith with the concepts of Greek philosophy. He was probably the first author who tried to construct a Christian system of metaphysics and for this he made an attempt to bring together the Bible and Neoplatonic thought. His work would in subsequent centuries remain very influential but also highly controversial. Origen studied philosophy under Ammonius Saccas (c.175–241) in Alexandria, whom Étienne Gilson considered as the founder of Neoplatonism and who also taught Plotinus. In line with the doctrine of his teacher, Origen was the first Christian writer who established in a philosophical manner the immateriality of God. He held God to be incorporeal and thus as unthinkable. For Origen, God is the supreme Good, beyond "being" itself.[20] Further, in accordance with his Neoplatonic formation, as for earlier orthodox writers, he considered the

17. Price, "Hellenization," 18.
18. Grillmeier, *Christ*, 90.
19. Justin *Apologia secunda* 13; PG 6:465–68; trans. Stevenson, *New Eusebius*, 62; Grillmeier, *Christ*, 91–94; Trakatellis, *Pre-Existence*, 109–11.
20. Gilson, *History of Christian Philosophy*, 36–37.

Cosmic Prayer and Guided Transformation

Son to be subordinate to the highest God, the monad.[21] More clearly than for Justin or Tertullian, however, Origen insisted in his major work *On First Principles* on the eternal generation of and co-existence of the Son with the Father. He further held that the Spirit is, in its turn, subordinate to the Son.[22] Origen recognized that the Holy Spirit "is an intellectual existence (*subsistentia*), with a subsistence and being of its own,"[23] and thereby also "the personal existence of the Holy Spirit";[24] this roughly at the same time period that the Latin Tertullian (c.160–c.220) in Carthage was writing similarly. Accordingly, for Origen, Father, Son, and Spirit exist as three distinct beings, that is, as three hypostases (ὑπόστασεις) or subjects (ὑποκείμενα).[25] The Son of God he identified with wisdom (σοφία) in continuation of 1 Cor 1:24 (but unlike Irenaeus, who, as we saw, identified it with the Spirit) and with the Logos (in continuation of John's Gospel, Justin, Clement of Alexandria, and others). He held that the Son, or Wisdom, or Logos, is the Father's mediator by whom he creates and communicates with his entire creation.[26] As Tollefsen points out, this wisdom contained the *initia*, *rationes*, and *species* of the whole creation; that is, the causes (ἀρχαί), principles (λόγοι), and kinds (εἴδη) of all that was to be.[27] The *logoi* would collectively have constituted an intelligible world in the Logos, as was earlier similarly held by Philo. Kattan explains that the notion that the *logoi* are contained within wisdom indicates that Logos is in a logical sense a capacity of God's Son that is ontologically prior to his ontological status as God's wisdom. (The *logos*-title reflects the revelatory function of the Son, since he makes the Father known and enables access to him, just as the human reason (λόγος) gives a mediating articulation of the intellect (νοῦς); whereas the wisdom-title would reflect the additional meaning of the Greek term *logos*, namely the thought of God and the with this corresponding divine activity.)[28] Origen held that God created everything out of nothing, while at the same time, that all existing beings had always been created and had existed collectively in an

---

21. Crouzel, *Origen*, 181–82, 188, 203–4.

22. Grillmeier, *Christ*, 140.

23. Origen *De principiis* 1:1:3 (this part of the text is preserved in the Latin translation of Rufinus); trans. Butterworth, *Origen on First Principles*, 9.

24. Ibid. 1:3:1; trans. Butterworth, ibid., 29.

25. Crouzel, *Origen*, 202.

26. Origen *De principiis* 1:2:1–3.

27. Ibid. 1:2:2; 4:4–5; Tollefsen, *Christocentric Cosmology*, 36.

28. Kattan, *Verleiblichung und Synergie*, 24–25.

God's Spirit and Creative Word

original unity (or henad) eternally in God; that is, "before" the present material world emerged. According to Origen's distinctive account, all the spirits of the pre-existent henad fell away from God, except for one spirit that remained in perfect adherence to him. As the spirits fell away, God graciously let them fall into matter as a remedy for their sin, for without it they would have kept falling further and further away. God then allowed the one spirit that did not fall away and that is the perfect image of the Logos, to enter into the material world, not as a punishment, but for the restoration of humanity as an expression of God's love; this spirit, the soul of Jesus, took on flesh while it remained in perfect union with the Logos.[29] As said, Origen's thought is original, but would in subsequent centuries be condemned on several counts.

At this point we can jump a few centuries ahead in time and take knowledge of the use of the *logos* concept in the works of Pseudo-Dionysius (sixth century AD) and that was adopted by Maximus. A key text is *The Divine Names* 5:8. I reproduce here the relevant extract in its full length in the translation provided by Colm Luibheid, for it is worth reflecting upon for some moments:

> The sun, as we know it, is one. It is a single illuminating light, acting upon the essences and the qualities of the many and various things we perceive. It renews them, nourishes them, protects them, and perfects them. It establishes the differences between them and it unifies them. It warms them and makes them fruitful. It makes them exist, grow, change, take root, burst forth. It quickens them and gives them life. Each thing therefore has, in its own way, a share of the one and the same sun and the one sun contains within itself as a unity the causes (τὰς αἰτίας) of all the things which participate in it. All this holds all the more truly with respect to the Cause which produced the sun and which produced everything else. The exemplars (τὰ παραδείγματα) of everything preexist as a transcendent unity within It. It brings forth being as a tide of being. We give the name of "exemplar" to those principles (τοὺς λόγους) which preexist as a unity in God and which produce the essences of things. Theology calls them predefining (προορισμοὺς), divine and good acts of will (θεῖα καὶ ἀγαθὰ θελήματα) which determine and create (ἀφοριστικὰ καὶ ποιητικὰ) things and in accordance with which the Transcendent One predefined and brought into being everything that is.[30]

---

29. Williams, "Origen," 138–39.
30. Pseudo-Dionysius *De divinis nominibus* 5:8; PG 3:824B–C; trans. Luibheid,

Cosmic Prayer and Guided Transformation

A first observation is that Pseudo-Dionysius envisions that the exemplars or *logoi* are contained within God; they are not (as was for Plato) ideas external to a Demiurge. It can also be noted that they serve not as mere passive models for creation, but they take on an active role within God for the production of the various created entities. Further, they are distinguished from the things that are being created in accordance with it, so that they are not identified, as for Origen, with the various spiritual beings themselves. They are being called "predefining, divine, and good acts of will," and Maximus will call them likewise "predefinitions" or "predeterminations" (προορισμός) and "divine wills" (θεῖα θελήματα).[31] According to the cited text, the exemplars that produce things are perceived to form a unity within God. The will of God for his creation may indeed be considered to be a unity, wherein particular intentions for particular aspects or entities of the created reality are consistent expressions thereof. This single-minded will of God need, however, not be assumed to be identifiable with the Son or Logos only. For the will of God is being shared in by the entire Trinity (*Divine Names* 7:4).[32] Besides this question of the relation of the *logoi* to the divine persons, there is the question of their relation to the things that emerge: are the *logoi* determining the created entities in every aspect of their existence? Despite Luibheid's translation that the *logoi* "determine" things, it does not appear that Pseudo-Dionysius held that they completely characterize every individual being; for every creature would then itself obviously be divine instead of contingent. What seems rather the case is that he held that for each entity there is provided a particular identity and place within the totality, and that there is no capacity that does not derive from God. The comparison with the sun is interesting in this respect. Despite what the text may again appear to confirm, Pseudo-Dionysius is not claiming that somehow within the sun is contained each and every cause for all that happens on earth. He is not positing a rigid determinism wherein every participating being and each of its movements is merely acting out a course of events set by the causes in the sun. What is being claimed is that none could happen without the sun, and that the sun provides warmth and light that energizes the various processes and creatures on earth. So also, and this in a much more sublime manner, the exemplars, or *logoi*, are claimed to have

Pseudo-Dionysius, 101–2.
    31. *Amb.* 7; PG 91:1085A.
    32. Kattan, *Verleiblichung und Synergie*, 40–41.

an active role in all that happens; they inform creatures, enable them to emerge into being and to live in accordance with their particular nature. Kattan brings to attention another text that appears to express a same perception: namely *The Celestial Hierarchy* 11:2 wherein there is mention of a supra-cosmic *logos* (ὁ ὑπερκόσμος λόγος) that is active in organizing the divine minds (οἱ θεῖοι νόες) according to essence, power, and activity.[33] Again at *Letter* 9:2 the *logoi* are being allied to God's providential creative activity,[34] just as in the here quoted text from *The Divine Names* they are being identified with the predefinitions, and the divine and good acts of will. This shows that, even though there has taken place a thorough assimilation of Neoplatonic concepts, we can still find here the notion of the efficacy of God's speech-act as envisioned in the Bible.

This brings us to the *logoi* doctrine in Maximus, which is far more extensive than that in any of his predecessors. I already mentioned that he follows Dionysius in considering the *logoi* constitutive of God's will. As such, Maximus would not deny them the status of divine realities, whether it is *logoi* that concern God's own existence or whether they concern the created realities. It is not inappropriate to entertain the following consideration: Since the *logoi* are constitutive of God's will they may be compared with the unspoken thoughts or spoken words of rational beings such as us. Our words and thoughts are brought about by ourselves, yet, they also determine our identity, the sort of person we are, our effects or actions upon other beings, and they influence the events that we encounter. Our words and thoughts are obviously very much part of who we are, they are inseparable from who we are, whereas we also exist prior to them (as causal and as earlier in time). We may apprehend likewise with regard to God, who is of course to a much higher degree in conscious possession of his own Self and of his thoughts and words than we are, while his words/Word much more perfectly than for ourselves express/es himself and belong/s to himself/the Word.

For Maximus the *logoi* are constitutive of the unity within the Logos or Son. As for what concerns their relation to the divine actions or energies (ἐνεργείαι; sing. ἐνέργεια), different opinions have been expressed.[35] *Book of Difficulties* (*Ambigua*) 22 shows that Maximus does indeed ally

---

33. Pseudo-Dionysius *De coelesti hierarchia* 11:2; PG 3:284D or SC 58:143; Kattan, *Verleiblichung und Synergie*, 45.

34. Pseudo-Dionysius, *Ep.* 9:2; PG 3:1108D.

35. Among those who identify them: Kallistos (Ware) of Diokleia, "Through Creation," 14; among those who do not: Larchet, *Saint Maxime le Confesseur*, 133.

the *logoi* to the divine energies, but without spelling out a strict identification. Perhaps it can be acknowledged, as Dumitru Staniloae comments, "The energies are not else but the principles [or *logoi*] in their creative and sustaining action towards creatures."[36] I also endorse Tollefsen's interpretation: "God is present in every natural process with his creative force. Instituting natural causality as such, he operates cooperatively to bring about what from eternity is conceived by him in his *logoi*."[37] This leads us to the lengthy *Ambigua* 7 wherein Maximus confirms: "For always and in all, the Word of God, and God, wants the mystery of his embodiment to be accomplished."[38] The perception I hereby adopt, and this in agreement with Paul M. Blowers, is that for Maximus this embodiment is respectively within creation, in the historical words of Scripture, and in Jesus' and other people's humanity.[39] This leads us to ask what this embodiment actually involves. It involves for people and for the various creatures a life in accordance with their particular *logoi* that God has for them. It is a life in accordance with the nature or kind to which a being is assigned and in accordance with the individual role that it is invited upon for the good of itself and others. Let us look at some other extracts from *Ambigua* 7 that clarify this further:

> With reason and wisdom (λόγῳ καὶ σοφίᾳ), he [God, the Logos and the Father] made and is making all things (τὰ πάντα) at the proper time, both the universal things and those that apply to each (in particular). For we believe that a *logos* of angels guides (προκαθηγεῖσθαι) their creation, (similarly) a *logos* of each of the beings and powers that fill the upper world [or heaven], a *logos* of human beings, and—in order that I don't have to mention it about each one—a *logos* of all that obtained their existence from God. . . . For all creatures are wholly affirmed in essence and becoming by their own *logoi* and those of the beings around them.[40]

Lars Thunberg considers this text in view of Maximus' refutation of the Origenistic doctrine of pre-existence and in view of his positive

---

36. Staniloae, "Commentaires," 473 (my trans.).

37. Tollefen, *Christocentric Cosmology*, 136.

38. *Amb.* 7; PG 91:1084D (my trans. of this and following texts of Maximus, unless indicated otherwise).

39. Blowers, "Analogy," 145.

40. *Amb.* 7; PG 91:1080A, 1081B.

evaluation of the created multiplicity.[41] God is bringing various things into being, each at its own time. According to Maximus, every creature has its own *logos*—or perhaps more than one—so that it receives being as an object of God's wisdom: each is created, not at random, but in an orderly manner. Each is a specimen (or individual being) of a species (or kind), whereby each comes into being and exists in a manner suited to one's kind according to an own particular hypostasis, or substantial existence. Therefore, at the level of individual being, each one's *logos* (or *logoi*) include(s) that what is shared with others of one's kind and what is particular, such as one's own time of being created. Moreover, actual existence in all its aspects takes place amidst other beings and is therefore conditioned not only by one's own *logos*, but also by those of many others.[42] Arguably, we may intimate from this that each individual being can only exist in co-existence with others and by being co-defined by their *logoi*, this for what concerns its characteristic constitution, its further development, and all aspects of its concrete existence. In other words, individual creaturehood and the individual's particular existence—which is not reducible to the species to which it belongs; that is, which is not a mere clone of the others—could perhaps be understood to be possible exactly through the co-existence of diverse creatures in various combinations. In addition, as can be noticed, Maximus reflects in terms of two overarching ontological levels with which we are well acquainted, namely that of the individual creature and that of the various species. The latter he closely associates with the concept of "essence" (οὐσία). The essence (or its *logos*) includes in its singleness the common characteristics of several creatures; it orders the created beings into a kind of their own, as is envisaged by its single *logos*. It is interesting to observe that the here provided quotation communicates to us an intricate interplay between unity and multiplicity, whether we look at it from the species level or from the particular creature level. It is a key insight of Maximus that multiplicity is realized in unity and vice versa, unity in multiplicity. This insight is highly significant in its own right, but it may also signal a warning that we be careful not too quickly to assume it self-evident that the species level is ontologically prior to that of the various specimens, and that therefore the *logoi* of the species are the more important ones and, hence, directly and irrevocably determined by God once and for all, pronounced within

41. Thunberg, *Microcosm and Mediator*, 74.
42. See also *Amb.* 15; PG 91:1217AB and *Thal.* 13; PG 90:296A or CCSG 7:95:9–13.

the divine communion before anything came to be. Certainly, as the text shows, Maximus holds that God has a *logos* for each of the spiritual beings and for the various kinds of earthly creatures. These *logoi* are being pronounced in such manner as to guide: there is no one-to-one determination; they enable species and individual creatures to emerge into being. Significant as well in the whole of Maximus' intellectual vision is the notion of creatures' becoming (γένεσις). The transition from non-being to being is not a sudden event, creatures overall do not emerge as with the touch of a magician's stick, their coming to be is a process enabled by God that involves the creature itself and all those around it. The process from becoming leading into being takes place within a reciprocal relationship of the Creator and the created order.

Searching in *Ambigua* 7 for additional clarification concerning the mystery of the embodiment of God and the Word of God, we find Maximus to comprehend as follows for what concerns the human being: "Every person who participates in virtue as a matter of habit unquestionably participates in God, the substance of the virtues."[43] And further down in the same treatise, "[A virtuous person] is a portion of God, as he exists (ὡς ὤν) through his *logos* of being, which is in God, and as he is good (ὡς ἀγαθός) through his *logos* of well-being, which is in God, and as he is God (ὡς Θεός) through his *logos* of eternal being, which is in God."[44] Maximus envisages here the process of life for the faithful with the triad being, well-being, and eternal well-being, to which corresponds a triad of *logoi*, (which at *Ambigua* 65 are envisaged as being contained within a single encompassing *logos*).[45] Failure to observe these *logoi* would alternatively lead towards ill-being and eternal ill-being.[46] The positive message that can be deduced from these few lines is that God's Word does not only guide the emergence of human beings into the world, but guidance is offered throughout life. God does not leave his creatures abandoned. These lines are concerned with the human, but Maximus envisages likewise for the whole of God's created reality.[47] Moreover, the idea that a creature neither strives merely to evermore correspond to its *logos* of being, as if merely overcoming a deficiency, that is, as if striving towards a restitution

43. *Amb.* 7; PG 91:1081D.
44. Ibid., 1084BC.
45. *Amb.* 65; PG 91:1392A.
46. *Amb.* 7; PG 91:1084D-85A; 1085C.
47. E.g. *Amb.* 10; PG 91:1192B.

God's Spirit and Creative Word

of an original unity as perceived by Origen, nor strives merely to attain a single universal *logos* while leaving behind its own *logos* or *logoi*, but instead strives to attain this manifoldness of *logoi* within God, allows us to see its movement, its process of existence, as itself positive and as towards a new form of being within God. The *logoi*, as expressive of God's will, guide the creatures towards a participation in life within God. The human being as well as the angelic beings are thereby given the task to orient the entire creaturely order towards God: their well-being cannot be self-centered, but is cooperative with God to promote universal well-being that takes place in harmony and thus by a same movement so as to attain eternal well-being in God, in whom there is no division, but who is love itself.[48] In this harmonious existence in God, the various creatures do not leave "being" behind, but attain it.

However, even a manifoldness of *logoi* does not adequately account for the process of life. As it is, human existence is not merely a smooth process of transition that is described by the *logoi*, from being through well-being towards eternal well-being. Although the *logoi*, constitutive of God's plan, are, according to Maximus, apparently unalterable, human beings, as a consequence of sin, realize the divine intention to variable degrees. Hence, Maximus adopts the concept of the *tropoi* that are indicative of the various modes of existence and therewith of the diverse degrees of orientation upon God in one's life. As such, for us humans they are associated with our responsibility. It is in *Ambigua* 42 that we find Maximus to explain about the *tropoi*:

> The principle of human nature (λόγος δὲ φύσεως ἀνθρωπίνης) involves soul and body, and the very existence of the nature that consists out of a rational soul and body, whereas a mode (τρόπος) is the disposition (ἡ τάξις) wherein it naturally acts and is being acted upon, which often changes and is altered, without changing at all the nature along with it. So it is for every other thing that occurs, when God desires to innovate something in its createdness, on account of his providence over the things preconceived and for the sake of giving an indication of his power that is upon all things and that penetrates through them.[49]

Although God, the Logos, and the Spirit are entirely present throughout creation and within every creature, yet, a creature partakes in this

---

48. *Thal.* 2; PG 90:272AB or CCSG 7:51:7–22.
49. *Amb.* 42; PG 91:1341D–44A; see also Dalmais, "L'innovation," 287–89.

presence in a particular manner that is appropriate for its created kind and it opens itself for him to various degrees of fullness from out of its imperfection according to its mode of existence. With regard to the modes that lead to eternal life, we need to take account of sin and Jesus Christ's redemption to fill in the picture. Because of sin, human beings became separated from God, from the Logos, and from the *logos* of eternal well-being with God.[50] With Jesus, however, there emerged a human being firmly established in obedience to God's Word. Jesus' very identity is that of God's Word, the Son; Jesus' humanity, though in every way the same as ours, belonged to Christ, the Incarnate Son. Maximus perceived that in Jesus, Christ came to renew or recreate the virtuous modes of living.[51]

Maximus took account of the distortions within the human sphere of a God given orderliness and movement towards him. He also acknowledged the distortions among the spiritual beings and the existence of demons besides the holy angels. From a contemporary perspective there is, in addition, a need to acknowledge the distortions within the wider created world. Maximus would not have been aware as we are, or to the extent that we are, of the existence of, for example, various harmful bacteria and parasites. He held that God brought creatures into being so that he might rejoice in his works and might enjoy their partaking in him.[52] It is, however, unlikely that Maximus would have held that certain species that are bound to cause much grievance give delight to God. It would have been rather odd if he had held that tsetse flies and various disease-causing bacilli can simply be ascribed to God's creativity in accordance with a *logos* (whether pre- or postlapsarian). For various microorganisms the parasitic mode of existence (*tropos*) is as it were inscribed in their genetic material. In comparison to Maximus' perception, it is therefore necessary to set another step further away from the idea of an all-embracing divine determination. This does not need to diminish belief that God pronounces his Word over the universal creation. The faith perspective that is subscribed to in this book upholds together with Maximus that God brings into being by his creative Word, that he guides towards life, towards well-being in harmonious co-existence, and towards the communion within him. Moreover, God remains not distant as he pronounces his Word, but he is journeying along with those being created.

50. Ibid., 1348D.
51. Ibid., 1344D–45A
52. *Char.* 3:46; PG 90:1029C.

God's Spirit and Creative Word

This leads us to complete these few pages on the *logos* doctrine in Maximus with an extract from *Questions dedicated to Thalassius* 15 where he explicitly affirms the omnipresence of the Holy Spirit: "The Holy Spirit is not absent from a single being and most certainly not from those that have somehow partaken of the Logos/*logos*. For the Holy Spirit contains (with himself) (Συνεκτικὸν) knowledge [or consciousness] of the existence of each; because, as God and Spirit of God, he is providently progressing through all[53] by power and he is stirring up the *logos* in each according to (the created) nature."[54] We have started this chapter with reflecting upon the Spirit that hovers over the dark waters of creation, going before the creative pronouncements of God, as it is narrated in Genesis. With this last quotation from Maximus, we have returned to the Spirit, who stirs up the *logos* in each.

A long chapter has thus been rounded off. We have reflected in some detail upon creation's emergence by the creative outreach of God, his Spirit, and Word. We have been invited by the biblical texts and Christian tradition upon the perception that universal existence has a thoroughly spiritual foundation and is guided upon a path towards a destiny in God. We have discerned that the multitude of entities that make up the emergent order are thereby not bereft of a contingent and authentic selfhood and agency, even though every capacity is lent by God. The created entities, both the intelligible and sensible ones, are invited upon a reciprocal Creator-creature relationship. In this chapter focus has been on the divine pole of the relationship, upon Spirit, and Word, for it is the divine that is at the origin of the created and every relationship. In the following chapter we will reflect upon cosmos so as to allow us in later chapters to appreciate the created order's contribution in the relationship with the divine, and the human purpose and responsibility therein.

---

53. Cf. *perichoresis* (this concept is discussed at ch. 8).
54. *Thal.* 15; PG 90:297B or CCSG 7:101:7–12.

3

Cosmos

ANCIENT HEBREW COSMOLOGY

JUST AS FOR THE previous chapter, the approach adopted in this chapter will have a historical character. For to understand something is to understand it in its context. For discerning the key elements of an emergent cosmology that can inform, guide, and encourage us in our present existence, it is necessary to take account of earlier cosmologies that still exert their influence and that enshrine insights of previous cultures. It is a matter of retaining what can be assessed as valuable and of discarding that what can be discerned as distorting a wholesome outlook upon reality. As we did for the previous chapter, we begin with the Hebrew Scriptures.

Our reflection upon Genesis 1 has already introduced us to the ancient Hebrew thought about universal creation and we have discerned the thoroughly spiritual foundation of all that is brought into existence. Other interesting texts for the purpose of discerning Hebrew cosmological thought are Psalm 104 and Job 26 and 38–42. There are various agreements between these texts and Genesis, but also notable differences. Whereas Genesis 1 is a rather sober account of God's creative activity, the latter two texts have retained some mythological elements and they are more descriptive. As such, the chosen vehicle of expression in Psalm 104 and Job is poetry. The use of poetry is significant in itself, for it makes an appeal not only upon the rational faculty, but also aims to engage the imagination and the entire intellect. It aims not only to inform us about the relationship with God the Creator, which is only possible to a very limited extent, but it also aims to draw us into that relationship, whole and entire.

It belongs, of course, to the nature of a Psalm to have a devotional and liturgical purpose. This, however, should not blind us to the significance of the fact that the various magnificent acts of divine creation brought to mind in the middle part of Psalm 104 are introduced and concluded with verses that jubilantly express praise and worship of God. Just as the origin of the created order is spiritual, its purpose and destiny is likewise spiritual. The purpose is a prayerful relationship with God. The Psalm does not envisage this worship to be the task of another time and another place beyond the present earth. It is an essential task for the present life on earth. The Psalmist lets us envisage, moreover, an earth that is purged of all that is evil (v. 35) and wherein all creatures can live in peace and devoid of suffering (vv. 9–18; compare Isa 11:6–9). He expresses the hope that God may rejoice in his works and that his creatures may rejoice in the fact of being alive and in their Creator (vv. 27–29, 31). Human beings are created by the same Spirit that gives life to all creatures and they are sustained by God amongst the other creatures and in dependence upon the fruits of the earth (vv. 14–15, 27–30). The specific task of humanity is to work within creation, to address God in meditation upon and worship for the various created realities, and to foster the Creator-creature relationship (vv. 33–34), desiring that God may continue to renew the face of the ground (v. 30).[1] A similar mindset may be discerned in Job 38–41. In magnificent poetry God is brought to speak about his various creative acts. Before Job and the reader's meditative eye are brought to mind the marvels of created reality: the earth and the seas, the pattern of day and night, snow, hail and rain, the stars that are ordered in the various constellations, the various animals with their amazing capacities and skills in their suited environments, and the great monsters that hide in the waters. After this meditative journey, Job exclaims, "things too wonderful for me, which I did not know." Job is thus brought to look beyond the reality of his own existence with its various, though real, sufferings. As Job is, the reader too is invited to meditate upon the all-embracing Creator-creature relationship. It is upon the confrontation with God during this meditative

---

1. Deissler, "Theology," 37–39.

journey that Job is asked to pray to God for others with the promise of being heard by him (42:8–9).

Genesis 1 let us envisage that God's creative outreach takes place through the breathing of the Spirit and the pronouncements of the creative words. Psalm 104 as well speaks of the Spirit as representative of God's creative touch and it speaks of God's wisdom in creating. In addition, God is depicted as more closely involved in the creative outreach than would appear from Genesis 1; he enters as it were himself within creation to continue his work. "Thou who makest the clouds thy chariot, who ridest on the wings of the wind, who makest the winds thy messengers, fire and flame thy ministers" (vv. 3–4). God's close involvement is also shown by elaborating on the fact that God's creative work is not completed in six days, but continues as he "makest springs gush forth in the valleys" (v. 10), "causes the grass to grow for the cattle, and plants for man to cultivate" (v. 14). God is continually looking after all creatures, even the wild animals, for "they all look to thee, to give them their food in due season" and to renew the face of the earth (v. 30). God is working and the human being is called to work with God within creation (v. 23). The insight that is here communicated is highly significant for a contemporary theistic outlook upon the event of creation. God's creative touch is not totally contained by instituting physical laws or by other nature laws that can be discerned. Universal creation and the emergence of particular beings takes place because of innumerable divine touches and because of a unique series of occurrences that have not automatically resulted from what went before. God is working and those that are being created, both human and other beings, contribute by their acts and behavior in the contingent development of the created order of which they are part and in the relationship with God.

This insight is complemented by the impression gained from Job 38–41. We can follow Raymond P. Scheindlin in his observation that God at first addresses Job angrily, after having been called upon to justify himself for Job's unjust suffering. God then starts to expound his mighty works to Job so as to show Job's incomprehension and smallness in the entire project of creation. But having begun his description of his works within creation, the angry tone of speech disappears as God is himself caught up in the contemplation of his works and of the various created entities.[2] The impression created by these chapters of Job coheres with the

---

2. Scheindlin, *Job*, 40.

insight that not all has been laid out as a mathematical design, but that there is marvel at various occurrences within the created order. The created beings in their particular situations can make a contribution within the cosmic whole that is worthwhile in God's eyes and that gives him delight.

In Genesis 1, Job 26, 38, and Psalm 104 we can find further details concerning the cosmic perception of the ancient Jews. The earth is envisaged as being firmly set on foundations (Ps 104:5), even though these foundations cannot be perceived to rest themselves on anything (Job 38:6). It is a flat earth that is covered by a firmament. Below the earth is the underworld, which is the abode where the dead continue in a shadowy existence (Job 26:5–6; 38:16–17; Ps 30:3, 9). The whole of earth and lower heaven is surrounded by the waters of the "deep" (Gen 1:6; Ps 104:6). Along the ends of the earth there are pillars that support the heavens beyond the firmament (Ps 104:3). The heavens contain the heavenly storehouses of rain, hail, and snow (Job 26:11; 38:22–25; Ps 104:13), whereas the upper heavens are the dwelling place of God (Amos 9:6; Pss 29:10; 32:13; 104:13). It is a worldview that is common to the entire ancient Near East and that is of a rather mythological character.[3]

Of greater relevance than the Hebrew perception of earth and heaven is the question whether spiritual beings and angels do indeed exist and whether they are, truly, ministers of God's word (Ps 103:20–21, as quoted in the previous chapter). It is a question that cannot be silently bypassed for a perception of a contemporary Christian cosmology. In the previous chapter it was noted that Proverbs introduces a personified wisdom, who is at God's side, who characterizes his creative outreach, and who being bestowed upon creation, represents responsiveness within creation that is cooperative with God. Wisdom is thereby not associated with any particular created entity. Its elusive and spiritual nature is particularly described at Job 28:12–28. The angelic beings, however, that feature at various places in Hebrew Scripture are presented as communicating a particular message, warning, or judgment from God, or they are sent to a particular place for assistance, where they become tangibly present and fulfill their ministry. Let us then survey the scriptural texts that give an indication of the evolving perception of the existence of beings in the metaphysical realm. In the Yahwistic storyline, which begins with the second creation story at Genesis 2 and which contains various

---

3. Keel, *Symbolism of the Biblical World*, 57.

Cosmic Prayer and Guided Transformation

mythological elements that are shared with surrounding cultures, there features the notion that there are lesser gods besides Yahweh, who form a heavenly court around him (Gen 3:22). The same passage mentions cherubim as guardians of the entrance into Paradise (v. 24). The story narrates that it is God himself who placed them there. They are imagined as winged creatures that are half human and half beast, like the two that were crafted from gold with outstretched wings in accordance with God's directions to Moses for overshadowing the mercy seat over the ark within the sanctuary in the tent (Exod 25:18–20) and like those that were later crafted from olivewood and overlaid with gold as guardians of the inner sanctuary within Solomon's Temple (1 Kgs 6:23–28).[4] The cherubim also feature at Ps 18:10; Ezek 1:4—2:25; and 10:15, where they are imagined as living creatures. In the same Yahwistic tradition at Gen 6:2 the lesser gods are called the sons of God. Likewise at Job 1:6 and 2:1 there is mention of the sons of God among whom is the satan. A heavenly court is also introduced at 1 Kgs 22:19–22 where the divine beings besides God are called spirits. The imaginary in these texts can be considered in connection with ancient myths, involving the belief in, among others, several gods and cherubim,[5] while the fragment at Gen 6:1–4 that narrates about intercourse between the sons of God and the daughters of humans may well refer to Greek mythology.[6] Besides these texts, the early texts of the Bible speak regularly of "the angel of Yahweh" (in the singular) either in the manner of a theophany, so that the spiritual being denotes God, "Yahweh," as tangibly present within the world, or as a messenger of God with an own subjectivity, who is empowered to speak and act in God's name, in such manner that it is God's own speech that is heard. Examples of these are Gen 16:7–13; Exod 3:1–6; 23:20–21; Num 22:22–35; Judg 6:11–23; and 1 Kgs 19:5–7. If we turn to Gen 18:1–2 we can notice that v. 1 narrates that Yahweh appeared to Abraham by the oaks of Mamre. In v. 2, however, the story continues by narrating that when Abraham looked up, he saw not Yahweh, which is quasi-impossible for a mortal being, but he saw three men standing in front of him. Gerhard von Rad (1901–71) considered that either Yahweh appeared with two companions that serve as an honor guard, or, as he held more likely, he appeared in all three of

---

4. Kessler and Deurloo, *Commentary on Genesis*, 57–58.
5. Rad, *Genesis*, 95; Jacob, *Genesis*, 33.
6. Kessler and Deurloo, *Commentary on Genesis*, 77–78.

them.[7] Later in the story, at v. 22, it is narrated that the men left Abraham and went toward Sodom, and in Gen 19:1, which begins what was originally a different story and tradition, two of them arrive by Lot, who is sitting at the gate of the city. After the men left Abraham, however, he still stood before God and draws near to him so as to engage with God in conversation. The fact that one of the three visitors apparently stayed somewhat behind indicates that to God belonged the first initiative for enabling the conversation. The scene illustrates that it is always God who enables the Creator-creature relationship. The conversation itself, however, is begun by Abraham. It is narrated that after the conversation God continues his way; apparently on the same road towards Sodom that his two companions took earlier. It can, however, not simply be deduced that the two men, or angels, who went ahead, left God behind, for whereas in their conversation with Lot they announce that they have been sent by God (v. 13), yet, they also speak in such manner as being God themselves (v. 21). The entire story is clearly very interesting in light of the later doctrine of the holy Trinity, wherein three divine persons are inseparably one God and wherein Spirit and Son are creatively active without leaving the presence of God the Father. But it is also interesting for what concerns the emergence of angelic beings in Scripture as it is developed throughout various texts. In Genesis itself we find the story associated with Jacob, wherein he saw in a dream several angels of God ascending and descending a ladder, erected between heaven and earth (28:12–17). Turning towards other texts, as we said earlier, in the books of the successive prophets it is the prophets themselves who speak God's word, even though they are not divine men but mortal men. In their visions there feature, moreover, spiritual beings that again are closely associated with God's majestic presence, but that are clearly distinct from him. An example is found in the vision described at Isa 6:1–9. It features two seraphim who each have six wings and who stand beside God seated on his throne. God is called "the King, Yahweh of the powers" (Isa 6:5; my translation). Next, in the vision of Ezekiel, there emerge four living creatures in the form of men, but each having four faces and four wings (Ezek 1:4—2:25). They are called cherubim (10:15), as at Gen 3:24, and they emerge from out of a gleaming bronze that is in the midst of the likeness of fire. The gleaming bronze and the fire are associated with the presence of God and as such the creatures stem from God. The fire is in the midst

---

7. Rad, *Genesis*, 199.

of them and, similar to the vision of Isaiah, above the living creatures is a firmament and the throne of the likeness of God. As each creature has a wheel beside it that contains its spirit and is full of eyes, they form as it were a living chariot for God. Interesting is that they move over the earth and that their four faces associate them with humanity and with the various realms of the animal kingdom. Turning then to the Psalms, we find mention of a multitude of angels, as in Psalm 103 that I quoted in the previous chapter; another example is Ps 91:11 at which there is mention of guardian angels. In the book of Daniel there feature again four living creatures. They do not emerge as in Ezekiel from the midst of God, but from out of the chaos of the sea, and they are not the ministers of God but beasts that assume a destructive power (Dan 7:1–8). Daniel offers an apocalyptic vision wherein a war is waged within the spiritual realm that extends throughout the entire extent of the created reality. In Daniel feature again the chariot of God, now surrounded by a great multitude of servants (7:9–10), the archangel Gabriel (8:16), and Michael, who is called one of the chief princes (10:13). Daniel also speaks of "one like a son of man" to whom is given everlasting dominion (7:13–14) and who is envisioned as the Prince of princes (8:25). Finally, the book of Tobit offers a touching narrative wherein Tobit's son Tobias is accompanied by Raphael, who towards the end of the story makes himself known as "one of the seven holy angels who present the prayers of the saints and enter into the presence of the glory of the Holy One" (12:15). He continues that he did not come from heaven by his own initiative to help Tobit and Tobias, "but by the will of our God" (v. 18). What I have offered here is not intended as a rigorous discussion of angelology in the Hebrew Scriptures, but it allows us to discern that just as the physical created realities are perceived as emerging with God's speech and as having an own subjective identity and freedom—yet without any capacity that does not ultimately stem from God—so also the metaphysical created realities have come to be believed in as emerging with God's speech, again as having an own subjective identity and freedom; a freedom wherein they can minister (justice) and bless, or become destructive. It would perhaps be interesting to explore further texts that introduce demons as spiritual beings that oppose God's intentions for creation, but it is probably not necessary here. Turning towards the New Testament, we find that angels feature abundantly in the Gospels from the Annunciation until the Resurrection and they feature within the events that are narrated of the early church. From the Gospels it appears that Jesus himself would have spoken about angels. A number of sayings mentioning angels that are ascribed to him in the Synoptic Gospels are related to the end time. An example of such a saying recalls the scene described in Daniel 7: "For whoever is ashamed of me and my words in this adulterous and sinful generation, of him will the Son of man also be ashamed, when he comes in the glory of his Father with the holy angels" (Mark 8:38; parallel Luke 12:9). In Matthew we find a saying that recalls the guardian angels that we found mentioned in Psalm 91, but that also harks back to the vision of the heavenly court just mentioned (Matt. 18:10). Whereas in John we find a saying that recalls Jacob's ladder: "Truly, truly, I say to you, you will see heaven opened, and the angels of God ascending and descending upon the Son of man" (John 1:51). Angels are written about in Paul's letters, in Hebrews and in subsequent Christian tradition.

I hold that it is possible to retain belief in angels and spiritual beings. A critical searching of Scripture for truth and belief in angels need not be mutually excluding. If it is granted that the created order is called forth within the communion of the economic Trinity, which is entirely spiritual, then the emergence of spiritual beings is not at all far fetched. If indeed the Spirit and God's creative speech are at the source of all entities, then spiritual beings can reasonably be expected to accompany the material ones. These spiritual beings that come from the divine persons are profiled as personal themselves. They are, conceivably, personal centers of intelligence that accompany visible reality and that are present as particular instances of wisdom. In the human being a capacity for intelligence is integral to our biological make-up, whereas in the ecologically viable communities, which are ensembles constituted by a variety of beings, such capacity may not be obvious, but can conceivably be associated with the totality; arguably, it can be attributed to focal personal beings within the spiritual realm who accompany these ensembles. This would accord with the inspiration offered by Maximus, as he envisaged that "while the intelligible beings are the soul of the sensible ones, the sensible beings are the body of the intelligible ones."[8] If, as suggested in the previous chapter, there is a creaturely reaching for communion with God, then the spiritual beings can be perceived as supportive of this.

---

8. *Myst.* 7; PG 91:685A.

Cosmic Prayer and Guided Transformation

ANCIENT WESTERN COSMOLOGY

Besides biblical and patristic thought, the first major period of Western cosmology is determined by classical Greek and Hellenic philosophy. Let us here focus on Plato's cosmology and say a few more words about Aristotle and the Stoics. We already devoted a few pages to them in the previous chapter in light of the *logos* doctrine, but here we want to take some more time to reflect on their overall cosmology and its significance for a contemporary Christian cosmology. These pages will thus closely correspond to our findings of the previous chapter, but looked upon from a somewhat different perspective.

For Plato, the truly real, the realm of pure intelligence and being, is the realm of the Ideas (τά εἴδη or αἱ ἰδέαι; sing. τό εἶδος or ἡ ἰδέα).[9] In *Timaeus* (28A, 30B, 31B, 37D) he reasons that these are contained in a single Living and Intelligent Being that is eternally the same.[10] He explains that when the Creator (ὁ ποιητής) (28C), or Craftsman (ὁ δημιουργός) (29A),[11] made the world (ὁ κόσμος), he kept his eye on the eternal (τὸ ἀίδιον) (29A). For, being good and thus devoid of jealousy, "he wished that all things should be as like unto himself as possible" (29E).[12] Francis M. Cornford explains that this Craftsman is for Plato not a religious figure, an object of worship, but a mythical symbol that represents a real element in the world that contributes to its ordering.[13] The visible world that the Demiurge thus created was to be an intelligent being, since of all that is visible, that possessing mind (νοῦς) is the most beautiful and perfect. Therefore, "in composing (ξυνιστὰς) the universe (τὸ πᾶν) he was joining (ξυνετεκταίνετο) mind (νοῦς) in soul (ψυχή) and soul in body (σῶμα)" (30B); or more accurately, body in soul (36E). Moreover, since the most perfect ideal world is not partial, but containing in itself all intelligible living beings (τὰ νοητὰ ζῷα), likewise "this universe contains us and all other creatures (θρέμματα) that have been formed to be visible ... he composed it a single visible living being, containing within itself all living beings that are by nature akin to it" (30D). Concerning the perfect Living Being, Cornford speaks of "the generic Form of Living Creature." He comments: "It is an eternal and unchanging object of thought, not

---

9. Plato *Republic* 7:1–4, 8–10; 10:1–2; Norris, *God and World*, 14–15.
10. Archer-Hind, *Timaeus of Plato* (text and trans.).
11. Or also God (ὁ θεός) (e.g., 30A, B, 32B, 34B), or Father (ὁ πατήρ) (28C).
12. My translation of this and the following extracts unless stated otherwise.
13. Cornford, *Plato's Cosmology*, 34–40.

itself *a* living creature, any more than the Form of Man is *a* man. It is not a soul, nor has it a body or any existence in space or time. Its eternal being is in the realm of Forms."[14] It is, however, the ideal, whose perfection the visible universe is to imitate. Cornford affirms that by Plato the Forms, or Ideas, which are the ideals, "are always spoken of as existing eternally in their own right."[15] Concerning the visible universe, Plato adds that this ought to be of a spherical shape, since that is the most perfect and regular, comprehending in itself all shapes that are (33B). He continues: "It needed not eyes, for nothing visible was left outside; nor hearing, for there was nothing to hear; and there was no surrounding air which made breathing needful. Nor must it have any organ whereby it should receive into itself its sustenance, and again reject that which was already digested; for nothing went forth of it nor entered in from anywhere; for there was nothing. For by design was it created to supply its own sustenance by its own wasting" (33BC).[16] Thereupon, Plato applies in some detail mathematics, largely borrowed from the Pythagoreans and their study of geometry and musical notes, as an intermediary between the undivided eternal ideal world and the world of divided material bodies. Among others, the orderly revolution of the planets is related to the immaterial Mind (35A–36D).[17] However, an attribute that the Platonic father found impossible to bestow perfectly upon the created image was eternity. He, therefore, "made of eternity that abides in unity an eternal image moving according to number, even that which we have named time (χρόνον)" (37D).[18] So, whereas the eternal Living Being simply *is*, possessing its existence perfectly and undivided, to the created image belong various portions of time, *was* and *shall be*. Accordingly, this constitutes a permanent distinction between the pattern and the image, between the two orders of reality, namely being and becoming (27D, 37C–38C). The Craftsman made the world soul (τοῦ παντὸς ψυχή) and diffused it throughout the whole and enclosed the spherical body in it (34BC and 41D). In fact, the material body of the world does not appear to have a separate origin, directly bestowed by the Craftsman, but evolves from the soul (34C). Next, the stars are created by the Craftsman and called heavenly or young

14. Ibid., 40.
15. Ibid., 41.
16. Trans. Archer-Hind, *Timaeus of Plato*, 101, 103.
17. See also Funkenstein, *Theology and Scientific Imagination*, 31–35, on the ideal of mathematization.
18. Trans. Archer-Hind, *Timaeus of Plato*, 119, 121.

Cosmic Prayer and Guided Transformation

gods (40A-D). With them has been initiated the reflection of the absolute Intelligence into the material world. The living creatures on the earth—those in the air, on the land, in the sea—are created by the created gods, that is, the Earth, Sun, Moon, and stars. Otherwise, if created directly by the Craftsman, these earthly creatures would be immortal and equal to gods (41C). Yet, the Craftsman sows some souls in the Earth, some in the Moon, and also gives one to every star. The stars are thereby given the task to weave a mortal body together with this immortal soul in the formation of living creatures (41C-E). In a first step, the souls are implanted in male human bodies. Those souls that live well can be delivered from their bodily form and return to their native stars where they may enjoy a blissful life; those that do not, are reborn according to a process of reincarnation as a woman; further punishment is the rebirth that results in a kind of animal; until finally after many rebirths these also can return to their star (41E-42D, 90E-92B). In the second half of *Timaeus*, Plato's attention turns to the human anatomy, to the three parts of the soul in the human being, and to the animals and trees that only share in lesser kinds of soul equivalent to the lower parts of the human soul (69C-77C). It describes the correspondence between the (human) microcosm and the macrocosm.

In summary, for Plato intelligence is the prior reality of which a reflection is present within all things that constitute the single living universe. The intelligence incarnate within human beings and earthly living creatures yearns for a permanent uninhibited blissful existence. The created universe is thus continuously being transformed into a harmonious cosmos, into a near-perfect image in multiplicity of the divine Oneness, remaining permanently distinct thereof, and this by way of, and culminating in, the upward movement of human souls towards the stars.

Many of the features of Plato's thought here expressed have influenced and contributed to the church fathers their Christology, anthropology, and cosmological outlook. An indication of this influence has already been given in the previous chapter. The influence of Plato can, in particular, clearly be discerned in, among others, the Latin Augustine, as well as in the vision of Maximus, which we have already touched upon.

As for Plato, so also for Christian teaching there are the two realms of being and becoming. We encountered them, for example, in the extract from Maximus' *Ambigua* 7 that we quoted in the previous chapter. Generally, for Christian teaching the realm of being is thereby not only characterized as living and intelligent, but as personal. Accordingly, the mediation is not analyzed mainly in terms of mathematical speculation, but perceived as the creative and salvific outreach of the divine persons themselves. At its best, Christian doctrine holds the transcendent and immanent aspects of the creative Godhead in distinction, yet without separation, so that by prayer and prayerful living we may touch immediately upon eternity, upon God. Fullness of life is within reach, already, here and now, both for human beings and other creatures, and not as the outcome of a process of reincarnation and eventually "de-carnation" that is reached within a distant star.[19]

The distinction without separation between the two realms of existence, which belong respectively to the divine and the created, is a most significant development within Christian doctrine through its reflection upon Jesus of Nazareth and the Word of God. Within orthodox Christianity, one came to discern that within Jesus—who is being identified as the Christ, the Son of the living God (Matt 16:16)—there holds a permanent distinction between the divine nature and the created human nature, yet that both natures, intact and whole, concur into *one* person, into one and the same Lord, Jesus Christ, who lived among his fellow human beings on earth, and yet, who was and is within the one Godhead. Christian tradition and magisterial doctrine testify to the way this mystery would have been realized: it is claimed that by the Father's providential care for creation, it is the Spirit who with the Virgin's consent informs her womb (Matt 1:18–25; Luke 1:26–38) and the Word that takes on flesh (John 1:14). At the core of Christian belief concerning the divine incarnation in Jesus is that God, as represented by the Spirit, was and is with and in Jesus throughout his life, that Jesus' very identity became expressive of God's Word, and that this wonder was made possible through Mary's, Joseph's, and Jesus' wholehearted cooperation with God. In parallel and in continuation with this event, at the realization of universal salvation, by God's initiative, creaturely being and intelligence is with its cooperation being impregnated with the divine, so that there arises harmony within the creaturely realm and with God (Pseudo-Dionysius spoke of "well-being"),[20] a harmony that by God's gracious gift is lifted up to a unified existence within God (Maximus, as we have seen, spoke of "eternal well-being"). It is clear that human beings, because of their capacity for the personal, have a significant role to play: for we also, need to let ourselves

---

19. Getcha, "Transfiguration," 23–31.
20. Pseudo-Dionysius *De divinis nominibus* 4:1; PG 3:696A.

be informed by the Spirit and, as Jesus, become another humanity for the Word,[21] so that we may contribute to our own and universal salvation. Thereby, this process of salvation is clearly a continuation, or fulfillment, of the one creative event.

For Plato soul is prior to body. The earth's body and those of individual creatures are woven around their respective created souls. While temporarily being clothed with a visible and material body, the souls are destined to leave their bodies behind in an everlasting existence unhampered by the material restrictions and entirely focused upon the divine mind. For Aristotle soul has no existence independent of body, but fully realizes its goal in union with the body (entelechy). Thereby, the soul-body is, as for Plato, informed by the divine mind that in an unresolved tension is both transcendent and immanent to it.[22] For the Stoics, as we saw in previous chapter, the divine mind is itself entirely immanent within the world.

If we then turn to the Judaeo-Christian tradition, we find that body and soul are held to form an indissoluble union within the creature. This is reflected in the Old Testament and in the entire Christ event;[23] it is upheld by the church fathers, and Maximus in particular. In this tradition, the divine mind is located in a personal God. (In comparison, Middle Platonism of the second century AD located the Platonic ideas in the mind of God, but it is a God who is engrossed in self-absorption, self-sufficient as he is, without any direct involvement with or concern for the created order.[24]) Created existence is not fully realized within the created realm as long as this is separate from God. It reaches beyond itself towards union with the transcendent personal ground of existence. God himself draws all things to himself and enables them to move towards him. We found this envisaged by Maximus with the notion of the manifoldness of *logoi*; it is also a key thought for Thomas Aquinas.[25] As such, Christian faith has in its reflection constituted a combination of elements of both the Platonic and Aristotelian schools, and also, by the informing Word and the Incarnation, of the Stoic school. To the extent that

21. This is clearly expressed in Elisabeth of the Trinity, "Prayer to the Trinity."

22. Van Peursen, *Body, Soul, Spirit*, 34–49, 104–19.

23. Ibid., 95–103.

24. Anatolios, *Athanasius*, 10–13.

25. E.g., Aquinas *Summa Theologica* 1a, q.2, art.3, (this art. contains the famous five ways); q.45, art.6; q.47, art.2a-3; q.105, art.3–5; q.115, art.1; Gilson, *Christian Philosophy of Aquinas*, 141–43.

Christian faith has been faithful to its own Judaeo-Christian inheritance, it has done this in such manner as to perceive the transcendent God as really knowledgeable of and directly involved with his entire creation in a dialogical manner. In addition, anticipating the discussion of a few pages below, it will be observed that (post) modern science lets us attribute to created existence not only soul that is as an *élan vitan*, a life principle, but soul that carries various degrees of immanent intelligence. A present day Christian perspective is thus somehow challenged to closely combine anew the Platonic transcendence, the Aristotelian entelechy, and the Stoic immanence, in such manner that the divine transcendence and immanence are held together in accordance with a truly personal notion of God.[26] But before turning towards our contemporary period, let us continue our journey through history.

THE MEDIEVAL COSMOS AND ITS SUBSEQUENT DISSOLUTION

The medieval cosmology as well was marked by a thorough interpenetration of Christian teaching and Greek philosophy. The first part of *Timaeus* was discovered in the twelfth century through the Latin translation (up to 53C) and commentary of Chalcidius, a fourth century Christian, and through the commentary of Proclus (412–485 AD), a Neoplatonic philosopher,[27] which gave an increased impetus to cosmological reflection. The medieval theologian obtained from Plato the notion that cosmology and anthropology are inseparable; the macrocosm and the human microcosm came to be perceived as complementary.[28] This and other aspects of Plato's cosmology would also have reached them more indirectly through the translated works of Greek church fathers and through Boethius' *Consolation of Philosophy* that was translated into many languages and was enormously influential in the Middle Ages. Yet, the medieval theologians rejected the belief in a separate world soul, even though many would wonder whether God himself could not be considered as the world's soul. Thomas Aquinas (1224/5–74) would deny that God is the soul of the world,[29] but rather held with Aristotle that God is

26. Anatolios, *Athanasius*, 13–25, 207–10.
27. Wildiers, *Kosmologie*, 24, 28; Brague, *Wisdom of the World*, 133–34, 138.
28. Brague, *Wisdom of the World*, 139.
29. Aquinas *Summa contra Gentiles* 1:27.

its unmoved mover. As for the question whether the planets are animated by a soul, Aquinas did not decide upon.[30] Whereas Plato's cosmology was thus influential, besides also the philosophical insights of Ptolemy, Pythagoras, and the Stoics, who related cosmology and ethical behavior, it was Aristotle's cosmology that was accepted as the overall picture and structure of the medieval cosmos. The only main aspect of it that was denied as contrary to the Abrahamic faiths, was the alleged eternity of the world, for it denied its creation by God.[31]

Every aspect of reality was seen to be part of a hierarchically structured cosmos consisting of God, the angels, the fixed stars and planets, the human being, the animals and plants. Whereas Aristotle's cosmos structurally consisted of fifty-five revolving concentric spheres with the earth at the center, in the Middle Ages a simplification was entertained. The latter consisted, with some variation regarding the outermost spheres, of the following: a spherical earth; seven spheres each associated with a heavenly body in the order that was found in both Plato and Aristotle, namely, Moon, Mercury, Venus, Sun, Mars, Jupiter, and Saturn; then an eighth sphere for the fixed stars; then non-astronomic spheres, namely, a ninth or Crystalline sphere associated with the angels, a tenth sphere or *Primum Mobile*, and the Empyrean.[32] As Edward Grant indicates, the planets were perceived to continuously revolve "in their ardent desire to come as close as possible to God."[33] In the meantime, the entire visible creation was held to have been made for use by the human being. Within the human society there were the distinctive classes: the clerical orders, the military, landowners, and the feudal peasants. The individual (whether powerful cleric or poor peasant) was destined for, or born in, a state and situation determined by God, as a wheel in a clock. The desires for understanding and mythic vision were often strongly intertwined, whereby the religious dimension was all-pervasive.

This medieval cosmos was not devoid of internal inconsistencies. The idea inherited from ancient times that the earth stood in the center of the universe and that the heavenly bodies circled around it appeared at first sight highly satisfactory for the human desire for order and harmony, and for the notion that the human being was most important in

---

30. Wildiers, *Kosmologie*, 85, 307 n. 22.
31. Grant, *Physical Science*, 60–61.
32. Ibid., 71–74; Wildiers, *Kosmologie*, 32; Randles, *Unmaking*, 1–31.
33. Grant, *Physical Science*, 71.

the universe. Nevertheless, Max Wildiers explains that there was paradox involved. He quotes the saying of the French thinker Blaise Pascal (1623–62) that shows the earth being held to be both "gloire et rebut de l'univers," the glory and the scum of the universe. Its glory because she was the place where the human being was living and where Christ came to enact his salvific work; its scum because she was perceived to consist out of the most imperfect matter. In addition, an even greater dubiousness was involved. For while the earth constituted the lower part of the hierarchical cosmic order, she was situated at the center of the universe. The dwelling place of God, the spiritual beings, and the fixed stars were found at the periphery of the circular cosmos, whereas the material earth was found at the center of the circle, which is unquestionably the most significant point of the circle, for it is the place where all radii of the circle come together. Worse still, it was thought that at the center of the earth hell was to be found (which is a perception continuous with that of the underworld within Hebrew cosmology). Hence, hell and the devil's throne stood in the middle of the universe, whereas God was at the periphery. It came to be realized that such cosmological perception amounted to a blasphemy.[34] The heliocentric worldview of Copernicus would resolve this contradiction. Moreover, not only the geocentric perception, but all aspects of the entire worldview would come to be challenged by various thinkers. Its overthrow, however, took place most of all due to the turn of historic events.

During the High Middle Ages, from the tenth through the thirteenth centuries, a steady population growth took place in Europe: from about twenty-five million in 950 to about seventy-five million in 1250. This period coincided with *the little optimum*, a period of warmer and favorable climate. From the late twelfth century onwards this period came to a close and until about the mid fourteenth century it got colder and wetter. This led to poorer crops. Land was also of increasingly marginal quality because of re-use. The result was that population growth could not be met by an increase in food production, and hence, an increased poverty and increased food prices. Peasants had to buy additional grain from the supplies of their feudal lords, which they had produced themselves. Famine came when crops failed, eventually widespread starvation by the end of the thirteenth and in the first decades of the fourteenth century. For example, in the years 1315–17 about 20 percent of the population

34. Wildiers, *Kosmologie*, 113–14.

Cosmic Prayer and Guided Transformation

of Ypres in Flanders perished. By 1320 many large urban centers lost up to 10 percent of their total population. People were reduced to eating dogs and cats, and in instances, apparently, resorted to eating the corpses of those who were hanged. Poor sanitation contributed to the spread of diseases. Very damaging were livestock epidemics that raged from 1316 to 1322. Profound social and economic changes took place: the structure of the feudal system was under strain, there was an increase in the power of merchants and of royal armies.[35] Then, in 1347, the Black Death, a combination of plague strains, entered Europe with an infected fleet at a Sicilian harbor. It spread across Europe from 1347 to 1351 and killed between seventeen and twenty-eight million people, between 25 and 45 percent of Europe's population. It is by many scholars considered *the* major turning point in the transition from medieval to modern Europe. As Robert S. Gottfried explains, "Depopulation virtually ended serfdom in western Europe."[36] The Black Death initiated a series of cyclic outbreaks of the disease until the eighteenth century. It also led to cynicism towards the clerics who were themselves in great numbers afflicted and who could not cure or banish the disease, while a number fled from their parishes. Yet, in light of the ever-present death, many people were also highly conscious of God's omnipotence and of their ultimate judgment. "Many Christians continued to follow their own path to salvation even after the plague had subsided and their priests had returned."[37] The pandemic plague that followed the Black Death struck every few years: about one hundred plague epidemics swept across Europe. The Great Plague of London in 1665 killed about one hundred thousand people (and basically ended with the Great Fire of London) and other cities were struck likewise.[38] Hence, negatively stated, a relaxation of the iron grip of the former clerical and feudal powers, that is, of the former hierarchy, took place not only by the work of a few thinkers.

In this wider context, Nicholas of Cusa (1401–64), Copernicus (1473–1543), Martin Luther (1483–1546), Johannes Kepler (1571–1630), Galileo Galileï (1564–1642), René Descartes (1596–1650), Isaac Newton (1642–1727), Immanuel Kant (1724–1804), Jean-Baptiste de Lamarck (1744–1829), and Charles Darwin (1809–82), are some of the

---

35. Gottfried, *Black Death*, 16–32.
36. Ibid., 136–37.
37. Ibid., 85.
38. Ibid., xiii–xvi, 77–103, 129–60.

Cosmos

great names that contributed to the dissolution of the medieval view and the liberation of, respectively, the individual, individual experience, and rational thought.[39] But as the former worldview collapsed, it was gradually replaced by the atomistic and mechanistic worldview of the rational sciences.[40] Thus, with the Enlightenment's positive differentiation of the various spheres of existence came also a fragmentation at every level of existence, individual, social, and cosmic, whereby the material instead of the spiritual was dominant. The progressive alienation of the human being within the cosmos was also accompanied by the introduction of various confused perceptions regarding God, namely, pantheistic, deistic, and atheistic.[41] Despite the human alienation within the cosmos and the reduced perception of the human as "the image of God," the transition from the Ptolemaic to the Copernican worldview was accompanied by an increased tendency towards anthropocentrism. The center of the universe had moved from the earth to the sun—and later the notion of center would dissolve in front of the uncountable galaxies—but this movement only took place for the material aspect. Copernicus himself had envisaged this shift of the center to include that towards a notion of the intellectual or spiritual dimension of the universe, yet gradually this latter aspect became seen as mere fantasy.[42]

Herewith, our survey of major periods of cosmological thought has brought us to the point where we can suitably return to the statement made at the very beginning of this book, namely that "in the West since the Enlightenment and until the beginning of the 1980s there had prevailed a notion of the universe that reduced it to a collection of material objects and that prevented the idea of a cosmos." I mentioned there with Brague that Eddington had an insight that signaled a new beginning for cosmology. Let us continue our journey and explore this further.

---

39. Wildiers, *Kosmologie*, 109–32, 167–70, 194–98; Randles, *Unmaking*.

40. Funkenstein, *Theology and Scientific Imagination*, 30–31, 41.

41. Van Peursen, *Body, Soul, Spirit*, 50–79; Nasr, *Encounter*, 51–80; Bohm, *Wholeness and the Implicate Order*, 1–24; Wildiers, *Kosmologie*, 137–70, 186, 211–12; Wilber, *Brief History*, 123–30, 261–77.

42. Nasr, *Encounter*, 66–68.

Cosmic Prayer and Guided Transformation

MODERN SCIENTIFIC INVESTIGATION OF THE PHYSICAL UNIVERSE LEADS INTO THE REALM OF THE METAPHYSICAL

It is a curious development that it is especially scientists who have given new impetus to a vision upon reality, akin to that of ancient times, whereby the material and spiritual dimensions of reality are closely, or rather indistinguishably, related. A famous early example is given by Eddington in his *New Pathways in Science* (1935):

> Let us now consider our answer to the question whether the nature of reality is material or spiritual or a combination of both....
>
> I will first ask another question. Is the ocean composed of water or of waves or of both? Some of my fellow passengers on the Atlantic were emphatically of the opinion that it is composed of waves, but I think the ordinary unprejudiced answer would be that it is composed of water. At least if we declare our belief that the nature of the ocean is aqueous, it is not likely that anyone will challenge us and assert that on the contrary its nature is undulatory, or that it is a dualism part aqueous and part undulatory. Similarly, I assert that the nature of all reality is spiritual, not material nor a dualism of matter and spirit. The hypothesis that its nature can be, to any degree, material does not enter into my reckoning, because as we now understand matter, the putting together of the adjective "material" and the noun "nature" does not make sense.
>
> Interpreting the term material (or more strictly, physical) in the broadest sense as that with which we can become acquainted through sensory experience of the external world, we recognise now that it corresponds to the waves, not to the water of the ocean of reality.... Like the symbolic world of physics, a wave is a conception which is hollow enough to hold almost anything; we can have waves of water, of air, of aether, and (in quantum theory) waves of probability.[43]

This passage is perhaps not so straightforward. It is clear that Eddington's consideration, which starts with a question, is about the ocean and the waves on its surface, not with a notion of wave that is part of a symbolic/mathematical description. Apparently, part of his intention is to illustrate that all we see with the eyes is but the visible manifestation at the surface

---

43. Eddington, *New Pathways*, 319–20.

of reality and that underlying and supporting this manifestation is an enormous depth of an intangible and spiritual nature. We can surmise about his fellow passengers; either they were speculating that the entire underlying ocean is simply layer upon layer of the same as we see on the surface and that there is nothing else to it; or they were colleague physicists acquainted with the results of quantum physics, and were teasingly answering by changing the intended meaning of the waves before their eyes around the ship, into the derived more generic sense of oscillations. Eddington wants to illustrate that all of reality is indeed an indivisible unity, not with a nature that presents itself readily to our eyes, not the surface-waves, but all is water; what is on the surface is well-considered the same as what constitutes the entire underlying volume. And indeed, with his colleague physicists, Eddington then explains that the foundation for his thoughts about the ocean lies in quantum physics. After the introduction of quantum physics, the fundamental entities of reality were no longer seen to be solid atoms but cloud-like geometrical patterns that indicate the probability of encountering a physical effect.[44] The embodied information and energy may present itself to us, depending on the particular aspect we focus our investigation on, as either material particles or symmetric fields of radiation, that is, patterns of oscillation at certain frequencies.[45] The ultimate or fundamental nature that underlies these manifestations escapes our gaze, both of our eyes and of our intellect, even though the embodied information can be represented and studied in symbols and mathematical equations. As Eddington's contemporary and colleague, James Jeans (1877–1946), expressed: "Thus we need hardly think of the waves as being located in space and time at all; they are mere visualisations of a mathematical formula of an undulatory, but wholly abstract, nature."[46]

The physical entities at subsequent levels of complexity, the elementary particles (or rather, vibrating "superstrings" or "M-branes"), atoms, molecules, inorganic crystals and organic cells, organisms, ecosystems, and galaxies, show evermore complex and involved combinations of oscillations or patterns of radiation. The late American professor of chemistry and music-lover, Donald Hatch Andrews (1898–1973), wrote a book

44. Finbar, *Organic Chemistry*, 28–33; Greene, *Cosmos*, 88–92.
45. Broglie, *Matter and Light*; Heisenberg, *Physicist's Conception*, 158–78; Davies, *God and New Physics* (concerning the two-slit experiment of Young); Laszlo, *Creative Cosmos*, 74–80; Greene, *Cosmos*, 177–99 (further variants of the two-slit experiment).
46. Jeans, *Mysterious Universe*, 150.

called *The Symphony of Life* (1966) wherein he described all reality as music; from single notes to entire symphonies. At the ultramicroscopic level this has been supported by the following theories: firstly, by string theory (in the 1960s), which instead of point particles posits the existence of one-dimensional vibrating filaments of energy; secondly, by superstring theory (since 1970s), which posits that besides the three large-scale space dimensions and the time dimension there exist several additional dimensions that at each point of the macro-space dimensions are curled up to a minute order of scale or that are large but escape present investigations, so that physical reality would be composed of ten spacetime dimensions (nine spatial and one time dimension); and thirdly, by the currently developed M-theory (since 1995), which instead of single-dimensional strings posits the existence of two-or-higher-dimensional entities that are called "M-branes" within a cosmic substrate composed of eleven spacetime dimensions.[47] The physicist Brian Greene exclaims regarding string theory, "If string theory is correct . . . at the ultramicroscopic level, the universe would be akin to a string symphony vibrating matter into existence."[48]

Eddington's image of the sea and its waves, which is also recalled by Jeans and later scientists,[49] invites us to make the observation that the scientific study of the physical reality has not led to a completely worked out and thus closed presentation of a material ground of reality—even though the various string theories and spin network theories[50] appear to be promising for a grand unified theory or GUT of the forces that make up the conventional physical description—but has opened up to a realm that eludes total comprehension, transcending the material manifestation. Moreover, neither is there so far a satisfactory comprehensive theory of the emergence of higher levels of complexity out of the physical ground of reality (a general evolutionary theory or GET).[51] This does not

---

47. Laszlo, *Creative Cosmos*, 46; Kauffman, *Investigations*, 259–61; Greene, *Cosmos*, 17–19, 327–412.

48. Greene, *Cosmos*, 347.

49. Jeans, *Mysterious Universe*, 139 (where he likens the universe with the surface of a soap-bubble), 155–56, 169, 187 (in these pages he considers the essence of the universe to be a reality of thought); Bohm, *Wholeness and the Implicate Order*, 242, 267; Laszlo, *Creative Cosmos*, 37, 87–89.

50. Kauffman, *Investigations*, 253–56.

51. This does not deny that significant contributions have been made in, for example, Kauffman, *Origins* and *Investigations*.

imply that the physicist or biologist is immediately prompted to conclude that the solution is found in a metaphysical realm, or with God. But to us, who are reflecting here from a faith perspective, it is an invitation to envisage a reality that does not starkly delineate the physical from the metaphysical; it points us to one cosmos that can include both realms.

Indeed, the immaterial waves referred to by Eddingon and Jeans and that function in mathematical theories, remind of the ancient Hellenic philosophies, of the *dābār* concept, and of the *logos* doctrine. We earlier found that Maximus envisaged that God's Word, which contains the *logoi*, is embodied in, among others, the words of Scripture. This is reflected in the fact that these texts can be read in more than one manner—there is the literal meaning that stays close to the immediate context wherein the author has written, and there are often the more spiritual or hidden meanings that have a wider application, this to the extent that these words contain truth stemming from God that is life giving. The waves of physical theory, not entirely dissimilar to the written words, give rise to a reality that can, as it were, be read or experienced in various ways; namely, as corpuscular and as oscillatory. Rising to the level of the envisioned symphony of macroscopic reality and of life, brought about by intricate combinations of, say, "superstrings" and conceived as being brought about in accordance with the mathematic wave-like conceptions, we are reminded of the *logoi* and the combinations thereof that Maximus conceived at the origin of various created sensible (or physical) and intelligible (or metaphysical or spiritual) entities.

This book is, however, not advocating a "God of the gaps," who would be deciding upon the outcome of every unpredictability (that is nevertheless accounted for by the current theoretical framework of natural laws) at the quantum level or at the bifurcation points (where the physical system can opt for various courses of events that are energetically equivalent) of non-linear macroscopic systems. Rather, God who truly is (Exod 3:14), creates the world as a whole by bringing it into being and by informing the whole and every entity through Word and Spirit. It is, however, not an *in-forming* that stringently determines every quantum or macroscopic event. According to the perception upheld in this book, God rather invites and guides every partial system at every level into an intra-cosmic harmonization and into communion with himself. There is, as contemporary science discerns, within the created order an inbuilt flexibility that eventually allows for free will and that enables a

Cosmic Prayer and Guided Transformation

truly creaturely co-creative outreach for what is natural and beyond the natural; it allows for prayer and divine answer.[52]

What then about participation in intelligence within the created order?

CONTEMPORARY SCIENCE FINDS EVERY FORM OF EXISTENCE TO PARTAKE TO SOME DEGREE IN A NOETIC FEATURE/INTELLIGENCE

God is believed in as creating an organized cosmos by speaking his word, by informing all things with an intelligible content. In accord with this, Gregory of Nyssa held that the human mind is intended to be governed by God, so as to mirror the divine beauty and goodness throughout the body. Moreover, reflecting with the science of his day upon the detail of phenomena such as grief and laughter, he perceived that the human mind/spirit/intelligence is not bound to a particular organ (either the heart, or liver, or brain) but expands its influence throughout the body.[53] Contemporary natural sciences appear to reconnect with this ancient insight of a non-excluding participation in intelligence suited to each one's creaturely nature and to every constituent (even though positive science does not pronounce itself on whether this mirrors the divine source).

The emergent scientific worldview leads Mariano Artigas, Professor of Natural Science, and Harold J. Morowitz, Professor of Biology and Natural Philosophy, to consider with regard to Pauli's exclusion principle for electrons, that there is a kind of noetic feature deep in physics.[54] Several other scientists and philosophers of science have detected a participation in a certain level of intelligence within physical reality.[55] Also in biology one finds that organic cells already possess a degree of apparent purposive behavior. Subsequently, basic organisms such as prokaryotes (that is, bacteria) and protoctists (that is, algae, slime moulds, and protozoa)

---

52. Polkinghorne, "Laws," 445–48; Drees, "Gaps," 223–37; Moltmann, "Reflections," 205–10; Peacocke, "Chance and Law," 140–42; Peacock, "God's Interaction," 277–87.

53. Nyssa *De hominis opificio* 12; PG 44:156C–64D; Behr, "Rational Animal," 228–31.

54. Artigas, *Mind of the Universe*, 90–91, 120–21, 130; Morowitz, *Emergence of Everything*, 101.

55. Dyson, *Infinite*, 297; Laszlo, *Science and Reenchantment*, 53, 62; Harding, *Animate Earth*, 87–90.

manifest a complexity of behavior in reaction upon external situations.[56] In the brain, the enormous complex combination of nerve cells, or neurons, opens up to self-aware consciousness.[57] Mind does then, however, not suddenly appear within the enlarged human brain—neither are neurons only found in the brain, but throughout the body—but has gradually emerged and developed within the natural realm. Furthermore, besides the brain, at other instances of great complexity in the physical realm, one comes to discern signs of the existence of associated organizing intelligence. Continuous with this, we can envisage complex patterns of form and energy that are not bound to any material manifestation, even though they may have an influence upon the material, that is, spiritual beings. As such, whether we start with an observation of the world (within and) around us, or with the particular revelations in the Scriptures that speak of angels, we are invited to a single view of the total reality, namely of an entire gamma of beings ranging from the "simplest" uncompounded material/vibrational towards the purely spiritual.

This notion of a universal participation in a noetic feature/intelligence, in combination with insight into the inseparability of the physical and the metaphysical as explored in the previous section, leads to the following general notion: at every level of the created reality we find that an entity can manifest itself in a dual manner. Such dualism characteristic of reality is not to be resolved into a duality, neither to be reduced to a one dimensionality. Instances of this dualism are the following: matter/energy; particle/wave; chemico-physical processes in the brain/thought; biological and chemico-physical processes within an organism, within ecosystems, and within the wider natural realm/mind; purpose-directed behavior and intelligence/soul; interactive existence/body; structure/organization; physical processes/spiritual dynamic; various partial realities combined/a whole; a sustained network of interdependent entities in harmony/cosmos.

The here suggested instances give expression of the dual character of reality. They may obviously invite much reflection and some couples may perhaps find an improved formulation. Resources that can inform and further stimulate such reflection include: Erwin Schrödinger, *Mind and Matter* (1958); Deepak Chopra, *Quantum Healing* (1989); Marian

---

56. Margulis, *Symbiotic Planet*; Morowitz, *Emergence of Everything*, 101–5.
57. Greenfield, *Brain Story*.

Stamp Dawkins, *Through Our Eyes Only?* (1993); Donald R. Griffin, *Animal Minds* (2001); Stephen Harding, *Animate Earth* (2006).

Sometimes both manifestations can to some extent (but hardly ever in their entirety) be observed directly with the senses, but often one is more or less observed directly, the other indirectly. Some entities may quasi-permanently be in a certain circumstance, which allows them to be associated with a particular (non-dual) manifestation of their existence. For example: a stone is usually associated with matter, even though this enshrines a quantity of energy. Even a stone, moreover, is only a quasi-permanent manifestation. For stones are eroded by weathering, and they may be partial realities within cyclical processes on geological timescales that contribute to life on earth and that are expressive of the activity of mind. Turning towards the other end of the spectrum, we find another example: namely, a spiritual being exists beyond the confines of space and time and is thus traditionally believed in as invisible and bodiless, even though, being not divine, it has a certain intangible form and can allegedly sometimes take on a visible body during a mission on earth so as to be seen and heard. For even spiritual beings lead an interactive existence and receive ultimate salvation through service, perhaps for life on earth, and through being cooperative for the establishment of a sustained network of interdependent entities in harmony wherein they are called to be an integral part.

Physicist and theologian Polkinghorne can be included among those sympathetic to the idea of there being a dual character of reality. He envisages "a dual-aspect monism, in which the mental and the material are conceived of as being opposite poles (or phases, as a physicist might say) of a single (created) reality. A key idea may well be that of complementarity."[58]

If, as Evagrius (345/6–399) held, prayer is an act of the intellect (νοῦς),[59] then, given that in one way or other everything contributes to, or partakes in, intelligence, and given that, moreover, everything has significance within God's creation, then this (condition of intelligence) does not imply that we can readily exclude any non-human existence from the great project of prayer. Furthermore, entertaining such perception is in

---

58. Polkinghorne, "Metaphysics," 154–55; in earlier writings Polkinghorne expressed himself similarly: e.g., Polkinghorne, "Laws," 444–45.

59. Evagrius *De oratione* 3, 36; PG 79:1168, 1173. Likewise Healy, "Prayer (Theology of)," 595–96.

accord with the scriptural notion that both the origin and the destiny of the created order are spiritual.

The ancient Hebrew and Hellenic cosmologies, as well as contemporary science, support the notion that an entity exists by the fact that it embodies certain information. It is, however, only by the intimate cooperation of many constitutive entities that created identities of a corporeal nature emerge with an own form that can interact intelligently with their surroundings. It is the emergence of such corporeal unities within the universe, and as constitutive of the universe, that I propose we now consider in more detail.

THE CORPOREAL UNITY OF THE UNIVERSE AND ITS SUITABILITY FOR INTEGRATED AND DIFFERENTIATED HARMONIZATION

The unity of the physical universe, at least that section of it that is within reach of human observation, has for long been discerned by the various natural sciences. The following paragraphs will illustrate this:

To begin with, there is Newton's Law of Gravitation, which describes the attractive force that material bodies exert upon each other. It is a law that was discovered for the planets and the Sun by Kepler, but that Newton posited to be applicable to all bodies of whatever size and this throughout the universe.[60] Consequently, Newton was confronted with the dilemma that this force seemed to mysteriously connect the various bodies in a single system without a sensible medium. He knew that promoting action-at-a-distance would have led him to be accused of introducing a return to occultism. He thus accepted that his gravity force required to be combined with a notion of ether that filled the entire space. Earlier, among others, Thomas Aquinas had posited, in alignment with Aristotle's αἰθήρ, the existence of a fifth essence (*quinta essentia*), which he believed to surround the physical universe, which was held to be constituted by four elements.[61] Later, Tycho Brahe, his disciple Kepler, and Descartes had all held various notions about the ether as filling the

---

60. Feynman, *Physical Law*, 13–34.

61. Randles, *Unmaking*, 19–24; Brague, *Wisdom of the World*, 178–79. Aristotle's inspiration would have been derived from *Timaeus*, 58D and *Phaedo*, (98C), 109C, 111B.

Cosmic Prayer and Guided Transformation

planetary space above the airy atmosphere.[62] Yet, Newton considered that it could not be a corporeal fluid, as Descartes posited, having a density, for this would inhibit the planetary movements. Because Kepler's astronomical laws described the planets as moving through a frictionless void. Hence, Newton sought association with Stoic philosophy, which, as we already encountered in chapter 2, posited a kind of subtly omnipresent spirit or fire, having the properties of a special kind of material substance.[63] This implied in the eyes of certain of Newton's readers an identification of space and God, which Newton himself, however, according to W. G. L. Randles did not want to overtly subscribe to. Nevertheless, as indicated by Randles, Edward Grant considers that Newton did conceive of God as incorporeal ether.[64] Alternatively, Amos Funkenstein and more recently Simon Oliver hold that for Newton space was a "sensorium," or a "sense organ," of God.[65] Moltmann dismisses this opinion and considers that instead Newton merely used the expression in a figurative sense.[66] Looked upon from a present-day perspective, Newton's struggles with the ether field were anticipatory to modern notions of force fields, in particular, regarding gravitation, Albert Einstein's gravitational field.[67]

A next significant step towards perception of the corporeal unity of the universe was introduced by Michael Faraday's (1791–1867) experiments at the beginning of the nineteenth century that led to the introduction of electric and magnetic fields. These concepts were later entwined by James Clerk Maxwell (1831–1879), which led to the idea of electromagnetic fields and the electromagnetic force. Subsequently, Einstein (1879–1955) introduced gravitational fields, while quantum mechanics introduced quantum fields to explain the nuclear forces. More recently, the unification of the electromagnetic and the weak nuclear forces into the electroweak theory has been accompanied by the introduction of the (still hypothetical) electroweak Higgs field. Prevalent in all this is the

---

62. Randles, *Unmaking*, 74–79, 130.

63. Toulmin and Goodfield, *Architecture of Matter*, 111–13, 217–18.

64. Randles, *Unmaking*, 129–32; see also Grant, *Physical Science*, 81–82.

65. Funkenstein, *Theology and Scientific Imagination*, 96–97; Oliver, *Philosophy, God and Motion*, 173–83.

66. Moltmann, *God in Creation*, 154–55.

67. Toulmin and Goodfield, *Architecture of Matter*, 217–21; Davies, *About Time*, 48–51; Pecker, *Understanding the Heavens*, 294–95, 387, 407; Greene, *Cosmos*, 8, 43–45, 68–72.

recognition of interdependence instead of localized effects; the recognition that everything is interconnected.[68]

Within our human sphere, the non-locality of events, in particular the reflection of light waves or photons by an illumined object, enables the techniques of the two-dimensional photographic plate, the time-inclusive film, and the three-dimensional hologram.[69]

The common origin and the interdependent emergence and sustenance of various entities (astronomical and biological) and kinds are postulated in natural evolution theories. For natural evolution (of the galactic, geological and biological spheres of reality) takes place as a continuous striving towards harmonious integration of various co-existent entities, which leads not to a lower order uniformity but to a higher order, or complex, structure as manifested by the inter-connectivity and variety of participant entities (such as make up an ecological system) and by organismically organized beings. Illustrative of this is the recognition that our bodies contain most of the common chemical elements, which were produced by the nuclear reactions in earlier generation stars that have since exploded. In addition, we can likewise reflect upon the complex molecules that are contained in our cells, upon the form of our bodies and upon our behavioral tendencies. All these situate us not only within humanity, but within the context of other earlier higher animals, of the totality of life forms, the earth's constitution, movement, and place in the solar system, and within the universe.

The idea that physical reality, including all manners of biological manifestation therein, forms a single and, moreover, comprehensible, system, at least for its material ground, has been pursued in the earlier mentioned search for a GUT and GET.

Physicists were also being challenged to attain a greater understanding of the universe's unity by the famous Einstein-Podolsky-Rosen thought-experiment. This experiment was proposed in 1935, formulated as a verifiable inequality by John Bell in 1969, experimentally tested by Alain Aspect in 1982,[70] and tested in another version of the experiment by physicists in 1997. The experiment turns out to show that two photons emitted by the same source in opposite directions and that travel unim-

---

68. Einstein, *Relativity*, 63–65, 74–78; Greene, *Cosmos*, 40–44.

69. Bohm, *Wholeness and the Implicate Order*, 182–86; Landsberg, *Cours élémentaire*, 329–46.

70. Espagnat, "Quantum Theory," 128–40; Bohm, *Wholeness and the Implicate Order*, 91–102; Barrow, *World within the World*, 145–50.

peded behave as a single physical system: the two particles are in so-called *quantum entanglement*. Changes imposed by the experimenters upon a photon at one side are instantaneously and automatically complemented by that on the other side. This excludes the exchange of an information-packet at light-speed (which is the maximum possible) by a mediating particle,[71] but rather suggests the existence of (a) higher ontological level(s), ultimately the workings of mind, relating both photons.

In agreement with this, quantum theory has discerned that no strict object-subject independence can be maintained. As such, the external reality that we perceive is co-determined by the very fact of our conscious observation, and we thus influence the movements of particles.[72] However, while as different people we each consciously look upon reality, we observe to large extent the same reality. This led physicist Schrödinger to argue that there is no plurality of consciousness, as is apparent, but that ultimately we all partake in a single consciousness (comparison with Carl G. Jung's proposition of humankind's "collective unconscious" suggests itself), and he searched for this perception association with, among others, the Upanishads.[73] But many physicists have since pursued as explanation for the difference between the quantum realm and that of the macro-world the phenomenon of *decoherence*: that is, the many photons and air molecules that continually bombard macroscopic objects disturb their wave function so that quantum interference does not occur. However, as Greene observes, it remains thereby unexplained how the collapse of quantum probabilities into a particular outcome effectively takes place through *decoherence*.[74]

An example of an atheistic interpretation of the observed unity of the universe is that of the physicist David Bohm (1917–92). In *Wholeness and the Implicate Order* (1980) Bohm proposed that things or material processes, and intelligence or thoughts, are both abstractions of "one undefinable and unknown totality of flux."[75] As Bohm envisaged: "The particle is only an abstraction that is manifest to our senses. *What is* is always a totality of ensembles, all present together, in an orderly series of stages of enfoldment and unfoldment, which intermingle and inter-

---

71. Clarke, *Living in Connection*, 54–58, 69, 246–51; Laszlo, *Science and Reenchantment*, 12–14; Greene, *Cosmos*, 99–123.

72. Greene, *Cosmos*, 181–99.

73. Schrödinger, *What Is Life?*, 86–90; *Mind and Matter*, 128–37.

74. Greene, *Cosmos*, 208–13.

75. Bohm, *Wholeness and the Implicate Order*, 69–70.

Cosmos

penetrate each other in principle throughout the whole of space."[76] What he considers to be fundamental is "the implicate order," which is "a process of enfoldment and unfoldment in a higher-dimensional space."[77] Referring to the image of Eddington presented earlier, Bohm presents this as his idea of space, containing an immense background of energy, so that the material manifestation we are acquainted with is rather like a tiny ripple on the surface.[78] It is a rather original suggestion, but as Polkinghorne observes, Bohm's idea includes a complete determinacy of physical reality.[79]

Without particular reference to the quantum-world, but to the irregular Brownian movement of a small particle suspended in a liquid, Schrödinger pointed out in *What is Life?* (1944) that in the macro-world the movements of many particles together result in the regular phenomena we are familiar with. Expanding this train of thought, he emphasized that the laws governing biological life cannot be deduced from the physical laws that govern inanimate matter, but that, on the contrary, the phenomenon of life is based on stability at the atomic level (allowing maintenance of genes).[80] Schrödinger then suggested, as we have seen, that it is an *I*, a person having mind, who guides and directs the atomic motions, yet without breach of physical laws at the micro-level.[81]

At a somewhat later date, the idea of various ontological levels has also been reflected upon by polymath Arthur Koestler (1905–85). Koestler introduced in *The Ghost in the Machine* (1967) the term "holon" "to refer to an entity that is itself a *whole* and simultaneously a *part* of some other whole."[82] He thereby envisaged the notion that reality consists of *holons* within *holons*. Accordingly, there are various interactive levels of reality containing *holons* that each possess a certain autonomy, a form, identity, and capacity, which cannot be found as the mere sum total of the parts.[83] The idea that the whole is more than the sum of its parts is, in fact,

---

76. Ibid., 233; and again at 257.
77. Ibid., 240.
78. Ibid., 242.
79. Polkinghorne, "Metaphysics," 148.
80. Schrödinger, *What Is Life?*, 78–80.
81. Ibid., 87.
82. Koestler, *Ghost*, 66.
83. Ibid., 72.

an idea that was held by the Stoics.[84] At certain ontological levels there may be situated several *holons*. The number of *holons* at a certain level is called by Koestler (after H. J. Simon) its "span."[85]

Reflection upon a higher ontological level as a kind of unifying field—that appears to be as a new step of a tradition of pursuit that included Aristotle's *aithēr*, the Stoics' fire, Newton's *aether*, and the physical fields of contemporary physics—has been taken further by Rupert Sheldrake in *A New Science of Life* (1981, 1985), where he presented the idea of (non-physical) morphogenetic fields. This idea, combined with that of *holons*, is being pursued in the new biology for addressing, among others, the problem how identical cells "know" to constitute a macroscopic organism by each activating the appropriate genes according to their location, and hence function, in the whole.[86]

The cooperation of various subsystems, which may be of different natures, and the coordinated phenomena they bring about is studied in the interdisciplinary new science of synergetics. This discipline is likely to lead to insights into the relationship between microscopic or particular subsystems and the macroscopic system or organism.[87]

Overall, lower ontological levels are increasingly perceived to contribute in the formation of higher, more inclusive, ontological levels that manifest their proper forms and more complex activity, even from a certain level onwards intelligence. Reciprocally, the higher levels draw the former levels into an integrated, yet differentiated, unity.

All this illustrates that the notion of unity has been crucial for the natural sciences in their pursuit of a better understanding of the physical universe. An integral part of insight into the corporeal unity of the universe is the perception that the universe forms a unity in view of its single origin. That is to say, for the scientist it is the physical universe that observes the *Cosmological Principle*, which states that it is the same in properties everywhere[88] and this in view of the big bang, a single superforce flowing from it, and non-localized physical fields. For the theist the single unifying origin of the entire universe is ultimately the creative

84. Funkenstein, *Theology and the Scientific Imagination*, 39.

85. Koestler, *Ghost*, 67, 384.

86. Koestler, *Ghost*, 146–50; Sheldrake, *New Science*; Harman and Sahtouris, *Biology Revisioned*.

87. Haken, *Synergetics*; *Advanced Synergetics*.

88. Funkenstein, *Theology and the Scientific Imagination*, 91; Barrow, *World within the World*, 204–12.

deity.[89] In particular, for Christians it is God the Father who creates by his only-begotten Son and by the Spirit, and who is also consciously present to it. All created reality receives being, as it were, through the creative vibrations of God's hovering Spirit, or breath, and of God's creative pronouncements that constitute a single Logos; and all God's works are realized in wisdom (Ps 104:24). There is one God, one Spirit, one Logos, one wisdom, and, hence, one creation.

Thereby, the unity at every particular instant in time of every then existing level of the universe that is becoming, is given a potential by God for a higher-order, more actualized, union. For the union between two groups of particles and, subsequently, of higher-order conglomerates at different corners of the universe is but meaningful when, informed by intelligence—originally the divine intelligence, and this conceivably through angelic mediation—they contribute to organismic structures and organizations, ultimately also of an all-encompassing sort, that carry a purpose. This purpose is to contribute in created intelligence and interpersonal communion. It involves a transformation from lower, more elementary levels of existence towards higher levels of existence and towards human beings, but concomitant with this, a transformation also of the encompassing universal totality towards participation in personal communion, even with God.

Hence, in view of the universal interconnectivity, it is likely that the mental abilities of human beings and their ability to focus their journey upon God and upon their transfiguration towards the personal, have bearings upon the entire universe and its transformation.[90] Further, in addition to the hierarchies that consist of *holons* (or *holarchies*, which is another word coined by Koestler) and that make the lower, more elementary, essential for the higher, more composed,[91] there are according to the Judaeo-Christian tradition the spiritual beings who are freely engaged with all other lower levels so as to provide information and orientation.

Let us reflect somewhat further upon the universe's suitability for integrated and differentiated harmonization. Such reflection should increase our comprehension regarding the assertion that the destiny and purpose of the created order is relationship with God. It will involve reflection upon the emergence of created entities that can interact

---

89. Funkenstein, *Theology and the Scientific Imagination*, 192–95 (regarding Newton's belief in God's omnipotence); Moltmann, *Jesus Christ*, 288.

90. Similarly, Rahner, "Christology," 161, 168.

91. Koestler, *Ghost*, 125–26.

intelligently and reflection upon transfiguration towards the personal. The approach adopted will let us once more return to the earliest period of the time-line and will let us travel from thence onward so as to obtain the broadest possible informed impression. As such, a first relevant observation is that simple uncompounded materials will under influence of physical forces such as gravitation and thermal movements tend towards an undifferentiated homogeneous equilibrium. Yet, because of the kinetic energy created at the universe's beginning, the material particles were blown in different directions. The heavenly bodies that later emerged under influence of gravitation have settled upon relative positions and velocities that allow their co-existence for very long periods and that allow for superstructures such as galaxies and superclusters.

Subsequently, in the oceans of the early earth, which contained a great variety of chemicals that were stirred by volcanic explosions and bombarded with electric discharges, a climate was formed that was suited for allowing complex molecular combinations without immediate dissolvement into a homogeneous liquid. In general, the complex organic molecules that have emerged on earth have tended to exploit their external circumstances so as to resist dissolvement.

Similarly, certain liquid crystals especially (which are omnipresent in biological systems) will under the right conditions and in a specific limited temperature range, form one or more so-called blue phases wherein the molecules take on highly complex macro-configurations.[92] Besides this curious happening, the emergence of order out of an initial disorder in the absence of organizing actions takes place in the so-called stochastization of non-linear dynamic systems.[93] Such systems form so-called dissipative structures in a situation far from equilibrium.[94]

It is, however, especially the hallmark of life to allow for highly organized entities that resist chaos, that are able to reproduce their information content and to give rise to new entities that evolve in a non-deterministic manner. Whereas dead matter will eventually always decay and lose its order, life knows to constantly renew itself. Our bodies are constantly renewed, whereas our clothes are worn down.[95] Similarly,

---

92. Crooker, "Blue Phases," 186–222.

93. Haken, *Synergetics*; *Advanced Synergetics*, 20–21, 341; Gapanov-Grekhov and Rabinovich, "Nonlinear Physics," 230–92.

94. Prigogine and Stengers, *Order out of Chaos*; Peacocke, *Theology for a Scientific Age*, 51–53, 64; Peacock, "God's Interaction," 268–72; Capra, *Web of Life*, 86–89.

95. Schrödinger, *What Is Life?*, 68–70.

Cosmos

entire ecosystems, the earth as a whole, and perhaps even the universe, manifest a self-regulatory capacity as is attributed to life and intelligence.[96] Under influence of these observations, the paradigm of the machine, prevalent in the previous modern period, has been replaced with that of the organism: especially by Whitehead who initiated this notion with his philosophy that he described as a "philosophy of organism."[97]

Life exists as a combination of constituents in a labile equilibrium. Survival is possible by upholding this situation. The chance of survival is increased by an increased variation and complexity, which increases the chance to react appropriately to external and internal changes. Life has thus led towards mind. While, as proposed by Schrödinger, vice versa, personal intelligence enables the process of life. There would therefore be a reciprocal dynamic initiated by the transcendent personal intelligence.

We can and need thus to go beyond the aspect of survival for properly appreciating the meaning of the emergence of created intelligence. For life not only maintains itself for the mere sake of being alive; it reaches towards a multifarious participation in the personal. Whereas the universe forms a unity in view of its single origin, which can be either scientifically or theologically perceived, it strives through its various developing manifestations of intelligence (from the universal to the local), as well as through the spiritual beings, towards an actual unification that involves the harmonization of all intelligence-bearing entities, without them conglomerating into a reality that carries a single undifferentiated experience of consciousness, so that all beings can become integral participant in the personal worship of God and relationship with God that is marked by love, joy, and every good virtue.

Life, as characterized here, allowing various constituents to come together into a stable, organized and shared existence, and thus into organisms, can thereby be seen to be an apt precursor to love, which brings the participants together into an intimate two (or indeed three)-oneness. Hence, life and love are closely associated.

The objective of physical science remained, however, the search for one formula/one law. It therefore needed to leave out of the equation any notion of feeling, virtues, and humanness. To allow for these the mathematical law has to be complemented with other dimensions.[98]

96. Lovelock, *Ages of Gaia*; Harding, *Animate Earth*.

97. Whitehead, *Science and the Modern World*, 80, 94ff., 129–30, 164ff.; Wildiers, *Kosmologie*, 237–43; Capra, *Web of Life*, 26–35, 187–88.

98. See also Feynman, *Physical Law*, 124–26.

Cosmic Prayer and Guided Transformation

Hence, arguably, it makes more sense to believe that there is a personal or beyond-personal reality at the origin of everything.

In this belief we can round off this chapter. We have so far been reflecting that Christian faith professes God to be personal and that the transformation towards participation in him is therefore a transformation towards the personal. We are thus summoned to look in the next chapter more closely at the meaning of the personal and person. But let us for a moment recapitulate this long chapter. The various cosmologies that we have explored have each of them aspects that are best discarded, but they can also be seen to have each contributed insight that is valuable for enabling continuation on the way towards a wholesome and truthful perception of the Creator-creature relationship. There is no need here to repeat ourselves concerning the insights of the Hebrew cosmology or of the Hellenic philosophers. As for the inheritance of the medieval cosmology, it includes the idea that the various beings, both those on earth, the heavenly bodies, and those of a spiritual nature, are organized in a hierarchical structure. In more recent times, it has been more clearly realized by some thinkers that every level of existence and every *holon* are equally essential for the entire web of creation and of life. The period of the Enlightenment has perhaps left us the positive inheritance of an appreciation for the individual and the particular. For life, love, and personal relationship with God are not only about different classes within humanity, and not only about various lower and higher species, but about particular beings that are touched by God, that touch him, and that each in their own place and manner contribute in various ontological levels of existence, ultimately in a single harmonious cosmos, and that each contribute in the creaturely desire to enjoy fullness of being in God.

4

Person

THE EMERGENCE OF THE CONCEPT "PERSON"

IN THE PREVIOUS CHAPTERS we have been reflecting that the creative process is not without direction or meaning, but that it reaches towards a multifarious participation in the personal. For at the origin of the created order and at its destiny is the personal God, who wishes by a dialectical process to bring the universe into being in an intimate communion with and within himself, especially through its personification within the risen Christ and this through and in the Spirit. It is key to the vision of Paul (Gal 3:28; 5:25; 1 Cor 6:11; 12:13; 15:28; 2 Cor 1:22) and later, at the end of the patristic era, of Maximus, whom we quoted in chapter 2 as having said that, "For always and in all, the Word of God, and God, wants the mystery of his embodiment to be accomplished" (*Ambigua 7*). With the objective of increasing insight into creation's multifarious participation in the personal in Christ and in the Spirit, we pursue in this chapter insight into the notion of a person and the personal. We will also reflect upon the place of human beings as regards the personal. We start with a reflection upon the emergence of this concept "person" with which we are so acquainted in our daily conversations.

The original meaning of the Latin word *persona* is associated with the "role" played by an actor in the Roman theatre who thereby took on

Cosmic Prayer and Guided Transformation

a "mask" or a "face." The word's meaning is equivalent to that of *prosōpon* (πρόσωπον), which originally indicated the face or countenance and as derived from this it meant in the theatrical setting again "mask." Scripture depicts God as entering into dialogue with people, as speaking by the mouth of the prophets, and as revealed in the face and life of Jesus. The word πρόσωπον thus occurred in Scripture in its original meaning with reference to God and came to indicate the fact of his presence (e.g., Mark 1:2; Acts 3:20); its Latin counterpart came to be similarly used with reference to God. Ratzinger (Pope Benedict XVI) concludes that "the idea of person expresses in its origin the idea of dialogue and the idea of God as the dialogical being."[1]

Staying close to the scriptural meaning of πρόσωπον, the Latin Tertullian (c.160–220) used the term *persona* for doctrine of the Holy Trinity. Tertullian held that the Father, Son, and Spirit partake in the one undivided reality and substance of God. He spoke of *una substantia* in *tres personae*, but the latter were not thereby understood to have an intrinsic ontological content.[2] Following upon these historical initiations, it is in the patristic reflection upon the co-existence of Father, Son, and Spirit, as well as in the reflection upon the mystery in Christ, that the notion of personhood in the modern sense emerged. In addition, antecedent and instrumental were the Israelite conceptions of the human individual as a psycho-physical organism that transcends the contours of the visible body and of God as at once both one and many.[3]

A further Western contribution in the development of the concept was made by Augustine, mainly in his work *On the Trinity*. This contribution has been partly positive and, arguably, partly negative in its effects. The positive aspect of his contribution is his insight that the divine persons exist both with their own selfhood and yet at the same time are directed towards the others; that God is thus constituted by a network of subsisting relations.[4] His *Confessions* indicate thereby the significance that he attributed to self-consciousness and other-consciousness in his notion of personhood. Zizioulas argues that the negative aspect of Augustine's

---

1. Ratzinger, "Retrieving the Tradition," 443.

2. Tertullian *Adversus Praxean* 12:6–7; text and trans. Evans, *Treatise Against Praxeas*, 102, 146.

3. Johnson, *Israelite Conception of God*; Johnson, *Vitality of the Individual*.

4. Augustine *De Trinitate* 5:6, 9–11; PL 42:913–14, 916–18; trans. Hill, *The Trinity*, 191–92, 195–96; Ratzinger, "Retrieving the Tradition," 444; Dorenkemper, "Person (in Theology)," 149.

Person

contribution is the positing of substance as a prior ontological category to the divine persons,[5] and this in continuation of his overt reliance upon classical Greek philosophy (Plato, Aristotle). LaCugna indicates that in *On the Trinity*, book 5, Augustine had indeed cited Father, Son, and Spirit in relative terms, but that in *On the Trinity*, book 7, he equates person with substance, (the person of the Father with the substance of the Father); that for God *to be* and *to be a person* are the same.[6] Zizioulas's critique is thus not sufficiently nuanced and is partial, even though the subject matter does indeed not seem to have been satisfactorily resolved in Augustine's work; Augustine's contribution was not a conclusive word on the matter. As regards the second half of *On the Trinity*, Ratzinger assesses that Augustine tried to understand the human being as an image of the Trinity whereby "he projected the divine persons into the interior life of the human person and affirmed that intra-psychic processes correspond to these persons." Complementarily, the human being as a whole is considered to correspond to the divine substance. As a consequence, whereas Augustine's was a valid desire to comprehend people's participating in the divinity, his work has contributed to a perception that (from the outside) God is encountered as singular (a divine "I") and that the Trinity is a reality within God's interior.[7]

Subsequently, in the sixth century, Boethius put forward a definition of the person that until recently prevailed in Western philosophy. Ratzinger explains that this definition is more to be criticized as remaining on the level of Greek thought, which reflects in substantialist terms. For Boethius placed the concept of person entirely on the level of substance;[8] according to his definition a person is "an individual substance of a rational nature"[9] and who, by implication, only in the second instance enters into external relationships. This definition, amplified by Augustine's individualistic perception of salvation has strongly contributed to the entire subsequent individualistic Western culture.[10] The definition was

---

5. Zizioulas, *Being as Communion*, 88.

6. Augustine, *De Trinitate* 5:7–10; 7:11; PL 42:916–17, 943; LaCugna, *God for Us*, 88–91; see also Fiddes, *Creative Suffering*, 139–40 and *Participating in God*, 34.

7. Ratzinger, "Retrieving the Tradition," 447, 454; similarly Fiddes, *Participating in God*, 36.

8. Ratzinger, "Retrieving the Tradition," 448.

9. Boethius *De persona et duabus naturis* 3: "Persona est naturae rationalis individua substantia"; PL 64:1343.

10. LaCugna, *God for Us*, 103, 250; Moltmann, *Spirit*, 93; Zizioulas, *Communion*

adopted by Thomas Aquinas, although in his comment he altered it to "a subsisting in a rational nature,"[11] and at another place to "some distinct subsisting in an intelligent nature."[12] Thomas further commented that what are distinct in God are relationships of origin, so that when the term "person" is used of God it means "relationship as subsistent substance—a hypostasis—subsisting in God's nature, and as such identical with that nature."[13] The notion of subsistent relationships is shared by the Western perception with that of the Eastern fathers, who, however, start from a trinitarian perspective and who thus can provide a corrective for the exaggerated Western individualism.

Significant contributions were made by the Cappadocian fathers, by the Council of Chalcedon, and by Maximus. The Cappadocians tried to understand personhood by deriving its notion not so much from the human—even though the co-occurrence of human individuals provided them an example of limited usefulness—but from considering the divine beings themselves. As such, they perceived that existence in relationship is not subsequent to a supposedly prior individual existence; that personhood takes place in communion, in freedom and is ecstatic.[14] Torrance points out that the concept of persons as substantive relations (οὐσιώδεις σχέσεις) was especially put forward by Gregory Nazianzen (c.330–c.390).[15] Zizioulas argues that the crucial contribution of the Cappadocians, and especially of Basil of Caesarea (c.329–379), was to provide the term "person" (πρόσωπον) with an ontological content, whereas through its former use in the world of ancient Greek theatre in the sense of a personage or "mask" played by an actor it had been devoid of an ontological content in Greco-Roman thought.[16] For Basil the aim was thereby to avoid the error of Sabellius, who could distinguish between the three

---

and Otherness, 1, 106, 150–51, 162, 168.

11. Aquinas *Summa theologiae* 1a, q.29, art. 3: "subsistens in rationali natura"; so also at *Summa theologiae* 3a, q.16, art.12: "persona significat quid completum et per se subsistens in natura rationali" / "a person signifies something complete and self-subsisting in a rational nature" (my translation).

12. Aquinas *Scriptum super Sententiis* 1, d.23, q.1, a.4 co.: "aliquid distinctum subsistens in natura intellectuali."

13. Aquinas *Summa theologiae* 1a, q.29, art.1, 4 (my translation); see also Velecky, "Divine Persons," 145–48.

14. Zizioulas, *Being as Communion*, 49; Zizioulas, *Communion and Otherness*, 9–10, 163–64, 166, 176–77.

15. Torrance, *Trinitarian Faith*, 239ff., 318ff.; Torrance, *Christian Doctrine*, 157.

16. Zizioulas, *Being as Communion*, 31, 36.

persons of Father, Son, and Spirit by holding that the one divine hypostasis metamorphosed as the need of the moment required.[17] The solution offered by the Cappadocians was to adjust the Nicene emphasis on the one *ousia* with the Origenist principle of three individuals with the formula, one *ousia* and three *hypostaseis*.[18] The term hypostasis, which had been identified earlier by Athanasius with *ousia*[19] and which in the West had been translated by *substantia*, could thus be identified with *prosōpon*.

The contribution of Chalcedon (451) was to clearly distinguish in its reflection upon the divine Son Jesus Christ the natural and personal levels of existence, and to identify divine personhood with the corresponding divine hypostasis. Aloys Grillmeier assesses, however, that even for the Council fathers the included expressions would have been devoid of a clear definition and only have been grasped intuitively.[20]

Maximus, in continuation of Chalcedon and of his spiritual guide Sophronius of Jerusalem (560–638), consistently argued that besides all other capacities, even the capacity to act and the capacity to will are part of the involved nature and not of the personal level. As such he clearly distinguished between the shared natural level and the subjective level of personhood unique to each person, at which level each remained perfectly free to make subjective decisions of will and to engage in relationship. Hence, while a divine person partakes in these capacities, which he co-possesses with the other persons and makes use of them, these capacities are not thereby descriptive of that person.

Jean-Claude Larchet and Zizioulas explain that the Greek fathers in general have cautiously avoided giving positive content to the divine hypostases.[21] As such, according to Zizioulas, "[Personhood] is only a 'mode of being' comprising relations (σχέσις) of ontological constitutiveness."[22] As such, for the human being, personal uniqueness

17. Basil *Ep.* 236:6; PG 32:884A–C; trans. Stevenson, *Creeds, Councils and Controversies*, 105–6 (NPNF altered).

18. Gregory of Nyssa *On the Difference between* Ousia *and* Hypostasis (preserved as *Ep.* 38 of Basil); trans. Wiles and Santer, *Documents*, 31–35.

19. Zizioulas, *Being as Communion*, 36 n. 23.

20. Grillmeier, *Christ*, 545, 551.

21. Larchet, *La divinisation*, 344; Zizioulas, *Communion and Otherness*, 165, 185–86.

22. Zizioulas, *Communion and Otherness*, 111, 173. We may also note the critique and subsequent defence of Zizioulas for distinguishing the person from the individual in his reading of the Cappadocians: Turcescu, "'Person' versus 'Individual,'" 527–39; Papanikolaou, "Zizioulas an Existentialist?," 601–7.

that is not extinguished at death is not guaranteed by a complex of qualities but by being taken up in the inter-personal communion within the Godhead.[23]

THE HUMAN BEING AS A LIVING BEING CAPABLE OF THE PERSONAL

As we set the next step of our exploration, we turn again to contemporary science, this time not physical or biological science, but anthropology and paleoanthropology.

Common views have been that the distinguishing feature of human being is language or tool making. A more recent opinion is that it is a symbolic capacity that allows us to recognize the presence of human intelligence, of human being. Scientists have been probing where along the lineage of hominids,[24] including perhaps the *Australopithecines*[25] and early hominines[26], these capacities have been clearly present. However, research has shown that certain present day ape-species and probably also other higher animals are not entirely devoid of these capacities.[27] Donald R. Griffin, a professor in zoology, argues that even weaver ants and honeybees are to some extent participant in conscious thought and feeling and thus are able to engage in symbolic communication.[28] Accordingly, it appears that it is not these capacities that are ultimate referents for human emergence and existence, and hence, for human intelligence. These are, of course, undeniably significant capacities for human being. Fiorenzo Facchini has argued that it is culture that reveals what is human in humans. Thereby, according to Facchini, at the very core of culture are projectuality—by which he means the capacity to plan or act intentionally—and symbolism. He further considers that there are cultural expressions related to biological needs and in the sphere

---

23. Zizioulas, *Being as Communion*, 56.

24. Hominids include various humanoid species from between 7 and 6 million years ago onwards.

25. *Australopithecines* ("Southern apes") include various species with which clear bipedalism emerged.

26. Hominines include all species within the genus *Homo* from early *Homo* around 2.5 million years ago onwards.

27. Gibson, "Animal minds, human minds," 7; McGrew, "Intelligent use of tools," 157–58; Lee, "Cognitive and behavioural complexity," 70.

28. Griffin, *Animal Minds*, 187–210.

Person

of social communications, but also in the spheres of art, religion, and ethics. According to Facchini, within the latter spheres "communicating means expressing the intimate thoughts of people without any particular reference to events or needs." He thus holds culture to express "human abstract intelligence and psychism." Facchini concludes, "'humanization' is mainly due to culture."[29] We already encountered such perception in Peacocke, whom I quoted in chapter 1. But I also mentioned there that I hold the human sense of purpose and intentionality, as well as the propensity to worship and prayer—which I acknowledge to be characteristic for humanity—as not representing a discontinuity in the evolutionary process. Let us try to explore this further.

All excavations that tell us about the emergence of full humanity seem to indicate that a sense of religiosity was already present.[30] A survey of the presently known tangible indicators of the humanoid awakening also indicates that even before a rational ability would have been fully developed, a mode of conscious self-aware existence as well as of conscious other-aware existence may have been present.[31] Arguably, already at an early level in human development, with language still in its elementary phases prior to well-developed articulate speech, there would have been expressed not only a rudimentary exchange of information content but also the at least partly self-possessed expression of emotion, anxieties, and hopes,[32] such as are contained in prayer.

I invite us to try situating these non-subsistence-related expressions in a wider context. With this purpose in mind, it is here considered that the emergence of hominids along a lineage marked by increasing mental ability and, more encompassing, the emergence of various creatures that contribute to an ecological ensemble and to a cosmos, are meaningful and purposive events and are thus not abstractly neutral. Moreover, it is here considered that these events of emergence involve the active participation of various created entities. Therefore, these events already hint to

---

29. Facchini, "Man," para. 3.

30. E.g., Mania and Mania, "*Homo erectus* at Bilzingsleben," 98–114.

31. See also Watson, *Lifetide*, 238 and Seybold, *Neuroscience, Psychology and Religion*, 84–85.

32. Marett, *Faith, Hope and Charity*; Hardy, *Divine Flame*, 156–75; Marshack, "Paleolithic Symbolic Evidence," 278–79; Marchack, "On Paleolithic Ochre," 188–91; Marchack, "Early Hominid Symbol," 457–98; Marshack, *Roots of Civilization*, 381; Masson and McCarthy, *When Elephants Weep*, 96–119; Marshack, "Paleolithic Image Making," 53–54; Tattersall, *Becoming Human*.

us that the emergence of some form of prayer and the emergence of care and joy were not subsequent, not even concomitant with, but antecedent to the event of humanization, of spoken language, and of conceptualization. The suggestion that some form of prayer, care, and other virtues, manifested itself prior to these lets us also consider beyond present conventional thought that the "praying" and "caring" subject is not merely or only the human being, but the entire involved created reality.[33] That is to say, the "praying" and "caring" subject would initially not have been attributable to a consciously praying and caring individual, but to an ensemble of ecological significant proportions. This idea can be linked to what we observed in the previous chapter as regards the notion of a universal participation in a noetic feature/intelligence and the notion of the partial manifestation of mind accompanying biological and chemico-physical processes within ecosystems and within the wider natural realm. We are, as it were, brought to revisit these notions, now with a particular awareness of the evolvement that has taken place along the time-line. The idea that is here being put forward can also be linked to that of Koestler's *holons*, which suggests reality to be organized according to various interdependent levels, and to the belief in spiritual beings, who can fulfill a ministry of guiding the ensembles and *holons*. Chapter 6 will elaborate upon these ideas, but mention of them has to be made here for situating the human being. What is envisaged is that prior to the emergence of humanity there were the purposeful ensembles consistent of various creatures and that with human beings there emerged purposeful ensembles consistent of a single organism, a single creature, albeit existent within the context of the various ensembles and *holons*.

In continuity of scriptural revelation, we are thereby invited to hold that "prayer," "care," "joy," and other virtues, both pre-human, non-human and human, are enabled by the Spirit of God. As such, the meaning of human life is not merely being invented in the process of humans' emergence but received. Accordingly, human being takes place by the supportive workings of the wider created reality and in the context of a relationship with God who conceives the human creatures and who receives their anxieties, aspirations, and very being. Here, we are obviously invited to differentiate ourselves from the late anthropologist Roy A. Rappaport's (1926–97) one-sided assessment in his last work *Ritual*

---

33. Cf. Hardy, "Another View," 74–82.

and Religion in the Making of Humanity (1999), "Humanity is a species that lives and can only live in terms of meanings it itself must invent."[34]

In agreement with Facchini's perception that "humanization" is mainly due to culture; in accordance with the mentioned archeological-based findings, and in light of the situatedness of humanity's emergence along the (horizontal) evolutionary chain and within the (vertical) context of purposeful ensembles within ensembles, the following suggestion regarding the nature of human being becomes sensible. Arguably, we can speak of human beings from when people stretched forth their hands and prayed, however rudimentarily; from when they danced with their hands in the air before God; from when they cared and learned to love; and from when they experienced joy. This proposal would seem to find support in Ratzinger's commentary on Genesis 1–3, *"In the Beginning . . ."* (1986, 1995), for he suggests therein that "human beings . . . are the beings that God made capable of thinking and praying."[35] Further support is found in theologian Margaret Atkins, who suggests the definition, "*Homo sapiens*: an intelligent mammal that prays."[36] It has, however, to be observed that the virtues of prayer, care, love, and joyfulness were not necessarily limited to modern *Homo sapiens*, our own species.

Some Paleolithic graves seem to provide some tangible indications that are suggestive for this opinion that some other hominine species had a share in these virtues. For example, it was found at certain burial sites of the Neanderthals (*Homo sapiens neanderthalensis*) that the corpse was ochered red, which eventually penetrated into the bones. The same practice was more commonly found in burial sites for people of our own kind in the Upper Paleolithic, which covers the period between about forty and ten thousand years ago. The applied red ocher probably signified to them in this context the color of blood, of life and vitality.[37] On the basis of this, burial gifts, and so forth, it can be suggested that the Neanderthals from perhaps one hundred thousand years ago, and perhaps people of our kind before them, already believed or hoped that their deceased would live on in one way or other. Another remarkable discovery was made in the cave of *Teshik-Tash*, Uzbekistan. Here a Neanderthal child was found buried at the Mousterian level, that is, at the level that contains

---

34. Rappaport, *Ritual and Religion*, 8; see also ibid., 391–95.
35. Ratzinger, *In the Beginning*, 48.
36. Atkins, "I think," 196.
37. André Leroi-Gourhan, *Les religions*, 60–62, 67–69; Waal Malefijt, *Religion and Culture*, 113–16.

the tool and art-culture of the Middle Paleolithic from about three hundred thousand to forty thousand years ago. The sepulcher was disturbed by an animal of prey, but it still allowed the observance of the remarkable fact that it was surrounded by the paired horns of five or six Siberian mountain goats.[38] This would seem to indicate a belief that, as in life, beyond death the human and the animal can be associated and interdependent in a somehow common fate. A third example is found in the cave called *Shanidar* in Iraq where several skeletons of Neanderthals were excavated, dating from about seventy thousand until forty-five thousand years ago. After careful analysis of the soil surrounding the grave of an adult man, palynologist Arlette Leroi-Gourhan (1913–2005) concluded that the corpse was buried on a bed of ramose branches and flowers more than fifty thousand years ago. The flowers provided the effect of a mixture of white, yellow, and blue, together with some green branches of woody horsetail. Ralph Solecki who guided the excavations, suggested moreover that all the selected flowers are long known to have medicinal value.[39] Significant also at the same site is the grave of an old man, between forty and fifty years old. His remains show that at some point in his life he had received a blow that fractured his left orbit, which would have left him at least partly blind. He further suffered from a withered arm with which he appears to have lived for several years. He also had deformities along his right side to his lower leg and foot. It is suggested that his survival over such an extended period would only have been possible with support of others within the group.[40]

It is possible that the mentioned virtues and abilities gradually emerged in *Homo heidelbergensis*, a late variant of *Homo erectus*, about five hundred thousand years ago, perhaps much earlier.[41] Given the very limited tangible evidence, it remains a rather speculative issue. But it appears suited that human being (that is, to be according to characteristics indicated as human) is not the exclusive capacity of a single species, that it is continuous with the created reality towards which it carries a task, and that the emergence of the image of God, who himself remains shrouded in mystery, is not sharply delineated from his wider creation.

38. Leroi-Gourhan, *Les religions*, 58; Waal Malefijt, *Religion and Culture*, 111.

39. Leroi-Gourhan, *Les religions*, 58; Arlette Leroi-Gourhan, "Flowers," 562–64; Leakey, *Mankind*, 153; Facchini, "Man," para. 4:3.

40. Tattersall, *Becoming Human*, 162.

41. Stringer and Andrews, *Human Evolution*, 72–75, 142–43, 148–51, 208; Mania and Mania, "*Homo erectus* at Bilzingsleben," 98–114.

Person

What certainly can be refuted is the position adopted by the physicist and Judaic biblical scholar Gerald L. Schroeder in his work *The Science of God* (1997). Schroeder acknowledges that various hominid species existed and that anatomically modern hominids lived about one hundred thousand years ago that displayed an advanced skillfulness and developed techniques such as cave paintings and agriculture, but he nonetheless holds that human spirituality and hence humanity would have emerged with the biblical Adam, whose creation he dates at about five thousand seven hundred years before the present.[42] In addition to the resources already mentioned, the following can usefully be brought into attention with regard to cave art that was practiced in the Upper Paleolithic and with regard to the spirituality thereby implied. So, once more I propose us to make an exploration into the past and to visit the people who were first found to have lived at a rock shelter called *Crô-Magnon* in the Dordogne region at about thirty thousand years ago.

The daily activities of the Cro-Magnons took place near the cave entrance, but their paintings and engravings could have diverse locations throughout the cave. They could either be situated in the entrance area where daylight could reach the paintings or throughout the dark corridors.[43] In some caves the decorations were in the corridors at depths of a few dozen meters. In some other caves they were placed over lengths of several hundreds of meters into the deepest recesses. For example, at *La Cullalvera* and at *Niaux* decorations were made unto fifteen hundred meters into the corridors, while there were side passages that could cause confusion for finding a way back or hide a dangerous animal, or there were natural obstacles that had to be negotiated. At *Rouffignac* decorations were made unto one kilometer into the cave, passing through hundreds of bears' dens of caves. Just as their remote ancestors had bravely taken control of fire, so these people were the greatest darers as they entered into the unknown dark tunnels, which they lightened up by their little lamps, where there was always danger of encountering a bear, and whereby they negotiated narrow passages, chasms, and steep climbs or descents.[44] The paintings themselves are sometimes placed at barely reachable places, at several meters above the ground or above a chasm, so that they were

---

42. Schroeder, *Science of God*, 135 fig. 7, 141–45.
43. Clottes and Lewis-Williams, *Shamans*, 53.
44. Leroi-Gourhan, *Dawn of European Art*, 45–50, 58–68.

Cosmic Prayer and Guided Transformation

made with the help of a long pole or with scaffolding.[45] In some caves, however, there are also spacious chambers not very far from the entrance that have been abundantly painted. These decorations would have been made by several people working together at various subsequent times and they would have been seen by relative large numbers of people; they were intended to be seen: for example, the Hall of the Bulls at *Lascaux* and the Black Salon at *Niaux*.[46] Others would, because of their location, have been visited by very few people. As such, there were representations of which the very act of application by the individual involved would have been most important; some obscure locations suggest that it was the fact of their being placed there that mattered most and not so much their being seen. Alexander Marshack's (1918–2004) microscopic investigations and careful photography of many animal representations and compositions of cave art show convincingly that a simple explanation, such as Abbé Henri Breuil's (1877–1961) initial interpretation of hunter's magic, even when this does indeed feature in association with certain of the represented animals, is by itself often an inadequate explanation. This had especially become apparent to the French priest and archaeologist Breuil himself and to others after the discovery of *Lascaux* in 1940. Marshack, and earlier, among others, Gertrude Rachel Levy (1884–1966), also proposed that of the earliest painted and carved human figures that are found with animals, none have weapons in hand, but rather, they are engaged in ceremonial. It does not, of course, mean that they were not hunters and killers, for they were.[47] It is, moreover, unlikely that the entire phenomenon of Upper Paleolithic cave art, including both wall paintings and mobile art, is explained by a single theory. Nevertheless, overall, it appears valid to observe that by their artistic expressions these Upper Paleolithic people illustrated their sense of the mysterious, of a sacred dimension beyond the visible reality that yet had its bearing on all existence and every aspect of daily living, that gave sanctity to the animal forms, that could be approached in ritual and prayer, perhaps be preferentially entered upon in the altered conscious states that would have been perceived to be part of a spiritual journey, and that provided meaning to their lives. They did not passively wait, huddled around a fire, until they

---

45. Levy, *Gate of Horn*, 7–16; Waal Malefijt, *Religion and Culture*, 127; Clottes, "Art," 210–13.

46. Clottes and Lewis-Williams, *Shamans*, 103.

47. Levy, *Gate of Horn*, 22–26; Marshack, *Roots of Civilization*, 272–74, 320–25; Zaleski and Zaleski, *Prayer*, 19–22.

were overcome by a mysterious feeling of a dread transcendent realm, but they went to encounter it in good hope and sought to evoke it by art and ritual in the deepest recesses of the earth and in the dignity of their bravery, individuality, and collectivity. Perhaps we may interpret from our theistic perspective that upon God's creative outreach and awakening action, Creator and creature entered here upon a mutual and consciously aware encounter; even though the human creature of the Paleolithic had been employing various techniques—involving ritual, various ascetic practices, drumbeat, the dark recesses, and hallucinogens (as is the case among present-day aboriginal cultures)—to enter into the spiritual realm by a state of altered consciousness.

Among the cave wall images of a clearly spiritual nature are those of people with hands raised high in prayer and worship. An inventory of these human figurines can be found in Johannes Maringer's article entitled "Adorants in Prehistoric Art" (1979). Renderings of a number of these can also be found in Marshack's magnificent work *The Roots of Civilization* (1972, 1991).[48]

Further cave wall images that have an overt spiritual character are those of sorcerers dressed as animals and/or the representations of mythical hybrid supernatural beings, such as those in the Aurignacian cave at *Chauvet*—whereby the designation Aurignacian indicates that it concerns art forms and stone tools within that particular European subculture of the Upper Paleolithic that is dated between circa thirty five and twenty nine thousand years ago. Such images have further been found in the Middle Magdalenian cave *Les Trois Frères* at Ariège in the Pyrenean foothills—whereby the designation Middle Magdalenian indicates the European subculture of the Upper Paleolithic that is dated between fourteen thousand five hundred and thirteen thousand years ago. Still more of such images have been found in *Laugerie Basse*, in *Gabillou*, and in *Lascaux* in the Dordogne.[49] It is noteworthy that one of the so-called "sorcerers" of *Les Trois Frères* is placed in an aperture in the upper part of the wall, three and a half meters from the ground, overseeing a cave chamber that is itself only reachable through a narrow passage from another chamber. The artist crawled up a sloping shaft that led to a narrow

---

48. Marshack, *Roots of Civilization*, 320–21, 388–89.

49. Leroi-Gourhan, *Dawn of European Art*, 34; 50–54; Marshack, *Roots of Civilization*, 272–273 Bahn, *Journey through the Ice Age*, 165–66, 180; Clottes and Lewis-Williams, *Shamans*, 45–46, 96.

ridge where he painted the figure.[50] The lower walls are covered with representations of animals. The solemn hybrid "sorcerer" has human legs and feet, perhaps human hands or possibly the front paws of a bear, the face of an owl, a long beard, antlers of a reindeer, the trunk and tail of a horse, and exposed genitals under the tail, that is, in the position where a feline would have it. The hide that covers the paws and feet is transparent so that the sense is created of limbs that are disguised. The dynamic of the body posture communicates that the figure is engaged in a dance or ceremony and this in association with the human beings and the animal creatures beneath. If the figure is intended to have a divine character, then it can perhaps be seen to hold incarnational capacities related to both the humans and the multitude of animal creatures. Or alternatively, it may represent the spiritual archetypal being of a human shaman, which would have been attributed a significance for fostering a harmonious relationship of both humans and animals with the supernatural spiritual beings and for fostering the former their ultimate ascent into the spiritual realm. Perhaps it is not too far sought to perceive here a distant adumbration of the biblical belief expressed at Ps 36:6c, "Man and beast thou savest, O Lord." The other hybrid representation (or anthropozoomorph) at *Les Trois Frères*, the so-called "little sorcerer," has the head, the horns, and the hooves of a bison and is also engaged in dance, not above but right amidst a multitude of animals. The few horned hybrid beings found in the Upper Paleolithic would in later cultures of the Bronze and Iron Ages in Egypt, Mesopotamia, India, and throughout Europe, become the horned gods and horned goddesses, among which for example the god Pan was one of several in Greece. Curiously, in later times, the early Christian seer John saw "a Lamb standing . . . with seven horns and with seven eyes" (Rev 5:6), which is a vision which would seem to have been directly inspired by Deutero-Isaiah's identification of the suffering servant with a lamb led to the slaughter (Isa 53:7), by Daniel's vision of one like a son of man who was given everlasting dominion (Dan 7:13–14), and by Christ who became the paschal lamb of the New Covenant (John 1:29; 1 Cor 5:7). Within subsequent Christian tradition, however, the horned gods of the old religions came to be identified with the devil. Nevertheless, I suggest that there is at *Les Trois Frères*, and probably also at *Lascaux* and elsewhere, already recognizably present an original spiritual notion such as we touched upon in chapter 2 and that we will return

50. Clottes, "Art," 212–13.

Person

to in chapter 8. In particular, this comparable intuition or belief concerns the idea that the informing or sustaining of all living beings takes place by a single transcendent or divine power and that this supernatural power makes possible harmonization of all living beings, among themselves as well as with the supernatural or spiritual beings, by human mediatory cooperation in life and ritual prayer. It is a perception that is central to a wholesome Christian belief.

With these observations our little exploration into the Upper Paleolithic has fulfilled its objective. Schroeder's assessment that human spirituality and, hence, human existence began five thousand seven hundred years ago is shown to be invalid. It is, moreover, not only Schroeder's opinion that is to be refuted.

The proposed perception regarding what defines human nature—namely, a capacity for a communal life and culture, which finds expression in, among others, the virtues of prayer, care, love, and joyfulness—also implies a refutation of the definition of Aristotle, which was adopted by Augustine and Thomas Aquinas, namely, the human being as *animal rationalis*.[51] It is to be recognized, however, that Aristotle's definition had been an improvement upon Plato's perception that the human being was essentially an immaterial soul that temporally was locked into a body. Aristotle's definition conceived of a common root, namely the received gift of being alive, in which human beings and other living beings partake, even though it pointed out the distinctive ability of our own particular species. It allowed us to perceive the human being as an intrinsic soul-body conglomerate. Yet, Aristotle's definition is, in its turn, to be improved. For human *being* involves a task that engages us entirely and not just our rational ability. The cruelty, injustices, blind self-absorption, mental aberrations, and sheer stupidity with which history is littered, make Aristotle's definition highly questionable. We may well be born as human beings, but this does not automatically imply that we will live as rational beings. It is too narrow a basis upon which to define and edify humanity.

The answer that has been given here regarding the emergence of human beings is consistent with the various sources of contemporary knowledge[52] and suggests that a human being is a living being capable

---

51. Augustine *De civitate dei* 9:13; PL 41:267; *De vera religione* 53; PL 34:167; Aquinas *Summa contra Gentiles* 2:59:15, 17; 60:2; *Summa theologiæ* 1a, q.91, art.3 (reply 2); q.96, art.2 (reply).

52. See also Fox, "Being Human," 32–45.

of the personal by the grace of God: *animal capax personae in gratia Dei tripersonae*. The virtue of prayer that like the other virtues is enabled by the personal, namely, by the Spirit of God, and that leads to the personal, is indispensable for realizing our humanity. As Kenneth Leech in his work *True Prayer* (1980) discerned, "Prayer is concerned with the unifying and integrating of the personality."[53] Arguably, the virtue of prayer that emerges gropingly within the visible creation springs up and comes to the surface in the context of humanity. Again, we can find in Leech a supportive assessment. "We move from darkness to light, from shadows to reality. . . . Prayer is an intensely human experience in which our eyes are opened."[54] It was pursued in the deep dark caves, led to the searching inspiration contained in the religions of all human cultures, and it was in great clarity made to shine forth in Jesus Christ.

The task that asks our attention after these thoughts is a clarification of the connection that I have implicitly made between the pursuit of various virtues such as have been mentioned and the capacity for personal existence.

A CHARACTERIZATION OF EXISTENCE THAT APPROXIMATES THE PERSONAL

In the previous section it was proposed that *human being* involves by definition a capability for the personal. The idea that is implied by this proposal is that the personal can to some extent be discerned in human individuals who try to live up to their humanity, yet, in the meantime, that the personal is also lying ahead of human beings as their anticipated ultimate goal. This goal, a complete appropriation of the personal, is only realized and, hence, found within a person. Accordingly, a human being, or any other created being for that matter, can only at best by approximation be identified as a person.

What is characteristic for an existence that increasingly tends towards realization of the personal? The following can be proposed:

1. It is an existence that is alive.
2. It is an existence wherein love, prayer, goodness, compassion, wisdom, and joyfulness become increasingly prevalent.

---

53. Leech, *True Prayer*, 40.
54. Ibid., 3.

3. It is an existence that is being increasingly imbued with an own effective willpower, thus enabling the realization of the mentioned qualities.
4. It is an existence wherein an unshared or individual side is complemented by a shared or common side; it is an increased realization of selfhood in self-giving communion.
5. It is an existence that takes place in the creative dialectic between the involved creature and the personal Creator.

Allow me to make some comments regarding these proposed characteristics. By its striving to attain the personal, created existence transcends its purely natural existence; it transcends the chemico-physical processes. Such existence can only be that of a living entity. As it was indicated in the previous chapter, created life exists as a complex order in a labile equilibrium and favors an increased complexity. Physical death, on the contrary, leads to decomposition, towards a purely temporal stable equilibrium, and towards an annihilation of the complex information content or form of the created entity, this unless the latter has been taken up in a higher-order continuation of being alive, beyond the merely physical. Correspondingly, by the transcendence beyond processes strictly tied to physical energy and the associated corruptibility, ultimately by transcendence towards the personal, the created existence perfects the dynamic of being alive by staying alive.

Concerning the various included virtues that I posit to be prevalent in an increasing realization of personal existence, it can be observed that they are strongly interconnected. The affinity of life and love has already been mentioned. In addition, being alive is a prerequisite for all these virtues. Love involves a being centered not upon the self, but upon another, and this is equally true for the other virtues, (through an emotional and/or intellectual involvement). Prayer could in theory perhaps be focused upon the fulfillment of a thing desired for the self, but this is, as will be discussed in chapter 5, certainly not characteristic of Christian prayer, that is, prayer that is expressive of the relationship with a loving God. All these qualities imply a degree of intelligence. Intelligence is especially at the fore in wisdom, for discernment in accordance with truth of the self, of ordered patterns in reality beyond the self, and for a *know-how* about life. An element of intelligence is certainly required in love, so as to distinguish between the own being and that of the other and so as to focus upon the other. Love is thereby most inquisitive. A degree of intelligence

Cosmic Prayer and Guided Transformation

is also prerequisite for the recognition and sustained focus involved in prayer, goodness, and compassion. Again, intelligence is required for the ability to be joyful, for being able to open up and rise beyond the needs and requirements of the daily. None of these virtues is exhausted by created beings. There is no moment in their existence when they can claim to have reached the end, the ultimate expression, of any of these. Finally, in addition to these, other virtues may conceivably be added. All mentioned qualities can only be sustained and brought to fruition by a sustained willpower as possessed by a free agent.

Towards the end of chapter 1 it was already suggested that personal existence does not take place in isolation, but involves both an individual or unshared aspect and a communal or shared aspect. For example, a human or angelic person-to-be has an own subjective self, but only finds meaning and fulfillment in an interaction with others marked by love, prayer, and so forth. By its very situatedness each such particular being has an own experience of life that cannot be entirely explained (that is, placed before another) and contained by another; that is solitary.[55] Yet, human beings are found in this very situatedness by sharing in a common humanity, or the angelic beings by sharing in one common mission. In the realization of the personal, it is obvious that the solitary and the shared dimension do not remain neatly side by side, but that the ones involved are wholly transformed while as yet remaining their own selves: a person is both *ekstasis* and hypostasis.[56] Surely, love includes as a constituent, in addition to intelligence and free will, a desire regarding the other that involves not only the intellect but that thrusts the entire self, all its powers, towards the other. Likewise, the other listed virtues cannot be exercised while remaining unmoved.

Finally, none of the personal virtues can be drawn, as from a well, from the own being in isolation. They are not natural powers intrinsic to created existence, even though created being is suited for their reception. In continuity of the foregoing paragraph it can be held that these qualities emerge in the context of a living relationship and that they are expressive of engagement in relationship. Christian believers hold that they require the workings or gifts of the Holy Spirit. In addition, they obviously require also the own active and free involvement. It is, thereby,

---

55. Shivanandan, *Threshold of Love*, 95–104, 108–9, 141–45; Clarke, "Incommunicability," 379–80.

56. See also Zizioulas, *Being as Communion*, 106; LaCugna, *God for Us*, 260–65, 188–89; Shivanandan, *Threshold of Love*, 143–46, 148–49.

Person

especially prayer that enables the continued working of the Holy Spirit in the believer and that is, vice versa, enabled thereby. It is especially by prayer that the faithful can journey in a focused manner towards God together with others, with whom and for whom they pray.

PERSONHOOD AND PERSON

It is in the divine persons that love, goodness, wisdom, and the other virtues are perfectly possessed. Thereby, Father, Son, and Spirit communicate themselves perfectly and entirely to each other, so that these virtues are their common possession. As such, the fullness of personal being is realized in the divine persons that constitute the Trinity.[57]

By their free participation in the creative process, by suffering, (which is related to both freedom and love),[58] by love, by the prayerful exchange, and by the exercise of the virtues, creatures are taken up in the divine and personal communion; they are effectively taken up into the Godhead. Their suffering [arguably], love, wisdom, and all other contributive aspects that we mentioned, become expressive of the divine mode of existence. As we discerned in Maximus, whom we explored near the end of chapter 2, it is in the divine mode (*tropos*) of existence that the creatures attain "being" in a harmonious co-existence. There are then no other real persons besides the three divine persons. This has similarly been expressed by Torrance. "In the strictest sense, God alone is Person, for he is a fullness of personal Being, and as such is the creative Source of all other personal being."[59]

Both movements, the divine willingness of taking up creatures in the divine communion and the creaturely participation in this have been reflected upon by Moltmann. In *The Crucified God* he envisaged that in the passion of Jesus Christ, God has assumed suffering human life and taken it up in his own eternal life.[60] Moltmann developed the same teaching in his later work *The Spirit of Life*, where he finds further support for this in Pope John Paul II's encyclical *Dominum et vivificantem: On the*

---

57. Lubac, *Catholicism*, 329.

58. Elphinstone, *Freedom, Suffering and Love*; Schroeder, "Suffering," 263; Southgate, *Groaning of Creation*, 35–39.

59. Torrance, "Soul," 116.

60. Moltmann, *Crucified God*, 65, 200–207, 212, 270–74.

Cosmic Prayer and Guided Transformation

Holy Spirit in the Life of the Church and the World (1986).[61] Moreover, as has been indicated in the introduction, both in *God in Creation* and in *The Spirit of Life* Moltmann considers that living beings are taken up in the divine communion through a process of reciprocal *perichoresis* of God and themselves.[62] Moltmann focuses thereby upon the significance of the Holy Spirit. "In the Holy Spirit the eternal God participates in our transitory life, and we participate in the eternal life of God."[63] There remains in this sentence, however, ambiguity as regards the inclusiveness of "we." Earlier on the same page Moltmann speaks about "the new creation of all things"; about the Spirit being "poured out upon all flesh," which thereby becomes spiritual; and about "the love of God which is 'poured out' in our hearts through the Holy Spirit." Taken together, it would seem that it is not only the community of the faithful that is envisaged by the "we" that is quoted above.

Turning towards Fiddes, we find that in continuation of Barth, he reflects in his books *The Creative Suffering of God* and *Participating in God* upon the identification of the divine persons as relations.[64] It is an interpretation that, as we found, is in concord with the conclusions drawn by both Zizioulas (Metropolitan John) and Ratzinger (Pope Benedict XVI). In continuity with this interpretation is, from a Roman Catholic perspective, the thought of both the feminist theologian Patricia Wilson-Kastner and the Brazilian liberation theologian Leonardo Boff as we find it represented by LaCugna: "The substance of God is the *perichōrētic* relatedness of three coequal persons. Like in all Latin-based theologies, substance is the principle of personhood . . . substance is conceived as dynamic interrelatedness."[65] The same perception is found by Torrance[66] and is critically reflected upon by Fiddes in his latter book as follows:

> There is, however, a problem with this way of thinking of perichoresis: it is possible to think of the circle of God's inner triune life as a closed circle, a self-sufficient dance. . . . But the stress upon the one substance—even as communion—means there is the danger of emphasizing the oneness and so the self-enclosure

61. Moltmann, *Spirit*, 62–64, 67–68, 70, 191–92, 213; John Paul II, *Dominum et vivificantem* 2:41.
62. Moltmann, *God in Creation*, 16–17; Moltmann, *Spirit*, 195–96.
63. Moltmann, *God in Creation*, 16–17.
64. Fiddes, *Creative Suffering*, 84, 139–42; Fiddes, *Participating in God*, 81, 89.
65. LaCugna, *God for Us*, 272.
66. Torrance, *Trinitarian Faith*, 236–40, 310–13.

Person

of God at the expense of the generous threefold richness.... [A] stress upon our *engagement* in God helps us to see the best in the insights of East and West. The Western theology of mutuality and reciprocity... makes most sense as a communion of subsistent relationships, that is as an interweaving of relational movements and actions in which we can become involved. We do not try to observe the persons on the "ends" of the relationships, but are drawn to share in the movements of the divine dance.[67]

A few pages earlier in the same book, Fiddes writes in light of John 17:21 that "salvation is conceived [by Eastern theologians] essentially as divinisation (*theosis*), which means not becoming God, but being incorporated in the fellowship of the divine life,"[68] and this through a process of *perichoresis*. It is a notion of divinization that we already encountered in Maximus in chapter 2 in light of our discussion concerning the mystery of the embodiment of God and the Word of God. As regards the idea of *perichoresis*, this will be elaborated upon in chapter 8, again with texts of Maximus. What can here still be noted is that Fiddes perceives that it is those who are praying who enter the movement of sonship (or daughterhood).[69]

From the Orthodox theologian John Meyendorff we learn that according to Gregory of Nyssa the divine image, although eminently present in the human mind (*nous*), cannot be truly realized within a single human being. Accordingly, it is in all humanity together, united in the harmonious co-existence of human beings (and as I think permissible to add: which takes place in unison with all created beings) and restored in God, that the fullness of goodness (and it can be added: of compassion and of every other virtue) is realized.[70] Thereby, it is in the attainment of the personal in fullness, which is the goal of the creative and salvific process, that the image is being realized by human beings, by their particular contributions and in their communion.

Zizioulas points out that for the human being it is on the basis of a relationship with God, "which is identified with what Christ in freedom and love possesses as Son of God with the Father," that human existence as personal is affirmed. In particular, according to Zizioulas it is through baptism that the human hypostasis is being identified with that of the

67. Fiddes, *Participating in God*, 78–79.
68. Ibid., 76.
69. Ibid., 42–43, 79.
70. Meyendorff, "Eastern Patristic Thought," 55.

Cosmic Prayer and Guided Transformation

Son of God, that people are born as person, and that their first biological hypostasis is replaced with the ecclesial hypostasis.[71]

The ideas advanced in these preceding paragraphs cohere with the following interpretation of Zizioulas by Papanikolaou:

> It is not that the Spirit was never active in creation before the birth of Christ, but with the "Christ event" the Spirit is active, on my reading of Zizioulas, in a new way. The activity of the Holy Spirit is now linked with the resurrection of Christ the fruits of which the Spirit makes present. . . . The resurrected Christ is the "corporate personality" who recapitulates all creation in himself. The Spirit's "new" activity renders the resurrected Christ present, and this not simply anywhere; but specifically, in the eucharistic worshipping community, where the people are gathered in praise and offer the world to be sanctified. It is in this act of the people, this *leitourgia*, that the Spirit breaks through history and *constitutes* the Church as the body of Christ, i.e., as the eschatological presence of the triune life.[72]

Undoubtedly, a significant source of inspiration behind this notion attributed here to Zizioulas has been Maximus. In chapter 8 we will have the occasion to give further first-hand attention to Maximus so as to discern in more detail his perception of the creaturely dynamic, the involved transformation, and the nothing-excluding hypostatic or personal union in the Son that is being reached. Another significant inspiration behind the here considered notion has most probably been Alexander Schmemann's description of human beings in the role of so-called "priests of creation."[73] For Papanikolaou envisages that people "offer the world to be sanctified." The downside of this, however, is that no hint is given whatsoever of an active non-human creaturely involvement.

When at the beginning of this section there has been mention of *creatures* that are engaged in striving towards the personal and that are being taken up in the divine and personal communion, there is involved an invitation to think not merely in terms of humanity but much more inclusively, and this in continuity of the Paleolithic and the scriptural witnesses. We have considered that intelligence is required

---

71. Zizioulas, *Being as Communion*, 56; also at Zizioulas, *Communion and Otherness*, 109.

72. Papanikolaou, "Divine Energies," 365–66 (the included italics are Papanikolaou's).

73. Schmemann, *World as Sacrament*, 16.

for partaking in the various qualities involved in personal existence. But earlier, in chapter 3, we also considered that all creatures somehow partake in intelligence, which for the lower animate and inanimate beings is obviously not entirely located within the confines of their individuality. Even human beings and all higher spiritual beings conceivably partake in levels of intelligence that transcend their individual confines, which is also hinted at in Gregory of Nyssa's notion of the human realization of the divine image.

The task of prayer has been seen to be indispensable for ascent towards the personal existence in God. The impression obtained from what has been discussed so far is that the praying creature not only orients its intelligent faculty towards God, but is in its entirety transported towards God. In the introduction and in the previous chapter it has been suggested that the great project of prayer transcends the confines of humanity and is shared in by all creaturely existence that is organized according to various ontological interdependent levels. In this chapter we have seen that the realm of "prayer" is extended into the past to the very beginnings of humanity, and it has been considered to extend even further back, so that human prayer emerged with humanity and that, vice versa, humanity emerged with cosmic prayer, which is the concept mentioned at the end of the introduction. The following two chapters will let us reflect further upon the virtue of prayer. In the coming chapter we will consider prayer within humanity and especially within Christianity; the chapter following will explore the participation of all creatures in cosmic prayer.

5

Prayer

PRAYER AS NATURAL TO HUMAN EXISTENCE

HARRY EMERSON FOSDICK (1878–1969), an American Baptist minister who wrote during the First World War his book *The Meaning of Prayer* (which was to be immensely popular in its many editions and translations), dedicates the first chapter to speaking about the naturalness of prayer. He quotes William James (1842–1910) as writing, "The reason why we do pray is simply that we cannot help praying."[1] A main justification for calling prayer natural is therefore, according to Fosdick, its universality; the fact that in one form or other it is found among all peoples, at all times and places. Fosdick immediately acknowledges, however, that a few thousand years ago Gautama the Buddha, the Enlightened One (sixth century BC), introduced a set of teachings and a way of life based upon a practice of meditation and self-control that dispensed with the idea of an absolute Being and, hence, with prayer. But Fosdick indicates thereupon that in Buddhist countries prayer is not absent. Indeed, Buddha's followers have not been able to avoid turning Buddha himself into a kind of God, whose colossal statues are the object of devotion and are visited with the expectation of some reward for merit. Buddhism also recognizes other deities that govern aspects of daily life, so that inadvertently Buddhism in

1. Fosdick, *Meaning of Prayer*, 19.

Prayer

its major traditions has become a religion wherein some forms of prayer are not absent, even if not strictly addressed to a personal God.[2] Another example given by Fosdick is the agnostic Confucius (551–479 BC), who did not want to have much to do with the gods even though he respected belief in a personal God. But again, while Confucianism disappeared as an official cult with the Chinese revolution of 1911, many Chinese and Koreans, amidst a combination of Confucian thought, Buddhism, and Daoism, burn incense in his memory and that of his followers.[3] The same thought as regards prayer's universality was also expressed, and this with mention of the same examples of Buddhism and Confucianism, by the late anthropologist Annemarie de Waal Malefijt (1914–82) in *Religion and Culture* (1968).[4]

A second justification for calling prayer natural is according to Fosdick that "prayer is not only universal in extent; it is infinite in quality."[5] It means that prayer is not outgrown by humanity that moves out of its early stages of development, or by the infant that becomes mature. Prayer has adapted with every culture, it evolves and becomes more sublime as the people or the individual is capable of it. When a well-developed mature and intelligent person moves towards his death, prayer is not to be left behind, but may reach an ever greater intensity and perfection, and the person with it.

A third justification that Fosdick gives is that "prayer is latent in the life of every one of us."[6] Even in our secularized and materialistic societies this may still be valid.[7] Many have perhaps given up praying to a divine person and they do not believe in a divine person, but as an overwhelming need emerges, or in a sudden unforeseen difficult situation, the opinion gives way to impulse and the individual prays,[8] often intermingled with all sorts of curses, for such is the pitiable state of many. However, it is probable that especially within Western societies there are

---

2. Ibid.; Smart, *World's Religions*, 57–86, 143, 424, 434, 452, 466; Harris, "Why," 7; Hawkins, *Buddhism*, 54, 80; Raj, *Essence of Buddhism*.

3. Fosdick, *Meaning of Prayer*, 19; Smart, *World's Religions*, 106–33, 448–50.

4. Waal Malefijt, *Religion and Culture*, 197.

5. Fosdick, *Meaning of Prayer*, 21.

6. Ibid.

7. Harrison, "Religious Person," 243–50; Seybold, *Neuroscience, Psychology and Religion*, 38–41, 84–85, 119–20.

8. Fosdick, *Meaning of Prayer*, 21–23. A colorful example can be found at Zaleski and Zaleski, *Prayer*, 331–33.

Cosmic Prayer and Guided Transformation

those who are so estranged from any religious culture and so impoverished in their personal selves that no words or expressions are available or sought for whatever the situation they find themselves in.

Towards the end of his book Fosdick lets us consider prayer as dominant desire. Even though we usually perceive prayer as a definite religious act that is performed at specific times when one decides to think of God, it can be seen in a more inclusive sense. That which we really strive after in our lives, that which we crave in our hearts, our dominant desire, that, so Fosdick lets us consider, is truly our prayer.[9] In this broad sense, Fosdick proposes that Columbus' search for America (or really for India) was prayer. Within this view, it is obvious that most people are praying, except perhaps again those so impoverished in their personal selves that they are devoid of any motivation or ambition. Similarly, Leech in *True Prayer* considers: "Prayer in itself is a human activity, something which we all do. At its simplest, prayer is longing, desire, the expressions of our deepest aspirations, joys, or sorrows."[10] Approached from this angle, it also shows that a formal speech to God that does not reflect what we really want, which is not in accord with our daily lives, may well be considered to be our prayer, but is not prayer at all. We can only truly pray in sincerity. Fosdick rounds off the topic by drawing our attention to *The Beatitudes* at Matthew 5 and notes that at first sight Jesus appears, surprisingly, not to have included anything about those who pray. Yet, Fosdick thinks them represented in one of the sayings, namely, "Blessed are those who hunger and thirst for righteousness, for they shall be satisfied" (Matt 5:6). Fosdick concludes: "Prayer is hunger and thirst. *Prayer is our demand on life, elevated, purified, and aware of a Divine Alliance.*"[11] It is valuable for our further reflection to keep in mind this perception of *prayer as a longing at the centre of our creaturely existence, sustained in the awareness of God's presence*.

Before we leave Fosdick's magnificent work, the following thought, which envisages prayer as extending beyond humanity, deserves to be noted: "Stones and clods are undisturbed by any sense of lack. The faintest glimmering of life, however, brings in the reign of want. Even in some one-celled amœba rolling about in search of food, the presence of life means a hunger which is the rudiment of prayer. And from these dim

9. This same idea has more recently been entertained in Ulanov and Ulanov, *Primary Speech*.

10. Leech, *True Prayer*, 7.

11. Fosdick, *Meaning of Prayer*, 175 (Fosdick's emphasis).

Prayer

beginnings of instinctive need to the spiritual demands of sage and saint, the extent and quality of a being's wants are a good measure of his life."[12]

Another person writing on prayer during the First World War was Friedrich Heiler (1892–1967), who was working on his doctoral dissertation in Germany. He began and ended his monumental work *Das Gebet: Eine religionsgeschichtliche und religionspsychologische Untersuchung* (1917) (published in English in 1932 as *Prayer: A Study in the History and Psychology of Religion*) with the observation that all religious people agree that prayer is "the central phenomenon of religion." As such, he found that the emergence and history of prayer parallels the emergence and history of religion.[13] He also asserts that the emergence of prayer and religion is to be discovered at the very emergence of humanity itself, when even human language was not yet fully developed.[14] It is an assertion that, as we saw in chapter 4, has become strengthened in light of more recent studies. Earlier, the English ethnographer Edward Burnett Tylor (1832–1917) considered in his study *Primitive Culture* (1873) that while prayer appeared not to be present in certain peoples with very primitive beliefs, the religious dimension of life continuously developed from primitive forms to the higher religions and that, as far as can be discerned, it has been and is found among all peoples.[15] As elaborated upon in the previous chapter, archaeological excavations have provided confirmation. Charles Darwin took up Tylor's idea of the universality and continuous development of religion in its broadest sense in his work *The Descent of Man* (1872; 2nd ed. 1874).[16]

In agreement with the findings of James, Fosdick, Heiler, and many others, the *Catechism of the Catholic Church* affirms that people of all ages up to the present have given expression of their quest for God—or, if we put it more generally, for the transcendent—in their prayers, sacrifices, rituals, meditations, and so forth, so that the *Catechism* wants us to think of the human being as "a *religious being*."[17] The *Catechism*'s last major section, which is devoted to prayer, has the first chapter under the title, "The Revelation to Prayer. The Universal Call to Prayer," and one of its

---

12. Ibid., 168.
13. Heiler, *Prayer*, xiii–xvi, 362–63.
14. Ibid., 3, 8–9.
15 Tylor, *Primitive Culture*, 2:362–74, 450–51.
16. Darwin, *Descent of Man*, 78–81.
17. *CCC*, no. 28 (italics are those of the *Catechism*).

Cosmic Prayer and Guided Transformation

first articles says, "In his indefectible covenant with every living creature, God has always called people to prayer" (no. 2569). With this sentence the *Catechism* refers to Noah, who amidst the animals was already being called into a relationship with God (Gen 9:8–17). It thereby wants us to realize that our prayer likewise suitably begins amidst the created realities that are a witness of God's concern for living beings and that the various creatures are being blessed through our prayer.

Recently, Philip and Carol Zaleski published a fresh phenomenological study of prayer in its various manifestations around the globe throughout humanity's history, *Prayer: A History* (2005). Earlier, Heiler, who while writing was in the process of leaving Roman Catholicism behind so as to become a Lutheran, had approached his subject with a rather restricted methodology; that is, he studied prayer as the oral and written expression of language in addition to the quiet absorption of the mystic, whereby he left aside as if unrelated the expressions of ritual, gesture, popular devotion, sacred art, and so forth.[18] Zaleski and Zaleski, pointing out Heiler's restrictive approach, have aimed to reconnect prayer to these various related expressions.[19] As is demanded by our times they also make a much more elaborate comparison between the spiritual endeavors in the various religions. Their assessment is: "All human beings long for the beautiful, the true, and the good, and every desire—for better crops or greater wisdom, for world peace or a good-night kiss—participates in this longing. We are constituted, by nature or divine gift, in such a way that this longing carries with it, as if its necessary companion, the impulse to pray. . . . Prayer lies in the ground of our being and connects us to its source, and every creative act bears, manifest or hidden, its imprint."[20]

The Zaleskis are thereby well aware of the greatly varying perceptions and experiences instilled by the various religions. They do not ascribe to the popular metaphor that "describes truth as a great mountain, and each religion as a path wending towards the summit, where all paths meet." They consider that the paths are quite different and that there are a multitude of peaks at the summit.[21]

---

18. Gill, "Prayer," 7368.
19. Zaleski and Zaleski, *Prayer*, 29–32.
20. Ibid., 31.
21. Ibid., 150–51; see also ibid., 306.

Prayer

CHRISTIAN PRAYER IN SCRIPTURE AND THE PATRISTIC TRADITION

For Christianity, as it evolved out of Judaism and worship in the synagogue, the Hebrew Psalms have traditionally assumed a very significant role in the expression of prayer, both in common and individual prayer.[22] In addition to this, Jesus himself regularly sought a quiet and lonely place to pray, so that Christian prayer is also expected to take on a very personal character. With regard to content, in continuation of the many examples in the Old Testament, including the various Psalms, different forms of prayer are discerned: adoration or worship, confession or the recognition of failures, intercession on behalf of other people or a certain cause, petition or asking for the satisfaction of various needs, thanksgiving, and the closely related praise of God.

Clement of Alexandria (d. c.214), trying to circumscribe it in a few words, says, "Prayer, then, to speak somewhat boldly, is converse with God (ὁμιλία πρὸς τὸν Θεόν)."[23] He clarifies that what matters is not our speech, but the outreach with all our heart to God, "For God unceasingly listens to all converse stemming from the heart."[24] Clement also perceives that as prayer is interiorized, becomes silent and intimate, it becomes constant and one with the whole of life.[25] All Christian spiritual writers after Clement, including, for example Gregory of Nyssa (c.335–395), adopted the idea that prayer is foremost "converse with God."[26] Evagrius, as I pointed out in chapter 3, qualified it to be "conversation of the intellect with God," or again, "the ascent of the intellect to God."[27] The latter definition is, for example, also found in John of Damascus (c.675–c.749), "Prayer (Προσευχή) is the ascent of the intellect towards God, or the requesting of good things from God."[28]

While the intellectual aspect is indeed a very significant and indispensable aspect of prayer, in general, the church fathers, in continuity of

---

22. *CCC*, no. 2585–88; Coyle, "What Was 'Prayer'?," 28.

23. Clement *Stromateis* 7:7:39; ed. Hort and Mayor, *Miscellanies book VII*, 69 (my translation of this and following extracts).

24. Ibid.

25. Ibid. 6:102:1; 7:35:6.

26. Nyssa *De Oratione Dominica* 1 and 2; PG 44:1119–47; Louth, *Wisdom*, 5; Phillips, *Concept of Prayer*, 41–80.

27. Evagrius *De oratione* 3, 36; PG 79:1168, 1173; Louth, *Wisdom*, 6–7.

28. John of Damascus *De fide orthodoxa* 3:24; PG 94:1089C.

Cosmic Prayer and Guided Transformation

Scripture (e.g., Deut 4:29; 6:5; 10:12; 11:13; 30:10; Josh 22:5; Pss 111:1; 119:2, 10, 58, 145; Mark 12:30 and parallel texts), have understood prayer to involve the entire person. As such, a well-known formula of Christian prayer in modern times expands upon the second definition of Evagrius by speaking of mind and heart, and adds moreover a motive.[29] For example, the *Catechism of the Catholic Church* expands upon the formulation by John of Damascus accordingly, even though it actually presents it as if an unaltered citation. "Prayer is the raising of one's mind and heart to God or the requesting of good things from God" (no. 2559). Prayer involves us entirely, body and soul, our mind and will, our desires and intentions. Shortly after providing this definition, the *Catechism* comments that "it is the whole man who prays" (no. 2562). In a later chapter the *Catechism* includes in its reflection on vocal prayer as an essential element of the Christian life, "We must pray with our whole being to give all power possible to our supplication" (no. 2702). A further suited comment upon the *Catechism*'s altered definition of John of Damascus is that such prayer is performed with the desire that God's will is done in our lives and in the world. This is exemplified in the *Our Father* by the petition that his will be done on earth as it is in heaven (Matt 6:10).

Benedict, writing in the mid sixth century, admonishes in his *Rule* for monks, "Let us stand to sing the Psalms in such a way that our minds are in harmony with our voices."[30] Taking to heart the saying at Ps 119:164, he wants his monks to praise God with psalms and hymns seven times a day[31] so that ideally the entire day and every moment of life would become sanctified. Concerning individual prayer he says, "If at other times someone chooses to pray privately, he may simply go in and pray, not in a loud voice, but with tears and heartfelt devotion."[32] Undoubtedly, the main message is that prayer and life are intended to flow in and out of each other, in accordance with our nature, involving our entire being, so that we may live evermore in God's presence.

The continuity between our prayer and life is also realized by having throughout the day a simple prayer in mind, such as the traditional *Jesus Prayer* that was already promoted by Diadochus of Photiki (c.400–486)[33]

---

29. Healy, "Prayer (Theology of)," 593.
30. Benedict *Rule* 19:7; ed. and trans. Fry et al., *RB 1980*, 216–17.
31. Benedict *Rule* 16:1; ed. and trans. Fry et al. *RB 1980*, 210–11.
32. Benedict *Rule* 52:4; ed. and trans. Fry et al. *RB 1980*, 255; similarly Benedict *Rule* 4:57; 20:3; 49:4.
33. Diadochus of Photiki *On Spiritual Knowledge and Discrimination* 59, 61, 97;

Prayer

and subsequently by the Eastern church. In the former rural Western societies where the Roman Catholic Church was found, thrice daily church bells stipulated the call to the silent recitation of the *Angelus*; at present it is mostly only the monastic churches that continue to ring the *Angelus*. In addition, Teddy Shovlin, my Scottish father-in-law, also rings it daily at St Machan's Parish Church near Glasgow, and hopefully there are still some other places.

A DEFINITION OF PRAYER AND CHRISTIAN PRAYER AND ASSOCIATED COMMENTS

Prayer proper takes place in the context of a relationship with a personal and living God.[34] It is instrumental for consolidating this relationship and for making it more intense and intimate.

This immediately implies that prayer is only meaningful, and not a self-deceptive activity, if God really exists and can receive a prayer. It also implies that God is not an impersonal Mind; as often we hear it said, "I believe there must be *something* to account for all that exists." It implies that God is not merely the organizing principle at the summit of an impersonal universe or in its immediate projected extension upon which we can philosophize without a need for our further life engagement, or which would be rather indifferent to our engagement. Rather, for contingent beings that receive being from a personal and living God, prayer and engagement cannot be optional, but are essential to their created existence.

In light of the foregoing observations, it appears valid to define prayer as follows: *Prayer is the deliberate, or willed, movement, or dynamic, with which human beings aim attentively to enter with all their needs, wishes and desires into God's presence. God is thereby considered as a personal God who is the ground and origin of theirs and every being, and with whom a two-way communication, a dialogue, is possible.*

Prayer is thus a longing for fulfillment, which is evermore realized into God's presence, where it is received as a gift. Prayer is by God's grace

---

SC 5bis: 119–21, 159–60. See also Leech, *True Prayer*, 53; Ware, "Origins," 175–84.

34. See also Tylor, *Primitive Culture*, 2:364; Heiler, *Prayer*, 357; Arbesmann, "Prayer," 588; cf. Phillips, *Concept of Prayer*, 30: "Not all prayers can be described as talking to God [In footnote: "Many Buddhist prayers, for example, cannot be described in this way"], but they are nevertheless claimed to be meetings with the supernatural or encounters with the divine."

effective for the actualization of this fulfillment, as those praying are themselves taken up in this movement by which they are being constituted and transformed. As already intimated in chapter 2 (where Maximus was found to envisage that humanity has a task of orienting the entire creaturely order towards God) and in chapter 3 (where Psalm 104 was found to situate prayer and worship in the context of universal salvation; where commenting upon Plato's two ontological realms we found that, as Jesus, we also need to become another humanity for the Word so as to contribute to our own and universal salvation; and where we discussed Koestler's interdependent *holons*), it contributes to the actualization of the entire cosmos. For, by their symbolizing capacity people may be capable of having some ideas about order, harmonious existence, unity, and so forth, but it is by their prayerfulness that its realization can take place in truth.

Prayer can thereby address God directly or indirectly by means of a mediator. In Christian prayer one relies on the mediation of the divine persons themselves. Christian prayer can address the Father through the Son, that is, in the name of Jesus, and by or in the Holy Spirit.[35] It can also be to Jesus, in the Holy Spirit. "No one can say 'Jesus is Lord' except by the Holy Spirit" (1 Cor 12:3).[36] It can also be to the Holy Spirit. As the *Catechism of the Catholic Church* teaches: "The traditional form of petition to the Holy Spirit is to invoke the Father through Christ our Lord to give us the Consoler Spirit.... But the simplest and most direct prayer is also traditional, 'Come, Holy Spirit,' and every liturgical tradition has developed it in antiphons and hymns" (no. 2671). Leech captures in a succinct manner what is specific about Christian prayer: "Christian prayer ... is prayer *in Christ*. And this prayer is rooted in, and arises out of, the Christian understanding of God."[37] Besides this, as W. Brede Kristensen informs us, it appears that not only within Christianity but also within the various religious traditions prayer is perceived to have a divine origin.[38]

It can further be noted that Roman Catholics are commended to call not only upon the divine persons, but to invoke the assistance of angels (*CCC* no. 334–36), the Virgin Mary (no. 2618–19, 2673, 2675–79), and those within the communion of saints (no. 956–57, 962).

---

35. LaCugna, *God for Us*, 122; *CCC* no. 2564, 2614–15, 2634, 2664, 2674.
36. LaCugna, *God for Us*, 123–27; *CCC* no. 2616, 2665–68, 2670.
37. Leech, *True Prayer*, 7 (Leech's emphasis).
38. Kristensen, "Prayer," 171–72, 175.

Prayer can either be offered by an individual or by a group of people as common or liturgical prayer. Liturgical prayer harmonizes and complements the prayer-expression of the participants. Ideally, it takes up the prayer of the individual in his/her outreach to God and incorporates it into the dynamic of the community towards God. Liturgical prayer realizes the religious culture of the local church and varies in its ritual expression according to the calendar, the various occasions, and so forth. It links the local community unto the worldwide church and its inherited tradition. It thus also assures the living link between the individual and the foundational revelations of the Christian faith.

Prayer is a very personal initiative. Yet, it is certainly not an individualistic or isolated event. On the contrary, as explored in the previous chapter, engagement in prayer is very much part of being a human and created being. It is for the greater glory of God, for the well-being of the one praying and for that of the entire creation.

In Christian prayer as taught by Jesus the aim is not so much to enter into God's presence with emphasis on the own fulfillment, but rather to place lovingly and trustingly one's entire being in the Father's hands, whereby the aim is to identify with his all-benevolent will.[39] Besides this, Kristensen points out that also in the prayer of many other religions, trust is a basic attitude.[40] Accordingly, when a faithful person who is rooted in this awareness is "praying for" a particular intention, it is a wanting to bring this intention, together with the own being, into God's presence.

Finally, prayerful silence has certainly a very different content for the one being silent in the various religions. We can recall the metaphor of Zaleski and Zaleski that was cited earlier in this chapter, namely, that there are a multitude of peaks at the summit. Yet, recognizing the particularity of a Christian mindset and of each individual, silence is a prayer shared by all religious people, among others, at death. There, when the mind quiets down, silence, with the diverse contents it encloses, is held in common with all beings.[41] Obviously, for the individual non-rational being this silence is by itself not prayer, but mere presence, with or without awareness of the imminent end. Overall, prayer is not so much found in words, rather beyond words. So also, as touched upon in the previous chapter, we ourselves are not so much found in mindedness, in reason,

---

39. E.g., Elizondo, "Jesus," 9–20.
40. Kristensen, "Prayer," 170.
41. Govaerts, "Dying Blackbird," 6.

and in symbol, but beyond it. With the risk of overstating it, prayer can be seen to have a dual manifestation, namely, in words and in silence, just as in chapter 3 we found created reality to have a dual character, on one side leaning more towards the physical, on the other more towards the metaphysical. Furthermore, one of the instances of dualism mentioned in chapter 3 is perhaps suitably recalled here: namely, physical processes/ spiritual dynamic. In prayerful silence the physical process is (both in the figurative and the literal sense) less pronounced than in vocal prayer, whereas the spiritual dynamic may be the more intensely sensed. It is the case that both manifestations are part of a wholesome prayer life.

In the following chapter the spiritual dynamic involved in prayer will be situated within the encompassing spiritual dynamic of the whole of creation. As human beings we are linked to this wider creation through our bodily presence. Hence, the body of the prayerful person is an interface between the spiritual dynamic of the wider creation and of the human soul. It is therefore valuable to be aware of the involvement of the body in the prayerful dynamic.

PRAYER THAT IS SUPPORTED BY THE BODY AND A HUMBLE LIFESTYLE

The involvement of the body, which supports prayer, finds expression in various positions. Mother Teresa was well aware of it and she invites as follows: "We shall make use of our gestures and postures in prayer to grow in the depth of prayer and contemplation of God by using them meaningfully and with devotion."[42]

For the early Christians the most common position for prayer, as it was for Jews and pagans, was to pray standing (Gen 24:13; Mark 11:25; Matt 6:5; Luke 9:32; 18:11–13) with arms raised towards heaven (Ps 141:2).[43] Another position, that is testified to by the psalmist (Ps 95:6), that we find practiced by Jesus in the garden of Gethsemane (Luke 22:41), by Steven before being stoned (Acts 7:60), and by Paul (Acts 20:36), is kneeling, whether with arms raised high, stretched out in the form of the cross, or with hands held together.[44] Around the end of the second

---

42. Mother Teresa, *Jesus, the Word to be Spoken*, 117.

43. Coyle, "What Was 'Prayer'?," 30–31.

44. Keel, *Symbolism of the Biblical World*, 17, 308; Coyle, "What Was 'Prayer'?," 30–31.

century Tertullian admonished the faithful in his treatise *On Prayer* to pray standing with arms spread out in the form of the cross, or alternatively to pray kneeling. Tertullian further advised to begin the first prayer of the day prostrate on the floor.[45] Perhaps, for ourselves what is important is the simple willingness to rise early (Ps 119:147; Mark 1:35; Luke 6:12) so as to pray and to dedicate some moments as is possible in a bodily position that induces alertness.

In the mid-twentieth century, the Belgian Benedictine monk Jean-Marie Déchanet was helped, and thus helped others, on a Christian spiritual path by striving after—in addition to the Eucharist and the Divine Office—a balance of *anima* (the subconscious aspect of soul, that which controls the body), *animus* (the conscious aspect of soul, that which thinks and reasons) and *spiritus* (the meta-rational, that which tends towards the higher virtues, God); first through his study of the works of William of Saint Thierry (c.1085-1149)[46]—himself influenced by both Eastern and Western fathers—and then on a more practical level through integration of elements of Yoga. The redemption of each of these three aspects of life is searched in a path of three stages or levels that leads towards perfection. Déchanet testified in one of his books, *La Voie du Silence* (1956), translated in English under the title *Christian Yoga*:

> The activity of the various vital currents really enters into play in prayer. An extraordinary sense of calm sinks into the mind, while from the depths of the soul there rises up towards God a silent concert, as it were, of praise and adoration. . . . It is less a concentration of intellectual faculties than a projection of the whole being towards Another. Nor is it a turning in of the spirit on itself—though in fact the spirit does become aware of what it is and has—but a silence in the spirit in which without saying anything, even to oneself, many things may be grasped and understood.[47]

The "silent concert" that rises from the depth of the soul hints at the symphony that is inherent to every physical entity as the configuration of vibrations associated with the various levels of its material structure and that together make up the symphony of the entire universe. It was mentioned in chapter 3 with reference to Andrews' work *The Symphony*

---

45. Tertullian *De oratione* 14, 17, 23; PL 1:1245-1304.
46. Déchanet, *Christian Yoga*, 1-2, 63-72; Déchanet, "Introduction," xxviii-xxxv.
47. Déchanet, *Christian Yoga*, 17.

Cosmic Prayer and Guided Transformation

of Life, which was written ten years after Déchanet published the cited text, and it was mentioned with reference to Brian Greene's *The Fabric of the Cosmos*.[48] A century before Andrews' book emerged, namely in 1868, the explorer, botanist, and nature-lover John Muir came to the awareness that "music is one of the attributes of matter, into whatever forms it may be organized."[49] He meditates that each created entity contributes its own tone or has its own voice: each wave in the seas worldwide; the wind as it moves through a particular landscape; a falling drop of water; the waving flower congregations and each tuned petal, pistil, and sculptured pollen therein; each bird, insect, and so forth.[50] From a theological perspective, talk about a "silent concert" resonates with Moltmann's reflection regarding the vibrating of the Spirit of God (Gen 1:2) that prepares for the Word in God's creative outreach:

> The Hebrew word *rahaph* is generally translated "hover" or "brood." But according to Deut. 32.11 and Jer. 23.9 it has rather the meaning of vibrating, quivering, moving, and exciting. If this is correct, then we should not think only of the image of a fluttering or brooding dove. We should think of the fundamental resonances of music out of which sounds and rhythms emerge. . . . In the quickening breath and through the form-giving word, the Creator sings out his creatures in the sounds and rhythms in which he has his joy and his good pleasure.[51]

Regarding Déchanet's silent way, it can be noted that to simply sit on the floor and search to enter into God's presence as an integrated being, as a human being, with a listening heart, though without a Yoga method, has also been central in the life project of other inspiring monks in the Benedictine tradition, namely, Thomas Merton (1915–68),[52] Henri Le Saux (Swami Abhishiktananda) (1910–73),[53]

---

48. See also Corey, *God and the New Cosmology*, 262, 285 n. 5 regarding the idea of "genetic music."

49. Muir, *Thousand-Mile Walk*, 199.

50. Ibid., 161–62, 199–200.

51. Moltmann, *Jesus Christ*, 288–89.

52. Merton, *Silent Life*.

53. Abhishiktananda, *Prayer*; Abhishiktananda, *Saccidananda*.

John Main (1926–82),[54] and Bede Griffiths (1907–93).[55] By their prayer and meditation they searched to integrate not only their own individual being, but to teach others and to engage with other faiths at their central quest for the Absolute, for interior and world peace. Some other Christians that have been able to inspire because of their daily prayer and meditation, each with their own charisma and vocation, are Brother Charles de Foucauld (1858–1916), who *post mortem* inspired the spirituality of the Little Brothers and Sisters of Jesus and various other religious institutes, Brother Roger Schutz (1915–2005), who founded the Taizé community in France, Mother Teresa of Calcutta (1910–97), who founded the Missionaries of Charity in India, and Catherine de Hueck-Doherty (1896–1985), who founded the lay-apostolic institute Madonna House in Canada. It is these institutes founded upon prayer that still attract young people and that therefore have recently to some extent been taking over the enthusiasm that once went to earlier founded religious institutes that are dwindling, that is, those wherein prayer, overall, has become a routine, and not sufficiently an outreach with all one's being towards God.

While a humble lifestyle and our body can support prayer, the complementary fact is that prayer can contribute to mental and physical health.[56] Within the medical profession itself there is an interest in the power of prayer as a significantly contributing factor to health and healing.[57] Further, prayer can contribute to a flourishing of the church and its religious and secular institutes, and conceivably foster the well-being of all creation.[58]

---

54. Main, *Word into Silence*.

55. Griffiths, *Golden String*; Griffiths, *Christ in India*; Griffiths, *Return to the Centre*; Griffiths, *Marriage of East and West*; Griffiths, *A New Vision of Reality*; Griffiths, *Universal Christ*.

56. MacNutt, *Healing*; Leech, *True Prayer*, 64, 163–70; Moltmann, *Spirit*, 190; Fiddes, *Participating in God*, 147–48; Theillier, *Miracles*; Zaleski and Zaleski, *Prayer*, 316–30; Gorbenko, "Prayer," 15–16.

57. Dossey, *Healing Words*; Lampmann, "Frontier."

58. Johnston, *Silent Music*, 132–37; Murphy, "Difference?," 235–45; Govaerts, "Prayer," 103–15.

6

Cosmic Prayer

NON-HUMAN PRAYER IN THE HEBREW SCRIPTURES

AS SUGGESTED IN THE foregoing chapters, it is not only human beings who are actively engaged in a relationship with God. This chapter will focus our minds upon the spiritual dynamic that is shared in by the various created beings in their particularity and in their collective, wherein humanity and human prayer can be situated as within its proper context. This situating of humanity was already undertaken in chapter 4, especially in the section on the human being as a living being capable of the personal. This chapter will provide further clarification as regards the place of the human being within the whole. We begin this exploration as we did in chapters 2 and 3, that is, with the Hebrew Scriptures. Can we find in the Hebrew Scriptures any support for non-human prayer?

Support is found in the Psalms, such as in Ps 103:20–21, which was quoted at chapter 2. Other Psalms that show non-human entities as involved in worship and prayer include Pss 19:1–6; 93:3–4; 96; 98; 148; and 150.

It can be recalled that in chapter 3 we read that Isaiah in the vision of his calling saw the seraphim that surrounded the divine throne. The prophet heard them proclaiming God's glory (Isa 6:3). This angelic worship has been adopted in Roman Catholic worship at the beginning of the

Cosmic Prayer

Eucharistic prayer following the Preface in a prayer called the Sanctus. In Isaiah we find, moreover, the prophetic expectation of a universal peace (Isa 11:6–9) and of the desert rejoicing, blossoming, and singing (Isa 35:1–2). These latter verses immediately precede the promise of God's coming so as to save those who await him (Isa 35:4) and the verses (Isa 35:5–6) that Jesus quoted to the disciples who came to enquire on John's behalf (Matt 11:5; Luke 7:22). Here also we find the prophet speaking of the Holy Way (Isa 35:8), after which the early Christian movement was called. This prophetic message we find reflected by Deutero-Isaiah:

> Behold, I am doing a new thing;
> now it springs forth, do you not perceive it?
> I will make a way in the wilderness
> and rivers in the desert.
> The wild beasts will honor me,
> the jackals and the ostriches;
> for I give water in the wilderness,
> rivers in the desert,
> to give drink to my chosen people,
> the people whom I formed for myself
> that they might declare my praise.
> (Isa 43:19–22)

As this text shows, the thriving or wasting of the people and of the various creatures is proclaimed as being very much interdependent. It is expressive of the covenant that, as Robert Murray has argued in his book *The Cosmic Covenant* (1992), is being taught throughout Scripture. It speaks of a God-given order that involves both human beings and the wider creation. It is narrated at Gen 9:8–17 as being established with Noah and his descendants and with every living creature. Whether there is order or disorder is co-determined by people's behavior, for they can either respect or scorn the covenant. When people behave irresponsibly and practice injustice and greed, and when they do not walk in God's ways, then this has repercussions for all creatures. When people recognize God as Lord of heaven and earth and when they act justly and responsibly, then the land gives its produce, the rivers flow and harmony is fostered within the created realm. The prophets repeatedly referred to this covenant. The prophet Jeremiah, for example, refers to it implicitly as he speaks of the land that is mourning to God because of human wickedness:

> How long will the land mourn,
> and the grass of every field wither?

Cosmic Prayer and Guided Transformation

> For the wickedness of those who dwell in it
> the beasts and the birds are swept away, ...
> They have made my pleasant portion
> a desolate wilderness.
> They have made it a desolation;
> desolate, it mourns to me.
> (Jer 12:4, 10b–11)

Other texts within the prophetic tradition that speak of the wider creation as either singing or mourning in God's presence include Isa 44:23; 49:13; Hos 4:1–3; and Joel 1:20.

Non-human prayer features also in the famous *Song of the Three Young Men in the Furnace*, which is found at Dan 3:52–90 in the Greek translation and in the Roman Catholic editions of the Bible, or it is found among the Deuterocanonical Books as part of the addition inserted after Dan 3:23. The included hymn of all creation, which is known as the *Benedicite* and which is found at verse 57 and following (or alternatively at vv. 35–68), draws heavily upon the Psalms, especially Psalms 103 and 148.

Around the same time as Daniel, approximately 200 BC, is the book of Tobit, wherein as part of the narrative there features at Tob 8:5, 15 prayer that summons the heavens, the angels therein, and all God's creatures to bless God together.

Finally, with Laurence Frizzell we may note the Qumran text "The Words of the Heavenly Lights" (4Q504–6) that contains a hymn wherein likewise the angels, the earth, and all creatures are admonished to bless God.[1] Other texts of the Qumran community that can be noted as illustrative of the belief in a cosmic covenant and that speak of creation in exultant prayer are the fragmentary *Apocryphal Psalms* (4Q88).[2]

THE PRAYER OF ALL CREATION IN CHRISTIAN TRADITION

Within the Christian Scriptures, in the writings of the church fathers, and in later writers, the notion of cosmic prayer is seldom prominent, but it

---

1. Qumran community *Hymns for the Sabbath Day*; Frizzell, "Hymn," 46; Vermes, *Complete Dead Sea Scrolls*, 379.

2. Qumran community *Apocryphal Psalms*; Vermes, *Complete Dead Sea Scrolls*, 314.

Cosmic Prayer

surfaces regularly; it is as a persistent current that runs rather unobtrusively along throughout Christian history.

Various aspects of the Christ event include a hint of cosmic prayer. To begin with, the Nativity Scene has in continuity of Matthew and Luke become depicted as involving the worship of angels, shepherds, magi, and this amidst the sheep, the ox, and the ass. Next, at the beginning of his ministry, Jesus would have been driven by the Spirit into the wilderness where he was with the wild beasts and where angels ministered to him (Mark 1:12–13 and parallel texts). A possible reading of the event is to perceive that Jesus' presence introduced a restored universal harmony, even drawing the beasts into its influence. At various occasions Jesus healed people in their body. Jesus was not merely concerned with immaterial souls, for in the Jewish perception the human being is a psycho-physical unity. Jesus was healing people entirely, both body and soul. He forgave those that came to him their sins so as to set them free for God, and he healed their bodies so as to enable them to live amidst their kin and in the world. By returning people to the world as fully healed, in body and soul, their gratitude and invigorated spiritual life can be of significance not only for themselves but also for those around them and for the entire web of creation wherein they are inserted. Another event within Jesus' life that hints at cosmic prayer is found in Mark and the other Synoptic Gospels where it is told that Jesus commands the storm wind and the sea expecting these natural elements to recognize God's Lordship that Jesus brought present (Mark 4:39 and parallels). This pericope is reminiscent of Genesis 1 where God expected the cooperation of the elements with his creative initiatives, and of Psalms 65, 89, and 107 where it is claimed that power over the natural elements belongs to God. Still further in the Synoptic Gospels we read that when Jesus died on the cross the wider creation joined in the mourning as darkness covered the land (Mark 15:33 and parallels; compare Amos 8:8–10; Isa 50:3). Finally, in the Apocalypse there is described the vision of the innumerable angels and of all sorts of creatures partaking in the heavenly worship of God and of the glorified Son, who is depicted as a lamb that has been slain (Rev 5:11–14).

The support for cosmic prayer in the Christ event has also been written about by me in a separate publication, where in addition I have discussed supportive texts from the church fathers and from the liturgy.[3]

---

3. Govaerts, "Transcendental," 29–41.

Cosmic Prayer and Guided Transformation

In the following I will instead bring us to reflect some moments upon the support found in Paul's letter to the Romans. Thereupon, I would like to provide some detail of a hymn that is ascribed to Gregory of Nazianzen, and then present some texts of later Christian history wherein a notion of cosmic prayer is present. Our journey continues here with Paul.

Complementary to the Gospels, we find in Paul a hint of both cosmic covenant and cosmic prayer at Rom 8:19–23. In these few lines there is mention of "the sons of God," that is, the faithful, "the redemption of our bodies," and of the whole creation (πᾶσα ἡ κτίσις) that groans together as it awaits deliverance and that "waits with eager longing for the revealing of the sons of God." For the idea of a cosmic interdependence and of a groaning creation Paul would have been directly inspired by Gen 3:17–19 and by the prophetic texts considered in the previous section. In the surrounding verses Paul says that at the present time the brethren suffer (Rom 8:18), and that they groan inwardly as they wait for their adoption by God (8:23; compare 2 Cor 5:2). This suffering for Christ that is here envisaged (Rom 8:35–36), whatever particular form it takes, and this groaning, Paul believes as not happening to humans in isolation as the result of haphazard situations. Their suffering is with Christ (8:17), and the Spirit himself intercedes for them with sighs too deep for words (8:26). Moreover, as Paul explains, the suffering of the brethren is to be seen as an integral part of the event of universal creation and salvation. Accordingly, the existent non-human creatures are not devoid of a destiny that is theirs, but are just as the faithful on a journey towards completion in God. As such, the created beings can be envisaged to long for glorious existence (8:21), delivered from the futility inflicted on them by humanity and malignant spiritual powers. Further down in the letter Paul expresses, as he did at 1 Cor 15:28, that everything receives existence from God and that through him everything finds in him also its end (Rom 11:36).[4] Ultimately, for Paul, everything is directed towards the glorification with one voice in accord with Jesus Christ, and through him, of God the Father (11:36; 14:11; 15:5–11; 16:27).

Gregory of Nazianzen writes at two places about the praise and prayer that is offered to God by various creatures. The first instance is found in his *Oration on the Nativity*,[5] wherein he expresses the idea that before humanity arrived on the scene, the heavenly spiritual beings

---

4. See also Ziesler, *Romans*, 220–21.
5. Nazianzen *Oratio* 38:11; PG 36:322C–23B.

Cosmic Prayer

as well as the earthly sensible beings were each praising God in their own realms. He envisages that with the creation of human beings there emerged a living being with a mixed nature, as a microcosm of the macrocosm, a worshipper mixed in nature for the greater glory of God. The second instance is a magnificent hymn to God, much in the same inspiration, wherein Gregory envisages a universal groaning in travail and prayer, as was envisaged by Paul before him and by Gregory's friend Basil. The hymn has been taken up in the French version of the Divine Office (*La Liturgie des Heures*, volume 4) for the Office of Readings on Wednesdays 1 of ordinary time.[6] An edition of the original Greek version can be found in *Anthologia graeca carminum christianorum* (1871).[7] An English translation based upon this anthology was made by Allen W. Chatfield (1808–96) in his book *Songs and Hymns of Earliest Greek Christian Poets, Bishops and Others translated into English verse* (1876), which has become entirely available online.[8] I provide here an English translation by myself:

> O You, the Beyond-of-all,
> is that not all that one can chant of You?
>
> Which hymn shall one pronounce, what speech?
> No utterance can express You.
> What shall the mind hold on to?
> No thought can attain You.
> You only are unpronounceable,
> for all that is spoken stems from You.
> You only are unknowable,
> for all that is thought stems from You.
> Every being
> that thinks or is without thought,
> renders You homage.
> For the common desires,
> the common groaning of being in travail,
> they present themselves before You,
> and the ensemble of beings
> prays to You.
> Every being

---

6. The first words of the hymn in *La Liturgie des Heures* 4: "O toi, l'au-delà de tout."

7. The first words of the hymn at Christ and Paranikas, *Anthologia graeca*, 24: Ὦ πάντων ἐπέκεινα.

8. Chatfield, *Songs and Hymns*.

that perceives Your watchword,
lets a hymn of silence ascend towards You.
Every being that remains, remains in You;
and among them together
Your divinity dwells.
Of all beings
You are the end.
Being one;
every being, yet none.
You are not a single being,
nor are You their totality.
You have every name,
and how shall I call You,
You who cannot be named?
What heavenly mind shall penetrate
the veils beyond the clouds?
Have mercy,

O You, the Beyond-of-all,
is that not all that one can chant of You?

Progressing on to the Middle Ages, we encounter *The Canticle of Brother Sun* by Francis of Assisi (1182–1226).[9] When Francis found flowers or anything beautiful, whether a forest, a vineyard, or stones, he apparently used to address these as if they were endowed with reason and encouraged them to praise their God and Creator.[10] It is in this spirit of holiness that Francis allegedly sang the *Canticle* towards the end of his life in a situation of distress, bodily suffering, and dispute among the brethren. The *Canticle* expresses the praise of God in name of the Sun, the Moon, the stars, wind and air, water, fire, and earth. As such, it recalls the *Benedicite*.

In the early modern period, a beautiful expression of cosmic prayer is encountered in Henry Vaughan's (1621–95) poem "The Morning Watch." It has been taken up in the English version of the Divine Office according to the Roman rite, among the poems that are recommended as being especially appropriate for the Office of Readings.[11] Vaughan's poem

---

9. Brother Ramon, *Franciscan Spirituality*, 138–39 (Italian text of the *Canticle* and trans. by Placid Hermann).

10. Ibid., 134.

11. *Divine Office*, Hymns and Religious Poems no. 98 (which can be found in each of the three volumes).

Cosmic Prayer

can also be found in *The Ark*, the journal of the society Catholic Concern for Animals, and is made available in the online archive of the journal.[12] In addition, I draw attention to William Wordsworth's (1770–1850) poem "Written in Early Spring" as approaching a sense of cosmic prayer. It can be found in the beautiful anthology *Field and Forest* compiled by Barbara Willard.[13]

Moving onwards in our exploration of writings within the Christian tradition that include a sense of the prayer of all creation we come to the spiritual classic *The Way of a Pilgrim*, which is the account given by an anonymous Russian pilgrim to a *starets* between 1853 and 1861. (A *starets* is a monk of a Russian Orthodox monastery who has had a long experience of the spiritual life and who is gifted to guide other people.) The story was printed at Kazan in 1884 and translated in English in 1930. In this we find again a passage that expresses an awakening awareness to the wider-than-human reality of prayer: "The trees, the grass, the birds, the earth, the air, the light seemed to be telling me that they existed for man, that everything proved the love of God for man, that all things prayed to God and sang his praise. Thus it was that I came to understand what *The Philokalia* calls 'the knowledge of the speech of all creatures,' and I saw the means by which converse could be held with God's creatures."[14]

About a century later, in a work on the prayer of Jesus, published in French as *La prière de Jésus* (1963) under the pseudonym "A Monk of the Eastern Church," Fr Lev Gillet envisages in accord with tradition that the wider creation is participant in a dynamic of prayer. I found the following extract translated by André Louf in "Prayer and Ecology": "The material universe murmurs Jesus' name in secret . . . and it is part of each Christian's ministry to express this aspiration, to pronounce the name of Jesus over the elements of nature: the stones and the trees, the flowers and the fruits, the mountains and the sea. This ministry enables the secret within things to be fulfilled, and to respond to this long, mute, unconscious waiting. We can transfigure the animal world as well. Jesus, who proclaimed that no sparrow is forgotten by the Father . . . did not exclude the animals from his generosity and his gracious influence."[15]

---

12. Vaughan, "Morning Watch."
13. Willard, *Field and Forest*, 84–85.
14. Russian pilgrim, *Way of a Pilgrim*, 45.
15. Louf (trans.), "Prayer," 135.

Cosmic Prayer and Guided Transformation

Next, in the *Dogmatic Constitution on the Church* (*Lumen gentium*, 1964) of Vatican II, at paragraph 36, the faithful are encouraged to deepen their Christian life and to learn how to associate with creation in their prayer life:

> For the Lord wishes to spread his kingdom by means of the laity also, a kingdom of truth and life, a kingdom of holiness and grace, a kingdom of justice, love, and peace. In this kingdom, creation itself will be delivered out of its slavery to corruption and into the freedom of the glory of the sons of God (cf. Rom. 8:21).... The faithful, therefore, must learn the deepest meaning and the value of all creation, and how to relate it to the praise of God. They must assist one another to live holier lives even in their daily occupations. In this way the world is permeated by the spirit of Christ and more effectively achieves its purpose in justice, charity, and peace. The laity have the principal role in the universal fulfillment of this purpose.[16]

Paragraph 48 of the same constitution is much in the same tone. It describes the church as "the universal sacrament of salvation" and envisages that "the human race as well as the entire world, which is intimately related to man and achieves its purpose through him, will be perfectly re-established in Christ."[17]

The vision of Isaiah of the desert rejoicing, blossoming, and singing (Isa 35:1–2), which was brought to mind at the beginning of this chapter, was referred to by Archbishop Oscar Romero (1917–80) in a homily that was preached for the suffering people of El Salvador on December 11, 1977, the Third Sunday of Advent, wherein he developed around the theme of "The Church of Salvation." He also refers to the groaning of creation that Paul spoke about and which has been recalled throughout Christian tradition. The homilies of Romero are made available in an English translation by The Archbishop Romero Trust; here follows the extract referred to:

> The liberation that the Church waits for is a cosmic liberation. The Church experiences that all of nature is groaning beneath the weight of sin. What beautiful coffee groves, what fine wheat, sugar cane and cotton fields, what farms, what lands God has given us! Nature is so beautiful! But we see it groan under oppression, under wickedness, under injustice, under abuse, and

---

16. Vatican II, *Lumen gentium* 36; trans. Abbott, *Documents of Vatican II*, 62–63.
17. Vatican II, *Lumen gentium* 48; trans. ibid., 78–79.

the Church experiences its pain. Nature looks for a liberation that will not be mere material well-being but God's act of power. God will free nature from sinful human hands, and along with the redeemed it will sing a hymn of joy to God the Liberator.

How beautiful is the song of freedom that we have listened to today in the first reading. The prophet Isaiah becomes a poet as he sings a song of liberation. *The desert and the parched land will exult; the steppe will rejoice and bloom. They will bloom with abundant flowers and rejoice with joyful song.*[18]

Moving on, we find a few years later another homily, preached in 1981 by the then archbishop of Munich, Joseph Ratzinger. Ratzinger had been present as a young theologian at Vatican II, which spoke of the significance of associating creation to us in our prayer. In addition, his German background may have contributed to an appreciation of the natural world. As he moved on in his appointment as Prefect of the Sacred Congregation of the Doctrine of the Faith, he would have been closely involved with the text of the new *Catechism of the Catholic Church* and other major papal writings. As such, he has been well aware of the rightful place of creation in Christian doctrine long before he became pope. The homily that I mentioned was given as part of a series of Lenten homilies in the Liebfrauenkirche in Munich. In this homily he expounds as follows: "Creation exists for the sake of worship. . . . The true center, the power that moves and shapes from within in the rhythm of the stars and of our lives, is worship. Our life's rhythm moves in proper measure when it is caught up in this. . . . Ultimately every people has known this. The creation accounts of all civilizations point to the fact that the universe exists for worship and for the glorification of God. . . . The danger that confronts us today in our technological civilization is that we have cut ourselves off from this primordial knowledge."[19]

We have in the meantime reached the long pontificate of Pope John Paul II, born Karol Józef Wojtyła (1920–2005), which lasted from October 1978 until April 2005. The *Catechism* that took account of the Second Vatican Ecumenical Council was published in Latin towards the end of 1992 and the English translation in 1994. It recalls *Lumen gentium* 36 for its teaching that "all creatures have the same Creator and are all ordered to his glory."[20] A little further it continues: "Creation was fashioned with

18. Romero, "Church," 6.
19. Ratzinger, *In the Beginning*, 28.
20. *CCC*, no. 344; noteworthy are also no. 337, 350, 1046.

Cosmic Prayer and Guided Transformation

a view to the Sabbath and therefore for the worship and adoration of God. Worship is inscribed in the order of creation" (no. 347). Elsewhere, the *Catechism* affirms: "Animals are God's creatures. . . . By their mere existence they bless him and give him glory" (no. 2416).

Next, in 1993, the pope was invited to participate in an interview proposed by Italian Radio and Television. The pope's busy schedule prevented the televised interview taking place, but he eventually answered the questions on paper and they have been published in the book *Crossing the Threshold of Hope* (1994). The pope was asked about his prayer life and his reply included the following, whereby he remained close to *Lumen gentium*: "According to the apostle [Paul], prayer reflects all created reality; it is in a certain sense a *cosmic function*." And the pope continued: "*Man is the priest of all creation*; he speaks in its name, but only insofar as he is guided by the Spirit. In order to understand profoundly the meaning of prayer, one should meditate for a long time on the following passage from the Letter to the Romans: 'For creation awaits with eager expectation. . . . For in hope we were saved' (Rom. 8:19–24) . . ."[21]

In the Apostolic letter *Light of the East* (*Orientale lumen*, 1995) the pope related again creation and the spiritual life:

> In the liturgical experience, Christ the Lord is the light which illumines the way and reveals the transparency of the cosmos, precisely as in scripture. . . . [C]reation is revealed for what it is—a complex whole which finds its perfection—its purpose—in the liturgy alone. . . . There creation communicates to each individual the power conferred on it by Christ. Thus the Lord, immersed in the Jordan, transmits to the waters a power which enables them to become the bath of baptismal renewal. . . . Cosmic reality is also summoned to give thanks because the whole universe is called to recapitulation in Christ the Lord.[22]

Finally, in a Wednesday general audience at the Vatican on January 17, 2001, the pope began with a reflection on Psalm 148:

> In the hymn of praise proclaimed a few moments ago (Ps 148:1–5), the Psalmist summons all creatures, calling them by name. . . . The believer, in a sense, is "the shepherd of being," that is, the one who leads all beings to God, inviting them to sing an "alleluia" of praise. The Psalm brings us into a sort of

---

21. John Paul II, *Crossing the Threshold*, 16–17 (the included emphasis is the pope's).

22. John Paul II, *Orientale lumen* 11.

Cosmic Prayer

cosmic church, whose apse is the heavens and whose aisles are the regions of the world, in which the choir of God's creatures sings his praise.

On the one hand, this vision might represent a lost paradise and, on the other, the promised paradise. Not without reason, the horizon of a paradisal universe, which Genesis (chap. 2) put at the very origins of the world, is placed by Isaiah (chap. 11) and the Book of Revelation (chap. 21–22) at the end of history. Thus we see that man's harmony with his fellow beings, with creation and with God, is the plan followed by the Creator. This plan was and is continually upset by human sin.[23]

In support of our theme, attention can further be drawn to a speech delivered by Bartholomew I, the Archbishop of Constantinople and Ecumenical Patriarch of the Orthodox Christians. The occasion for the speech was an environmental symposium organized in California in 1997, a few weeks before the meeting of world leaders in Kyoto, Japan. Part of the address is as follows:

> People of all faith traditions praise the Divine, for they seek to understand their relationship to the cosmos. The entire universe participates in a celebration of life, which St Maximus the Confessor described as a "cosmic liturgy." We see this cosmic liturgy in the symbiosis of life's rich biological complexities. These complex relationships draw attention to themselves in humanity's self-conscious awareness of the cosmos. As human beings, created "in the image and likeness of God" (Gen 1:26), we are called to recognize this interdependence between our environment and ourselves. In the bread and wine of the Eucharist, as priests standing before the altar of the world, we offer the creation back to the creator in relationship to him and to each other. Indeed, in our liturgical life, we realize by anticipation, the final state of the cosmos in the Kingdom of Heaven.[24]

The ecumenical patriarch continues to be a spokesman for the environment and all his addresses on the environment can be found on the website of the Ecumenical Patriarchate of Constantinople.

In chapter 1 was already mentioned the contributions made by some theologians towards the notion of the prayer of all creation. Here I will restrict myself and refer to one more theologian, namely Diarmuid Ó Murchú, who has been writing several books on the need for a renewed

23. John Paul II, "God," para. 1.
24. Bartholomew, "Speeches," para. 8.

Cosmic Prayer and Guided Transformation

spiritual awareness. In *Religion in Exile* (2000) he reflects as follows: "Our desire to pray, and our need to pray, is not merely a divine gift bestowed by special grace. Every moment of every day the universe to which we belong, and the planet we inhabit, pray in us and through us. God's creativity, which impregnates the whole of creation, is forever trying to break open the doors of the human heart."[25]

A DEFINITION OF "COSMIC PRAYER" AND ASSOCIATED COMMENTS

The reflections on prayer undertaken in chapter 5 were about human prayer. Yet, the definition of prayer was formulated in such terms that prayer can readily be envisaged to be encompassed by a wider spiritual dynamic that is integral to the being that is shared in by all God's creatures. In chapter 3 on cosmos it was hinted that all created beings partake in manifestations of intelligence; that intelligence can be discerned at various levels of complexity. The idea was put forward in chapters 3 and 4 that the universe is in a process of constant transformation, striving through these manifestations of intelligence towards a harmonization and towards an increased participation in the personal. We also considered that everything is informed and guided by the Word or Son and by the Spirit and thus, in accordance with the scriptural teaching, is invited unto a dialectical relationship with the Creator.

In light of the previous chapters, therefore, the following definition of "cosmic prayer" can be put forward. The support found in authoritative writings throughout the Judaeo-Christian tradition provides encouragement to propose such definition and to entertain belief in the vision that it enshrines. The remainder of this chapter may provide further clarification.

Cosmic prayer is the longing for communion with the Holy Trinity and for transformation towards personalization within the Trinity (1) by meaningful ensembles of unconscious entities and/or of faintly consciously (self-)aware animals that behave intelligently,[26] (2) by representative individual human beings who are themselves guided by this encompassing dynamic, through a virtuous life and natural contemplation and through illumination already offered within ecclesial institutes (wherein sacramental

---

25. Ó Murchú, *Religion in Exile*, 104.
26. The subject is here still the ensembles.

Cosmic Prayer

gifts are passed on) and possibly elsewhere, (3) by invisible spiritual beings who exist in close conjunction with the visible realities.

As suggested in chapter 4 in the section on "Personhood and Person," the transformation towards personalization within God occurs in virtue of a process of universal harmonization or incorporation, whereby the various ensembles and entities cohere within a unity that is both immanent and divinely transcendent to the universal created reality in a manner that accords with the intrinsic features of the natures and with the situations of the created entities. As such, the various particular manifestations of (imperfect) cosmic prayer lead into the single multifarious cosmic prayer that perfectly expresses the prayer and love of the divine persons.

Moreover, just as Scripture says that God has loved the brethren first (1 John 4:19), so the divine persons also have, as the first, willingly been desiring to take up divinized creatures within the divine inter-personal communion. As we proposed in chapter 2, God has allowed for the emergence of creatures with an own identity, but every capacity they partake in stems from God. The created entities mentioned in the here provided definition are the authentic subjects of cosmic prayer, but the capacity thereto is enabled by God. It can be envisaged that God bestows a *logos* that instills the capacity to pray and hope in love, whereby he wants to lead to eternal well-being. It is the task and responsibility of the ensembles, human beings, and spiritual beings to realize the divine intention in such mode of existence (*tropos*), in such orientation upon God, that the various suited *logoi* and the one(s) here mentioned are appropriated in such manner that they come to live within God's embrace and power.

PARTICULAR MANIFESTATIONS OF COSMIC PRAYER

In this section I provide explanation as regards the three categories of being referred to in the proposed definition of cosmic prayer. Let us look at each category in turn. To begin with, it is envisaged that the "praying" subjects can be indicated as "meaningful ensembles that behave intelligently." What are these ensembles and what signs can we discern of their alleged engagement in cosmic prayer? It is to be acknowledged that cosmic prayer just as prayer is a rather elusive reality. Even for human beings, prayer is not always readily observable. This applies even more so for creaturely entities that we understand only very partially.

Cosmic Prayer and Guided Transformation

We need to contemplate with insight to distinguish cosmic prayer. The meaningful ensembles that behave intelligently are to be related to Koestler's *holons* discussed in chapter 3. So, where is it that we can observe in one way or other such *holons* or ensembles? It is those ensembles that can be recognized as allowing for such cooperation among their constituent entities and such receptivity of the divine informing that it has resulted in a form of self-transcendence and in a transformation towards an increasing participation in the personal. These are the ensembles that display a complexity of behavior and a purposive behavior that qualifies them as meaningful and as behaving intelligently. It is these also that indirectly can be envisaged as being engaged in cosmic prayer. The following can be listed as examples of such ensembles:

1. The Milky Way, which from early onwards would have consisted of hydrogen atoms, each made up of a proton and an accompanying electron, and wherein stars formed that enabled nuclear fusion into helium atoms and some of the other chemical elements.

2. The solar system, which began with interstellar dust that included a variety of atoms, and wherein these atoms were being organized by the force of gravitation into a system that contains the Sun at the center wherein are found most of the lighter hydrogen atoms, and the circling planets made up of a great variety of chemical elements; and wherein the continuing nuclear fusion provides the energy that enables chemical reactions to take place.

3. The early earth with a liquid surface and a developing atmosphere, which from early onwards (from about 4.5 billion years ago) contained inorganic molecules, in which developed simple organic molecules, later more complex ones, and early life forms.

4. The earth from about 3.5 billion years ago and onwards, which despite periods of higher and lower temperatures has, overall, maintained global temperatures within a limited range that allowed continuation and development of life on its surface, this despite an increasingly hotter Sun.

5. The same earth at whose surface photosynthesizing microorganisms contributed from around 2.5 billion years ago and onwards to the establishment of an oxygen-rich lower atmosphere that has remained roughly constant in the proportion of its various gases for

about the last 350 million of years, allowing for the development of more complex life forms.

6. The various developing local ecosystems in the oceans and seas and on dry land wherein life forms developed of varying complexity.

7. The ecosystems of some valleys in East and South Africa that were the cradle for early hominid species (from around 7 million years ago and onwards) and later for anatomically modern people (about 160,000 years ago).

All these are examples of ensembles that have realized a potential for self-transcendence. In general, examples on earth of "ensembles that behave intelligently" are what can be termed "ensembles of ecologically significant proportions."

It can be observed, though only indirectly so, that the macro ensembles that have manifested a form of self-transcendence have, as cooperative with the divine informing by Word and Spirit, allowed for a development at the micro level towards complex behavior, towards life, towards increasing freedom, towards conscious awareness and the ability to be compassionate, to care, and to love. As it were midway between the micro and the macro level there have emerged creatures that are capable of what we consider to be a personal existence: namely human beings, who, though autonomous in their behavior, are greatly dependent for their existence upon all other levels of existence, both at the macro and micro level. As I have mentioned in chapter 4 at the section "The Human Being as a Living Being Capable of the Personal," I suggest that human beings have emerged at that point of the development at which the intelligence of the individual bodily creatures was able to reach a certain threshold so that these creatures by themselves constituted as it were ensembles that behave intelligently. The "praying" subjects within the visible creation were then no longer only the macroscopic ensembles at various levels, one within the other, such as we listed, but also individual human beings,[27] who of course emerged very much as creatures who are sustained by the encompassing social and ecological networks. It is proposed therefore that, as our emergence itself, also human prayer has come about in the context of the wider existential dynamic that is cosmic prayer.

---

27. See also Allchin, "Theology," 147–48.

Cosmic Prayer and Guided Transformation

It needs further to be pointed out that the earth from about 3.5 billion years ago and onwards has been manifesting such regulatory and stabilizing capacity as is characteristic of life.[28] For, as I explained towards the end of chapter 3, life takes place as a combination of constituents in a labile equilibrium. Hence, the name Gaia has become established within part of the scientific community to indicate the whole planet as a single living being from then onwards. In this light, Gaia could equally be said to constitute an ensemble by herself. I have, however, refrained from giving explicit mention of Gaia besides human beings in the definition of cosmic prayer. Gaia can be seen as included among the ensembles that make up category (1). Moreover, even though Gaia is understood as nurturing the life forms within her, she is not comprehended as representative of the ensembles in such manner as to assist orienting universal existence upon personal being in God by virtue of the faculty of conscious awareness.

Moving on towards a consideration of the cosmic prayer of the representative human beings, it can be asked who it actually is that prays. Who or what are human beings? In the previous chapter in the section on "Prayer that is Supported by the Body and a Humble Lifestyle," we found that mention was made by Déchanet of the silent concert that rises from the depth of the soul, which finds its origin in "the vibration of the Spirit of God," as Moltmann reminds us, or again, according to Andrews, that rises from the material constituents of the human and every physical body. All these insights appear also in line with the teaching offered in the *Pastoral Constitution on the Church in the Modern World* (*Gaudium et spes*, 1965) of Vatican II, paragraph 14, which continues in light of the insights of *Lumen gentium* and which draws on the *Benedicite* for its reflection on the dignity of the human person and, in particular, on the human body as good and honorable. In this reflection it takes as a starting-point: "Though made of body and soul, man is one. Through his bodily composition he gathers to himself the elements of the material world. Thus they reach their crown through him, and through him raise their voice in free praise of the Creator."[29]

Our physical human body is actualized by about, in very rough estimate, one hundred trillion cells (that is 100,000 billion or 100 million million cells) that each contain a full genetic code that encodes common

---

28. Lovelock, *Ages of Gaia*.

29. Vatican II, *Gaudium et spes* 14; trans. Abbott, *Documents of Vatican II*, 212.

human features and other features that are specific to each of us.[30] Each living cell "knows" thereby without our conscious involvement to perfectly play its role so that we can exist and function as a single organism, as a human being. In addition, we can only exist healthily by virtue of the manifold microorganisms that are contained by our physical bodies in symbiotic relationships (that is, relationships of long-term association): there are, among others, eyelash mites, fungi and protozoa, as well as entire communities of bacteria in our mouth, pharynx and intestines that synthesize essential nutrients and that contribute to immunity against pathogenic bacteria; while others appear to be neither harmful nor beneficial to us.[31] In total, there are about five hundred to one thousand different sorts of bacteria within us, outnumbering our cells by, in estimate, a factor twenty. According to Patrick Holford up to two kilogram of our body weight comes from bacteria. Or, as Lynn Margulis indicates, in estimate, 10 percent of our dry weight consists of symbiotic microorganisms.[32] We are not our soul, we are not our body, neither are we our genetic code, or a mere sum total of our cells, or a collection of bacteria, but we emerge as, and to some extent consciously so from, this multiplicity in unity. Moreover, every seven or eight years (seven for women and eight for men) all one hundred trillion living cells that make up our body at any given time have died and their place has been taken by new cells. The old cells are expelled from the body, as we renew our entire blood every three to four months, as we regenerate our liver every six weeks, as we renew our skin surface every four weeks, as we shed about sixty hairs a day, as we blink our eyes, whereby we dispose of hundreds of cells along the tear ducts, as the interior lining of the mouth is washed down into the stomach and digested every time we eat, as about seventy billion cells a day are scraped of the walls of the intestine by passing food, and so forth. Every exterior touch and every interior event that involves us mentally takes its toll.[33] In a young adult as many cells will be replaced as are being lost, but in a mature adult there is a constant drain. All this takes place while we continue to exist as an identity of human nature. Further, we

30. E.g., Ridley, *Genome*, 6.

31. Clegg and Clegg, *Man against Disease*, 14–15, 115–16; Sonnerwirth et al., "Indiginous Bacteria," 808–16; Holford, *Improve Your Digestion*, 46–47.

32. Holford, *Improve Your Digestion*, 45; Margulis and Sagan, *Acquiring Genomes*, 18–19.

33. Watson, *Romeo Error*, 38; Watson, *Lifetide*, 105; Toolan, "Praying," 456–57; Waxman, "Secret," para. 3.

would not be able to come into existence as human beings in isolation. Our physical and mental make-up is to a considerable extent determined by whom our parents are. Our personality is largely influenced by our bodily characteristics and by talents, as well as by race and culture, by education and by particular persons and situations encountered, and for some of us by religion. All this is undeniably the case, even when in the meantime we are not entirely and irrevocably determined by these.

When *I* will, desire, pray, or love, it is really I who do so, yet I am thereby enabled by the Holy Spirit and by the Son. Or again, it is really I who do these things, yet my cry or outreach gathers in and harmonizes the dynamic of my living constituents and gives a particular expression of a section of the broader human society of which I am a part in the search for fulfillment and for the non-subsistence-related transcendent and divine reality.

However, this is still but part of the story. For, while we human beings obviously exist in virtue of our cells and symbiotic microorganisms that are contained within us, the natural constituents outside us are equally necessary for our existence. All our cells live in virtue of a constant supply of oxygen, water, nutrients, and minerals supplied by the blood, and in virtue of waste products that are deposited in the blood and excreted through the kidneys, the liver, the large intestine, the lungs, and the sweat glands. This, in turn, is only possible, among other things, through the stable constitution of the lower atmosphere that contains 78 percent nitrogen, 21 percent oxygen, water vapor, and low amounts of carbon dioxide, noble gases, and others. The very constant amounts of nitrogen and oxygen have been established by ancient forms of life; they are under the constant influence of the various present life forms, and have so far been maintained by the earth's (Gaia's) regulatory intelligence, informed as it is by the divine Word and Spirit.[34] If we then shift our perspective, as evolutionary biologist Lewontin invites us to, from our internal to our external life sphere, it can be perceived that we exist with our human features as particular partial expressions of the earth's "life" as a whole and of its partial ecological systems that surround us at our various locations.[35] We can obviously repeat this consideration in light of the earth's temperature regulation, in light of gravity, of solar energy and light, of plant and animal life, of water, and so forth.

---

34. McElroy, "Atmosphere," 305, 312, 315–17.
35. Lewontin, *Triple Helix*, 41–68.

I exist somehow as an *I* at the interface of internal worlds at the cell, molecular, atomic, and ultra-minuscule levels that escape our gaze, and of external worlds at the ecological, earth, solar system, Milky Way, and universe levels that equally escape our gaze. At this interface I am not only expressive of the "life" of these "worlds," but also, in light of Christian revelation, of the "love" and cosmic prayer divinely inspired into these worlds. In support of such an outlook Ratzinger (Benedict XVI) expresses "that we human beings are not bounded by the limits of our own little 'I' but that we are part of the rhythm of the universe,"[36] which he follows with pages on "creation and worship," of which I have quoted earlier in this chapter. In a comparable mind-set David S. Toolan speaks of "the cosmic symphony'" and considers that "we are members of the orchestra."[37] If we, alternatively, fail to be this, it is to be attributed to our self-alienation, because of the constant lie with which we are bombarded by the consumer society and because of the mental closure of many religious leaders for a truthful and real life-promoting spiritual awareness. But besides this, such failure is also at least to some extent attributable to the individual's own negligence and/or unwillingness.

Let us then consider the invisible spiritual beings as forming the third category of created entities capable of cosmic prayer. In chapter 3, where we considered the existence of spiritual beings, it was already suggested that they are capable of the personal and that they may be involved as focal personal beings for the ensembles within visible reality. Accordingly, cosmic prayer can be attributed to each of the holy angels. However, while human prayer is supported by the body and thereby rather obviously continuous with the various created dynamics, as was discussed in the previous chapter, angelic existence and prayer are probably in a more subtle, more hidden manner dependent upon the visible creatures for the attainment of completion and salvation in God.[38] Complementary, the spiritual beings include, as Scripture suggests, a supportive task for human well-being and prayer (Rev 8:3–4),[39] and arguably, in addition, a supportive role for all creatures.[40] We just saw that we are but conscious for a small proportion of our total existence, and that human prayer

---

36. Ratzinger, *In the Beginning*, 26–27.
37. Toolan, "Praying," 463.
38. *CCC*, no. 340.
39. *CCC*, no. 332–36.
40. *CCC*, no. 331, 344, 350.

primarily connects with the cosmic prayer through the unconscious body and subsequently through a consistent fostering of this intrinsic interdependence by engagement upon a spiritual path that involves the manner of living and natural contemplation. Spiritual beings, however, are entirely conscious and can by God's will, conceivably, be orienting the more or less unconscious dynamic of ensembles of visible beings that are rather extrinsic to them; perhaps similar to the relation we have to our own bodies. Indeed, if angels exist, and this not a few but in exceedingly great multitudes (Dan 7:10; Matt 26:53; Heb 12:22; Rev 5:11), it may be expected that they have significance for the entire visible creation embedded in matter.

On the downside, if we recognize that the holy angels can cooperate in orienting the dynamic of the creaturely ensembles and those therein, then we may not lose sight of the existence of the devil and the malignant spiritual powers with which Jesus and Paul held themselves to be contending with (e.g., Mark 9:25; Matt 13:38–39; Luke 10:17–19; 1 Thess 2:18; 1 Cor 15:24) and which allegedly want to distort the creaturely dynamic towards God. Yet, their power and influence has been limited by God and Christ within those adhering to them (e.g., Mark 7:29; Matt 12:50; 13:19, 23; 1 Cor 15:23; Rom 8:19–21, 38–39; Col 2:13–15; Jas 4:7–8).[41]

COSMIC PRAYER IMPLIES A PRONOUNCEMENT ABOUT GOD

Recognition of cosmic prayer implies that God is held to be the God of the entire universe. In addition, since prayer actualizes a relationship between two subjective realities that are not identical, the proposed existence of various manifestations of cosmic prayer implies that God is not to be equated with the universe or any part of it, which ultimately addresses him. This even while the whole created reality or certain sections of it, whether in their present or in their deified situation, may be considered to possess personal qualities that are received as a result of God's all-pervading presence. It immediately excludes any pantheistic notion.

It also excludes any deistic notion. For prayer that is addressed to a living and personal God involves a real interaction. It implies that God is present to creation and not at a distance from it. It takes us beyond the theology of Thomas Aquinas. For, whereas Thomas held God to be

---

41. Govaerts, "Prayer," 104.

present to creation,[42] he failed, as mentioned at the beginning of chapter 1, to envisage a real interaction between the Creator and the created order. Recognition of cosmic prayer includes the perception that the course of the emergent cosmos that is being created by God's continuous creative initiative is being effected and affected by spiritual beings, by human prayer and life, by the creaturely cooperation in the act of life, and by every micro- and macroscopic composite or single entity that by its existence makes a contribution. It implies that God is creating and transforming in the present. It does not mean that God is as one working in the dark, but as one who untiringly takes all constantly changing factors perfectly into account to achieve his will for the cosmos. It takes us also beyond Augustine, who held God to be an unsurpassable organizer,[43] yet, as was mentioned in chapter 1 at the same place, as not entering upon a truly intersubjective dialectical relationship with those being created. Recognition of cosmic prayer does not degrade God to such impersonal impotence, but takes account of the belief in the biblical God, the God with whom Abraham palavers in front of Sodom, a God worthy of worship.

Finally, recognition of cosmic prayer implies, of course, the exclusion of that other modernist trend, namely atheism.

COSMIC PRAYER IMPLIES A PRONOUNCEMENT ABOUT THE UNIVERSAL CREATION

The proposal that cosmic prayer is truly existent envisages that it is not only the angelic and human beings—that is, those traditionally called "rational"—who have an active significance and role in the relationship with God, but every living being and every existent entity (as they are part of encompassing ensembles that involve intelligence) and the entire universe. Accordingly, it envisages that there exists a real dialectic in the creative process. (Dialectic is here understood as the continuous interactive process that involves both Creator and creature.) Hence, it does not fit the hypothesis of creationism (old or new), nor that of unqualified intelligent design, but favors the idea of a guided transformation.

Again, as such, the proposal that cosmic prayer is truly existent is irreconcilable with an all-comprising providence wherein the particular

---

42. Aquinas *Summa theologiae* 1a, q.8, art.3.
43. Augustine *Sermones* 125:4–6; PL 38:692–93.

significance of the dynamic of prayer is, in distinction of other creaturely acts and happenings, for the (human) creature, besides the meritorious faith act of addressing God and its granting satisfaction of fulfilled piety, merely its educative (and thus intellectualist) value as was held by Augustine.[44]

Similarly, as can be found quoted and commented upon by Fiddes, according to Thomas Aquinas, "Our motive in praying is . . . that we might obtain that which God has decreed will be obtained by prayer."[45] Hence, for Thomas the reason for the divinely supported effectiveness of an act of prayer is not very different from that of any other act, whereas I hold it to be crucial, in addition to God's prior grace, for the occurrence of a real reciprocal divine-creaturely relationship ad hoc and the manner wherein this occurs.

Finally, cosmic prayer, if real, implies that universal, inanimate, animate, and human existence is not exhausted within certain time limits, but enters upon the eternal realm and has a teleological destiny reached in God.

COSMIC PRAYER AND COSMIC LITURGY

For the last section of this chapter I propose us to compare the concept "cosmic prayer" with that of "cosmic liturgy." It may be recalled that the latter concept was already encountered in this chapter in the quotation from Patriarch Bartholomew, who has undoubtedly borrowed it from von Bathasar's book on Maximus, *Kosmische Liturgie* (1941, 1961) that was mentioned in the introduction. Before entering upon the comparison of the two concepts, some more background to this idea of a cosmic liturgy is called for.

A first general comment is that the dynamic towards a new creation and towards a newness of life harmonious in God's presence has been perceived in light of the human liturgy. In this more inclusive idea of the Christian liturgy, all creation is perceived to be involved in an act of praise and worship. As we observed earlier in this chapter, this perception has in recent times been especially promoted by Pope John Paul II and by Patriarch Bartholomew.

---

44. Augustine *De sermone Domini in Monte* 2:12–14; PL 34:1274–75 (ref. provided at Zaleski and Zaleski, *Prayer*, 100, 374 n. 8); *De civitate dei* 5:10, 11; 21:24.

45. Aquinas *Summa theologiae* 2a2ae, q.83, art.2; Fiddes, *Participating in God*, 121.

Supportive of this idea of an inclusive liturgy has been the notion of a "cosmic liturgy" introduced by von Balthasar in his study of St Maximus. In particular, von Balthasar speaks of cosmic liturgy with regard to the effectiveness of the ecclesial liturgy, the holy synaxis, for drawing the entire world into a transformation towards union with God.[46] Besides this, von Balthasar recognizes that significant for this cosmic transformation is the prayer of the faithful as an expression of worship and love, not only in words but also in actions. Von Balthasar reflects that prayer is made effective by a virtuous life that is in service of all creation; it offers the world to God.[47] This resonates with the reflection entertained at the end of chapter 5. It is a notion that has become known by Schmemann's expression that indicates faithful people as "priests of creation." Also Thunberg's study on Maximus presents von Balthasar's term "cosmic liturgy" in the broader context of human mediation for the unification of all creation through a virtuous life and through contemplation.[48] It can further be observed that the term "cosmic liturgy" has also been mentioned by Mircea Eliade (1907–86) in his comparative study of religions, when he considers what has been lost in "the Christianity of the industrial societies and especially the Christianity of intellectuals." Eliade means by it, a (human) way of living Christianity with a "feeling of the sanctity of nature" and also "the mystery of nature's participation in the Christological drama,"[49] a meaning that is close to Paul's cosmic perception and not so much tied to the human ecclesiastical liturgy as by von Balthasar. Also Moltmann's perception of "cosmic liturgy" is fully acceptant of an active contribution by all creatures in the praise of God.[50] Such perception is closest to that put forward by Maximus himself. The term was also used by Swimme and Berry in *The Universe Story*, again without overt dependence upon preceding authors. They mean by it the phenomenon of the universe's existence itself, wherein they consider celebration to be omnipresent. "Celebration is omnipresent, not simply in the individual modes of its expression but in the grandeur of the entire cosmic process."[51] They do, however, thereby not make mention of the

---

46. Balthasar, *Cosmic Liturgy*, 322.
47. Ibid., 329–30.
48. Thunberg, *Microcosm and Mediator*, 397.
49. Eliade, *Sacred and the Profane*, 178–79.
50. Moltmann, *God in Creation*, 71; Moltmann, *Jesus Christ*, 289.
51. Swimme and Berry, *Universe Story*, 264; see also Berry, *Great Work*, 19.

Christ event or of a transcendent deity. Instead, they present the universe as an *autopoietic* or self-organizing process.[52] Even though in a later short essay Berry returns to speaking of, among others, "praise of the Divine" and "the Divine indwelling."[53] It can further be remarked that the concept of *autopoiesis* was first developed by the biologists Humberto R. Maturana and Francisco J. Varela in the book *Autopoiesis and Cognition* (1980). They mean by it the organizational capacity common to all living systems.[54] The concept certainly has its valid place in natural science; but from a faith perspective the concept cannot validly be applied to the universe in such way that it is presented as self-sufficient without any reference to the divine Creator. This little survey has shown that in the way the concept of cosmic liturgy has been employed, the swing has turned from an overly anthropocentric approach to Christian faith towards a nature-centered approach that thinks it best to leave talk of God out of the picture.

The immediately foregoing may heighten appreciation of the merit of the concept cosmic prayer. In what follows a number of reasons are brought forward as to why cosmic prayer promises to be a valuable complement to the idea of a cosmic liturgy.

1. In our perilous times, we wish to keep in mind—as did *Lumen gentium*, Archbishop Romero, and Pope John Paul—Rom 8:19–22, which perceives creation in anxious anticipation of better times, of liberation. Creation is not only a celebratory event, but a suffering and groaning in hopefulness. Though Berry was acutely aware of the destruction of the created reality by people, McFague criticizes him for having insufficiently incorporated this awareness by placing all emphasis upon celebration.[55]

2. We intend not only to consider the large scale dynamic, that is to say its overall sum total, but to be attentive upon the particularity of the various individual created beings. We want to let each creature be its own center in its relationship with the Creator, this not in isolation, but as contributing to and being supported by the all-encompassing cosmic dynamic. It is proposed that cosmic prayer takes comprehensive account of this.

52. Swimme and Berry, *Universe Story*, 53–54, 226–27, 238.
53. Berry, "Christianity's Role," 133–34.
54. Capra, *Web of Life*, 98, 157, 163.
55. McFague, *Body of God*, 70–71.

3. In addition, this concept allows us to adhere closely to the priority of the divine Word that is spoken within creation. As such, it allows us to perceive the entire creation, which is obviously to a large extent material, as at heart spiritual.

4. It envisages that in supplement and support to the liturgical expressions of the world religions, the human and especially also non-human prayer sounded in the existences, lives, and volitions of the created beings can go beyond the temporal and allow the beings themselves to be lifted up by God towards human and cosmic union, whereby the created beings or their prayer-existences become ever more included in the divine communion.

5. To perceive human prayer as a manifestation of cosmic prayer encourages us to pay attention to both the shared *cosmic* dimension of prayer and to our individual disposition of and contribution to *prayer*. As such, human prayer that is tuned into the cosmic prayer is destined to lead into the personal Son and Spirit (as was explored in chapter 2 and at the end of chapter 4), who exist by both a shared and a particular irreducible side. Such perception of the context and meaning of prayer also encourages a practice of prayer, both common and individual, wherein the individual (personal) prayer and the liturgical participation (in praise and intercession) are mutually supportive and in balance.

6. Finally, the concept cosmic prayer offers a broader take upon the notion of stewardship.

In light of this chapter it can be noted that prayer and cosmic prayer make sense only in the context of a truly dialectical Creator-creature relationship. They exclude the delusion of a universe that is developing without any divine involvement and that is self-sufficient. They also exclude an alleged all-inclusive determinism. Their complementary concept is that of a guided transformation. It is the subject of the next chapter.

7

Guided Transformation

GUIDED TRANSFORMATION TOWARDS PERSONAL EXISTENCE THROUGH COSMIC PRAYER

IT IS USEFUL FOR gaining insight regarding the co-occurrence of natural processes and divine guidance to consider once more, "Why does transformation take place?" Even though according to Richard Dawkins we are only supposed to ask the "how" question.[1]

Darwin thought the answer was small chance mutations. With the discovery of DNA and the genetic code in 1953, Francis Crick (1916–2004) and James Watson provided a support to the idea of chance mutations.[2] Since this discovery, neo-Darwinists have been interpreting that transformation takes place because of a miscopying of the genetic code. Accordingly, they hold that there is no preferred directionality inscribed within nature, no motivation except survival. The fact that human beings are around with conscious awareness, an ability to love, to be gentle and compassionate, together with all other creatures, would ultimately be merely the result of an accumulation of natural occurring mistakes and the subsequent unstoppable and addicted drive to multiply those genes that constitute the own species. Accordingly, human consciousness

1. Dawkins, *River out of Eden*, 97.
2. Ridley, *Genome*, 13.

Guided Transformation

would have come about as an epiphenomenon of purely physical processes and of the inherent dynamic of life processes, even though it has since then actively contributed in changing the face of the earth.[3] Another question that presents itself is then, of course, "How did life begin in the first place?" Physicists thought to provide an explanation in terms of mathematical laws: these laws tell us that the change of one or more physical factors is accompanied by the change of other factors. But again no preferred directionality or motivation is given thereby, except the maintenance of a certain equilibrium or balance. Just as biologists look to the genetic code for answers, so physicists try to discern the elementary material entities and the laws they adhere to, for explaining all that has happened since the beginning of the universe. All these provide explanations that are contributing factors, yet by themselves unsatisfactory. Present approaches try to consider the totalities: the organism, the ecological community, or the multiscalar recombination (that is, at multiple scales of space and time) of the physical entities for the emergence of functional relationships.[4] Again, these approaches are very valuable, yet inadequate by themselves.

Alternatively, some scientists have argued for a version of the theory of *panspermia* ("seeds everywhere"), that is, the theory that life has been seeded on earth from elsewhere in the universe, either as free floating bacteria (Lord Kelvin, Svante Arrhenius, and Fred Hoyle) or in the head of an unmanned spaceship from an extraterrestrial civilization (Francis Crick).[5] All these approaches, even the latter, suppose an enclosed system and self-sufficiency within the earliest material manifestations, the chemical mixture, the simplest life form, the past and present. Even though, as we saw in chapter 3 with Eddington, quantum physics points away from an enclosed system.

Further, mention has to be made of the many-universes hypothesis (which does not necessarily exclude belief in God). Physicists have tried to come to terms with the extraordinary combination of apparently extremely fine-tuned physical constants that account for the characteristics of physical forces and materialization as they are, so that our universe can exist and evolution could take place towards the emergence of galaxies,

---

3. E.g., Dawkins, *River out of Eden*, 104–5, 135–61; Margulis, *Symbiotic Planet*, 4, 72–85.

4. Caldwell, "Post-modern Ecology," 279–81.

5. Crick, *Life Itself*; Hoyle, *Intelligent Universe*, esp. 83–107, 158–61.

Cosmic Prayer and Guided Transformation

solar systems, planets, life, and reflexive consciousness.[6] So as to account for the extraordinary initial conditions, some physicists that aim to see the physical order as totally self-sufficient have proposed that the big bang cannot have been an absolute beginning, that there must have been prior events, a prior history. In one form or other, the hypothesis of a *multiverse* (or *Metaverse*) is made so that our universe is considered to be one among innumerable others, each originating in a big bang with certain initial conditions. In combination with this, certain scientists have suggested that information can be stored (or memorized) and carried over from prior or simultaneous existent universes (though strictly spoken time-reference would be meaningless), so that the *Metaverse* is as it were a continuum in which our universe is embedded.[7] These searchings are very interesting but highly speculative. The *Metaverse* reintroduces, among others, a kind of ether-like field (besides the empirically verifiable physical force fields) that acts as a trans-universal memory and that informs processes within the universe and among universes much as a well-willing conscious and intelligent agent might do.

In this book, instead, is upheld the belief in the existence of a personal divinity, existent as three persons, who is at the origin of contingent created reality and who guides it towards personal existence, in particular towards the interpersonal communion within God. It is also suggested in this book that personal existence is already participated in to various extents by various ensembles and individual creatures, both spiritual and sensible. The envisaged transformation is that whereby each entity becomes increasingly participant in the personal and lets itself, its entire existence, be fully illumined by the divine persons.

In chapter 3 it was considered with reference to Koestler and to the new science of synergetics that various beings contribute to higher order systems wherein they are being integrated, which carry information and intelligence. The emergence and existence of the higher order within the human being, which is situated at the personal level, can be perceived to be surrounded, embedded, and enabled by the non-human integrated and differentiated systems. Hence, the human sense of purpose and

---

6. Barrow and Tipler, *Anthropic Cosmological Principle*, 408–12; Rees, *Just Six Numbers*.

7. Hawking, *Black Holes and Baby Universes*, 111, 115–25; Laszlo, *Science and the Akashic Field*; Laszlo, *Science and Reenchantment*, 23–90; Quincey, "Metaverse Story," 109–20. For assessment of the hypothesis: see also Davies, *Mind of God*, 190, 215–20; Rees, *Our Cosmic Habitat*, 157–81.

intentionality, as well as the human propensity to worship and prayer, are situated exactly at the upper part of the central axis of the process of natural evolution; it is an axis leading towards personalization, worship and prayer, and along which God's transforming guidance is being informed and appropriated within the entire created reality, which thus is longing for the manifestation of the personal, the truly human, and its personal Creator God.

The creaturely desire towards the personal occurs for the inanimate entities, such as pebbles, as an inherent tendency, which is immediately given, to be resistant or resilient and, yet, to let itself be molded, so as to contribute to a varied ecological and geological ensemble. It is rather counterintuitive to attribute to a pebble a tendency that is expressive of a creaturely desire, but there is some support in the fact that the Greek Orthodox theologian Nikos A. Matsoukas (1934–2006) used the same terms when interpreting the cosmology of Maximus: "Even a stone, following the exemplary reason (*logos paradigmaticos*) of the divine will, tends towards being, it desires being."[8] For the large-scale ensembles the tendency and capacity for the personal results in harmonious co-existence of its contributors and in the bringing forth of organic complex living beings. For the animate beings the creaturely desire towards the personal occurs as a desire for life and for self-realization in accord with their own nature, and this concomitant with a desire for belonging to the group that makes up the species or with a desire for taking up a place within the wider ecological community.[9] For highly evolved animals, these partial desires for self-realization and belonging are, arguably, accompanied by an underlying desire for a harmonious existence wherein a liberating peace is attained, an experience of being able to live in accord with the own will. To greater or lesser extent such individual animals already adumbrate all higher values, including devotion, care, love, and compassion, wherein the drive towards both self-realization and belonging is fulfilled.[10] For the human and angelic beings these contributing desires are being sustained by their greater mental capacities and willpower, and thus lifted higher to the plain of the personal values. They express these desires for themselves and others in prayer that addresses God and

---

8. Matsoukas, *La vie en Dieu*, 120 (my translation).
9. E.g., Tinbergen, *Social Behaviour in Animals*.
10. E.g., Lorenz, *King Solomon's Ring*.

in their working for other individuals and for the ensembles as their respective natures allow.

The tendency, or desire, or motivation of created realities for the personal is impressed by God through Spirit and Word. This does not contradict the recognition that the human bodily characteristics have emerged more or less continuously out of—and, as has been described in the chapter on cosmic prayer, as expressive of—the encompassing created reality. For the Spirit and Word of God animate the process towards personalization as well as the created entities themselves with the active involvement of these very entities. We ourselves, human beings, are touched by God and touch God, not only indirectly through other creatures as was envisaged in the Pseudo-Dionysian hierarchies, but also directly, whereby each in his/her particular circumstances is offered and enabled to make a specific contribution in the process of personification.

Hence, arguably, there is merit in the teaching of the Roman Catholic Church that besides the natural evolution of the body, the soul as principle of animation and intelligence is directly bestowed by God.[11] It is a teaching that accords with Gen 2:7 and further, among others, with the positions taken by Maximus[12] and Thomas Aquinas.[13] In accordance with this teaching, the soul is instrumental for formation of the body, which simultaneously with the soul emerges through the support of prior existent created entities and intelligence-carrying ensembles. The subsequent development, either for good or for bad, of both a creature's body and soul takes place by its own desires and efforts, which are both intrinsic and being inspired. It can be noted that the Catholic teaching and the interpretation of the phenomenon of life offered by quantum-physicist Schrödinger, as discussed in chapter 3, cohere.

As appears from all this, in the movement towards God, which is a movement towards the personal, each created entity is offered to partake in the cosmic dynamic towards this. Human beings as well as the angelic beings can thereby become centers of harmonization. For we are to become channels of peace, love, prayerfulness, goodness, wisdom, and joyfulness so that harmonization may take place. Thus we may offer ourselves and surrounding creation to God. And reciprocally, surrounding creation, empowered by Spirit and Word, offers itself and us as well as a

---

11. Pius XII, *Humani generis* 36; CCC, no. 362–66, 382.
12. *Amb.* 42; PG 91:1324C; trans. Blowers and Wilken, *Cosmic Mystery*, 87.
13. Aquinas *Summa contra Gentiles* 3:75, 88(§5)–90.

Guided Transformation

cosmic prayer. Concomitant with this cosmic prayer, guided transformation takes place that leads towards the personal wherein the created realities attain a liberating peaceful existence.

DIVINE PLAN AND NATURAL EVOLUTION

Once more we consider the position of Darwin, who did not present his evolutionary theory as an unbeliever.[14] Darwin did not deny that the primary cause of creatures' existence is the divine Creator. He neither, therefore, denied that there is purpose in life or that there is a teleological principle. However, he thought that God's creative act was completed for all life by the working of physical and biological laws that he called forth at the beginning of creation and life, and that every future development that God willed to happen was already implicitly contained by these laws. As such, his thought was continuous with the prevalent perception of deterministic physical laws governing a mechanistic universe. Such perception, characteristic of modernity, had been initiated by Immanuel Kant (1724–1804), who already had even expressed the idea of natural evolution (but without Darwin's one-sided emphasis on a struggle for survival).[15] Earlier, Thomas Aquinas, whose philosophical theology can be discerned as having contributed to this development, thought that every effect within creation was the result of the divine primary cause (Thomas's unmoved mover) and subsequently of a created secondary cause. Hence, Darwin wrote in an intellectual climate that regarding the Creator-creature relationship was largely overshadowed by the Thomistic notion of the all-directing eternal law of which the Newtonian laws came to be perceived as a reflection in the physical realm. As such, Darwin thought to exclude the notion of special divine interventions for every species—God as *deus ex machina*—by taking on a deistic notion. Darwin effectively held that the divine plan for particular creatures scattered along natural evolution history was so elusive that teleology or purpose was not a factor that needed to be taken into account for understanding creation or life, but was, on the contrary, a mere impediment for the increase of scientific insight.[16] But failing in his turn to give importance to a real dialectical Creator-creature relationship, his theory carries no

---

14. Darwin, *Descent of Man*, 79.
15. Kant, *Critique of the Power of Judgment*, 286–88.
16. Darwin, *Origin of Species*, 1st ed., 488–90; 6th ed., 428–29.

explanatory force. Within a more consistent vision the divine plan and outreach is effectively *to touch upon every being*.

Another issue regarding divine plan and natural evolution, which is not unrelated, is that it would be a grave mistake to think of the transformation that occurred on the way to humanization as that of an isolated hominoid species. All the various species at a certain time are so interdependent that it is not merely one species that adapts to external circumstances, but the total collection of geological and biological forms present in a cohabitation that interactively transforms towards a renewed ensemble. Beyond this, the transformation occurs even in dependence upon astronomical circumstances.[17] Such a perception has been promoted by Richard Levins' and Richard Lewontin's idea of dialectical evolutionary biology as presented in their book *The Dialectical Biologist* (1985). However, since these authors—as well as the late Stephen Jay Gould (1941–2002)—write from a Darwinian and Marxist-influenced perspective, they opt for a dialectical materialist, non-teleological approach.[18] From our faith perspective we hold that a transformation takes place towards personal existence. But keeping to our main train of thought, the significance of this close interdependence is that our human existence could and can only take place under very specific conditions of external reality. The divine plan would thus not only have included a transformation of the hominoids, but of all the creaturely realities that together are involved in the process towards humanization and personification. In accordance with our earlier reflection regarding the differential harmonization of visible reality and life, it is therefore reasonable to assume that the various created realities are being taken up towards a multifarious personified existence. Moreover, if this is the case, transformation towards the personal is then not a lifting of the human soul out of the entire created reality, but ultimately an all-affecting process of entering into God's presence.

INTELLIGENT DESIGN AND CREATURELY FREEDOM

In his reflection upon the first verses of Genesis at *Confessions* book 11, Augustine quotes Ps 104:24 to express his marveling at the manifestations of God's wisdom throughout creation; in particular, the great diversity of creatures and their constitutions he believes to be designed with wisdom.

17. Dar et al., "Life Extinctions," 5813–16.
18. Gould, *Ever Since Darwin*, 21–27; Clark and York, "Dialectical Nature."

Guided Transformation

The same thoughts can be found to have been expressed by Maximus.[19] The same observations, but now with exceeding great detail, are in the present day upheld by theistic scientists to refute the total reliance upon general laws and random chance by Darwin and the neo-Darwinists. The mathematician William A. Dembski has, arguably, presented objective criteria that allow us to discern the presence of intelligent design.[20] In accordance with these criteria, the physical laws themselves and the physical constants therein can, arguably, be seen to be the result of a prior super-intelligence; this can likewise be applied to the combination of astrological events and subsequent intricate combinations of the elementary chemical components in the liquid oceans upon the early earth that led to the emergence of life. So also, for example, the constitution of cells and their incredibly complicated internal processes that result in the ability to duplicate, or the existence of the incredibly complicated optical-sensitive cell, are without credible explanation in the absence of overt reliance upon intelligent design.[21] Another very appealing example presented by biochemist Michael C. Behe is the rotor mechanism of a bacterial flagellum, which is exceedingly similar to an outboard motor that allows the body to be propelled forward without letting unwanted outside fluids find their way in.[22] Or again, medical practitioner Geoffrey Simmons describes in his book *What Darwin Didn't Know* (2004) how the overall constitution of the human body, the incredible delicate constitution of every organ and the capacity for skills and intelligence, require the intricate cooperation of its one hundred trillion cells and all bacteria in a manner that he calls mind-boggling.

But not all that happens needs to be part of the divine plan, or all that exists be expressive of intelligent design. Indeed, such interpretation would frustrate the very objective of creaturely existence, namely, a creation-inclusive personal communion within God, which takes place in cosmic prayer and freedom. Does it ultimately matter when and where a certain leaf falls to the ground or where a nut drops; and subsequently, whether or where a tree grows from a particular nut? When a hundred mice are chasing each other through the undergrowth does it ultimately matter which mice mate with each other? Biologist Lyall Watson explains

---

19. *Amb.* 15; PG 91:1216AB; *Thal.* 13; PG 90:296B or CCSG 7:95:22–24.
20. Dembski, "Third Mode," 17–51.
21. Meyer, "Evidence," 115–18.
22. Behe, "Evidence," 123–24.

that the mice do not know one another; there is no hierarchical order among them and so it does not even matter to the mice themselves with whom they mate within their group.[23] And is it necessarily divine purpose that a certain young man meets a certain young woman—or rapes her—or that a certain sperm at a certain time meets a certain egg? When a particular rabbit comes in front of a tree, it may continue its way by hopping into a bush left or right of the tree, unknowing that along the right side a fox is ready to grab it. Need these events be contained in the divine plan? In my assessment, they are not contained in it or by it. For both foxes and rabbits are being sustained and want to live; while God does not need to (pre)determine and want the killing of a particular rabbit. If God would have (pre)determined all events, then God would indeed be coldhearted, cruel, and unworthy of worship. Or, for example, in the case of untimely and violent deaths of innocent human beings, are these necessarily (pre)determined by God? Again, in my assessment, they are not. This does, however, not prevent God influencing the course of events; in particular, for example, as the answer to a prayer that expresses reliance upon him (e.g., Ps 113:9).

Despite the signs of intelligent design, can there not be, besides the creative activity of God and his holy angels, such wild-running chanciness within creation (emerging from, among others, the quantum-vacuum jittery, which was mentioned in chapter 2, and the dissipative structures, which were mentioned in chapter 3), such "planless" combination of circumstances, and such crawling, swimming, hopping, mating, and so forth, as well as such distorting influences exerted by malignant spiritual forces,[24] that has led to various gruesome creatures? It seems that the natural circumstances and the evolving ecological systems bring forth all imaginable and unimaginable kinds of creatures as in a gone-crazy grand-scale all-try laboratory.[25] Yet, most species are well adapted to live within the complex tightly woven web of relations that exist almost everywhere on earth and that they contribute to. The manifold life forms are closely interdependent, allow local and global adaptivity of life, and constitute despite individually gruesome creatures a large-scale harmony and beauty. In light of this, and of humanity's emergence and so far continued existence, which are enabled by the global web of life forms, the

---

23. Watson, *Lifetide*, 128.
24. Pendergast, "Evil," 840–45.
25. See also Dillard, *Pilgrim*.

idea is here being upheld that with unsurpassable inventiveness creatures are being incorporated in the divine plan. For example, as proposed by Lynn Margulis, parasites could have played a significant role in the process of what she calls *symbiogenesis*, which involves the fusion of two organisms into a new type of organism.[26]

Nevertheless, the path of natural evolution does not value highly individual lives. This appears not only from particular chance events such as were mentioned, but also from various inherited characteristics of established species. Ian Tattersall gives an example in his book *Becoming Human* (1998) regarding the second egg of the ground hornbill of southern Africa. Tattersall explains that this bird lays a second egg a week after the first, with the result that by the time the younger chick hatches the older chick is strong enough to dispose of it.[27] Christopher Southgate refers in his book *The Groaning of Creation* to Holmes Rolston III's book *Science and Religion* (1987) for the same example concerning the white pelican, with the explanation that the second egg or chick is as an "insurance" in case the first chick would not develop and thus it has a function in the species' continued existence.[28] Moreover, numerous individuals and entire groups (even among human beings) are victims of genetic aberrations.

Whereas Christian belief can envisage that transformation according to the divine plan takes place along the path of natural evolution, it is most unlikely that the divine plan and purpose is fostered by *all* steps that occur along this path or that it calls for species such as the various types (species and subspecies) of trypanosome (parasites) (*Trypanosoma brucei brucei, T. b. gambiense, T. b. rhodesiense*, and *T. cruzi*) and the different species of tsetse flies (of the genus *Glossina*) and blood sucking bugs that transmit them,[29] or for leprosy-causing bacilli (*Mycobacterium leprae*), or for the closely related tuberculosis causing bacilli (*M. tuberculosis*),[30] or for the various species of tapeworms (*Cestoda*), blood flukes (*Schistosoma* species), and hookworms (of the genus *Nematoda*).[31]

26. Margulis and Sagan, *Acquiring Genomes*, 12–14.

27. Tattersall, *Becoming Human*, 96.

28. Southgate, *Groaning of Creation*, 46; Holmes Rolston III, *Science and Religion*, 137–39.

29. Clegg and Clegg, *Man against Disease*, 178, 217–19; Lumsden, "Protozoa," 563–88.

30. Wolinsky, "Mycobacteria," 723–42.

31. Clegg and Clegg, *Man against Disease*, 220–38.

Cosmic Prayer and Guided Transformation

If the divine plan would be fostered by all these then it certainly would not be the plan of the compassionate Father revealed by Jesus Christ. It is to be mentioned, however, that the Jewish Scriptures narrate that even these species God may let appear or disappear at will and take up in his plan (e.g., Exod 4:4–7; 8:16–17, 21–24; 10:12–19; Num 12:9–10). Jesus, the Incarnate Word, did not cause leprosy—which is considered "uncleanness" in the Scriptures—to appear, but when implored made it to disappear by his will (e.g., Mark 1:40–42).

On the positive side, let us consider that, in accordance with the explanation offered in the first section of this chapter, the creaturely tendency, or desire, or motivation that contributes to the various expressions of the cosmic prayer also contributes in the realization of the divine purpose.

As this section has shown, the theme of intelligent design and creaturely freedom is hardly separable from that of divine providence and creaturely contingency. A few more words are called for about this very closely related theme.

DIVINE PROVIDENCE AND CREATURELY CONTINGENCY

I propose us to begin with the following two considerations regarding the contingency of human decisions. Firstly, often we need to make a choice between two or more options. It can occur that two options appear of equal quality; that neither option has a moral advantage over the other. We deliberate our choice rationally and thus consciously. This may, however, remain indecisive for important matters of which we cannot evaluate all factors involved. We will then try to tap into our intuitive wisdom, which is rather situated at the unconscious level, to make a right choice, a choice we are satisfied with. It thus appears that we may decide upon our course very much as other creatures are doing, who for the overall direction of their lives may nevertheless be also consciously guided through the service of spiritual beings. This again indicates that we are not separate from the universal creaturely dynamic towards God. In deciding upon a course the human being and other creatures make choices that are theirs and that need not have been determined or decided upon for us by God. Secondly, by faith it is possible to believe that

Guided Transformation

when we have chosen a particular path, God will be with us on our path and steer it by if we want him to do so (e.g., Josh 1:7–9; Ps 139:8; Jonah).

As already touched upon in the previous section, contingency is not restricted to creaturely decisions but unavoidably concerns the very existences of particular creatures, which are the result of decisions by earlier generations and of a combination of various other contingent factors. As such, the very human being that I am with a particular shape of nose, face, body, habits, talents, and shortcomings, need not be predetermined by God. Indeed, adding our earlier consideration regarding young or not so young man and woman, decisions this or that way, sperm and egg, and so forth, it implies that my very existence—or Adolph Hitler's or Joseph Stalin's for that matter—need not be predetermined by God and be a necessary part of his providence. I, along with all creatures, am a contingent being, even though God sees me, my entire life, and all that exists, and knows me through and through (Heb 4:13). As such also, whether there are five billion healthily and peaceably living human beings or ten billion unhealthily living, poverty ridden, and suffering human beings on this planet is a human responsibility and task bestowed by God. It is our responsibility within the means and possibilities available to us to learn about God's will, the cosmic prayer, and to take heed of them in our actions. It is our responsibility whether we live greedily and selfishly, or take thought for our integrity in the context of universal existence and for the being of others.

The issue of contingency goes to the heart of cosmic prayer that is truly constitutive of a dialectical relationship with God, which excludes a static divine providence. But are the Scriptures not saying just the opposite of such an idea for at least the human sphere?

Ps 139:13–16 speaks of God forming King David in his mother's womb and seeing all his days in advance. I argue that God does not and need not see in advance, for he is not bound to a particular time; instead, in faith it can be held that God is undividedly present to King David's birth, life, and death, as well as to all existence in time. In addition, I already confirmed in chapter 2 that God *in-forms* every human form and every existence. It is thereby not excluded that King David's life was subject of a distinctive divine involvement in view of his prominent role in salvation history.

Let us then also take notice of 2 Kgs 20:1–11 that tells the story of King Hezekiah's prayerful pleading for healing whereby, as the story goes, he influenced God's word regarding his fate, which was subsequently altered.

Interesting is Isa 54:15 where the prophet is said to proclaim in God's name: "If any one stirs up strife, it is not from me." There are other times when it is prophesied that because of the wickedness of the leaders of the people, because they do not take care of the poor and the weak, and ignore justice, that the enemies give expression of God's anger. But here in this instance it is proclaimed that any eventual trouble is not God's doing.

Absolutely central regarding divine providence is the saying at Ps 32:10: "Steadfast love surrounds him who trusts in the Lord."

In the New Testament, the divine providence alluded to in 2 Thess 2:13 and Eph 1:4–5 (which both happen to be letters of disputed origin) requires attention. This verse of 2 Thessalonians states that from the beginning God chose the brethren that are addressed by the letter to be saved. The RSV translation signals that some ancient authorities have an alternative reading for "from the beginning." But even if we keep to the said reading, can we make sense of it? In the exposition of this book it has been upheld that God in his eternal existence intends there to be people who believe in him and who enter into a personal relationship with him. God has guided the evolving creation towards this. It is God's choice and initiative to let there be such people who can believe in him for the sake of their salvation and that of the wider creation unto eternal life. When therefore the letter addresses brethren who confirm their belonging to God, then this has been made possible because of God's prior gracefulness and because of his presence that travels along during their life journey. It is in this sense that God has chosen the faithful. It is a reading that does not contradict creaturely contingency. The indicated verses of Ephesians can be read in a like manner.

All this means that, as a contingent being, I, the faithful, and other creatures, can truly give delight to God by our prayer and worship.

DIVINE CREATION AND CREATURELY INVOLVEMENT AS COOPERATIVE IN A DIALECTICAL PROCESS

Guided transformation is not a concept that is intended to replace the idea of divine creativity, but to complement it and provide specification.

Guided Transformation

God, though not bound in time or in space, creates in time and space in a differentiated manner by his undivided Word and Sprit by an undivided act. He thus creates at a particular place or for a particular being for subsequent times; this in a manner that needs not be predetermined, for God is entirely free.

The idea that is here being suggested is that when entities (ensembles and single creatures therein) that are being created come to belong to and within God, they can effectively participate in the process of their becoming, color the creative outreach of the Word itself, modulate by their receptivity the flow pattern of the outpouring Spirit, and hence influence the way they, their eventual offspring, and the wider created realm are being further created.[32] Consequently, it is here that can be situated the merit of the Greek patristic idea of unification with God in the energies. Since early times, Eastern theology has distinguished God's essential being (οὐσία) from his actions (ἐνεργείαι) or energies. For, according to Gregory Palamas (c.1296–1359), without a real distinction between divine essence and energies it would not be possible to distinguish between the processions of the divine persons and the act of creation.[33] Hence, a sharing in the divine energies still preserves God's innermost being from participation and thus upholds the distinction between Creator and creature. But as this and foregoing chapters have made clear, this is but part of the story, of the mystery of faithful humanity's and creatures' unification with God. In the next chapter, we will enter deeper into this mystery with Maximus.

The reflection that we have entertained in this chapter considers a reciprocal relationship initiated and supported by the divinity. Before moving on to the next chapter, it may be interesting to give some extra attention to situating this exposition with regard to that of some well-known theologians. As was presented in chapter 1, in the section on "The New Theology," a real reciprocity has been defended in Moltmann's theology and this as part of "an intricate web of unilateral, reciprocal and many-sided relationships."[34]

Peacocke as well envisaged a reciprocal Creator-creature relationship; this in terms of a "top-down" and "bottom-up" causation.[35] Pea-

---

32. Cf. Moltmann, *Spirit*, 195–96, 212; *CCC* no. 306–8.
33. Lossky, *Mystical Theology*, 73–74.
34. Moltmann, *God in Creation*, 14.
35. Peacocke, *Theology for a Scientific Age*, 53–55, 157–63, 171–77, 220–21.

Cosmic Prayer and Guided Transformation

cocke thus allows for a real contingency. "The future of the quantum or complex system is genuinely open and genuinely new states of the system occur."[36] For the human-divine relationship he considers that there is "interaction, dialogue even, between human decisions and actions, on the one hand, and divine intentions and purposes, on the other."[37]

Further, as we quoted in chapter 4 in the section on "Person and Personhood," Fiddes elaborates in his book *Participating in God* on those that are praying as "being incorporated in the fellowship of the divine life."[38] He promotes a dynamic notion of every inter-trinitarian relationship and a real and mutual Creator-creature relationship. For this he refers, following Moltmann, to the idea of *perichoresis*: "The idea of perichoresis in the Trinity kept alive, within the theological system itself, a challenge to the image of a dominating God whose power lies in immobility and in being secure from being affected by the changing world. The challenge was especially acute where perichoresis was understood in the sense of mutual movement (circumin*cessio*)."[39] He then complements this insight with the notion of divine action as persuasion. "[The relations in God] are actions in the sense that when we are involved in their movement, we are persuaded and moved to certain ends, caught up in their momentum."[40] Both in *The Creative Suffering of God* and *Participating in God* he comes to the conclusion that a relationship that affects both God and creature, a relationship created by a God who loves and is changed by those whom he loves, implies "a kind of contingent happening in the divine life."[41]

I am to large extent sympathetic to the views of Peacocke, Moltmann, and Fiddes here represented. But while these authors hold thereby that in one way or other it implies that there is in God both an eternal and a temporal aspect, I differ from them in regard to this, as was already expressed in the first section of chapter 1. God may be believed in as interactively engaged with the entities that he is creating without thereby being inserted within space and time (or its equivalent, Einsteinium space-time). Accordingly, there is no temporal aspect in God. God

---

36. Ibid., 129.
37. Ibid., 158.
38. Fiddes, *Participating in God*, 76.
39. Ibid., 74–75.
40. Ibid., 133; see also 146.
41. Ibid., 175; see also Fiddes, *Creative Suffering*, 66–68.

enables, as Creator, the existence of the creaturely order and those therein—that is, the entire emergent creaturely fabric and the co-emergent space-time—and is thus believed to be prior to them. This perception is supported by the images used by Jesus when he spoke about the kingdom. These suggest that it is a dynamic reality and not simply a realm at a particular locus (as regards space and time). As narrated in John's Gospel, in the story of Jesus and the Samaritan woman at the well of Jacob, Jesus speaks of a spring of water in the faithful welling up to eternal life (John 4:7–15). Later on in the conversation Jesus would have added that there will be a time, and already is, when true worshippers will not worship on this or that mountain, but will worship the Father in spirit and in truth (4:20–24). As narrated in the Synoptic Gospels, Jesus compares the kingdom, among others, with the hidden life and growth power of a seed, a seed, moreover, which hardly has any substantial foundation and yet, which is so vigorous that it profoundly affects the lives of various creatures (Mark 4:26–32 and parallel texts). This seed that is being sown is the word of God (Mark 4:14; compare Gen 1:3 and Isa 55:10–11). This teaching of Jesus suggests that the kingdom is a most elusive, yet very real reality, capable of taking everything up in its sphere of influence and transforming all. This accords with what we found in chapter 2 regarding the manifoldness of *logoi* in Maximus, which lead beyond the merely natural, and with the envisaged personal destiny as at another ontological level from that what is naturally given. The kingdom and the realm of eternity as the realm of divine perfection are found at an ontological level that transcends space-time and the purely natural capabilities. It is not the purpose to enter here upon a philosophical discussion of eternity, but God can be envisaged as being (eternally) perfect God and can be professed to be in his personal existence beyond any conceivable goodness; God is, in mainstream Christian tradition, believed not to increase or decrease in vigor, wisdom, love, or any other virtue (Ps 102:25–27). God needs not be infected with the changeability that is part and parcel of the physical and moral maturation of the imperfect by his creative and salvific engagement. God's interactive engagement with creation, such as we have been considering, is the actuality of an extremely multifarious touching (or speech-act) and being touched, as well as of the creaturely entities, personified, being adopted into the undivided and indefinable wholeness of the living and divine communion. This divine actuality and this adoption of the contingent and created take place at an ontological level that transcends space-time. It therefore implies a differentiating dynamic in God, albeit atemporal and nonspatial. But besides this, there is in God already the dynamic process that is implicit in being a living and personal God.

With these thoughts the chapter can be concluded. This last section has been a suited preparation for focusing our minds upon the theme of the following chapter, which makes us dwell further upon the destiny of the created reality in God.

8

Personal Existence in Christ and in the Spirit

PARTICIPATION IN THE LOGOI

THE *LOGOI* WERE DISCUSSED in chapter 2 in order to obtain a more detailed notion of the divine speech that is creative. It was thereby found that in Maximus' doctrine of the *logoi* it is envisaged that they not only let creatures emerge, but that by them God guides the creatures towards a participation in life within him. In this present chapter we are invited to reflect further upon the destiny that is reached in God. It is not the purpose of this section or of this chapter to study the doctrine of the *logoi* in more detail, but rather to comprehend better that participation in them leads the created order to participate in that mystery in God for which the universe is called into being.

Let us begin by noting that Maximus' discussion develops insights from the Pauline letters as regards the cosmic significance of Jesus Christ, the Incarnate Word of God. Paul envisaged for the end-time the replacement of the entire cosmos with a new creation that is completely dominated by Christ's rule. This conviction, as was mentioned in chapter 2, also shines through in Mark's presentation of the significance of Jesus' final week in Jerusalem. As Paul perceives it, at the completion

Cosmic Prayer and Guided Transformation

of creation's renewal, God is envisaged to become "everything in all (τὰ πάντα ἐν πᾶσιν)" (1 Cor 15:28; my translation). In addition, Paul spoke of the faithful as collectively forming the body of Christ (1 Cor 10:16–17; 12:12–27; Rom 12:4–13), whereby appears to be conveyed an identifying of the ecclesial body with the eucharistic body of Christ. Each would therein attain a reality of union with the risen Christ to the extent of identification (1 Cor 6:15–17). A number of sayings attributed to Jesus in the Gospels are supportive of such identification (Mark 9:37, 41; Matt 10:40; 18:5; Luke 10:1, 16; John 13:20). Or again, with the parable of the sheep and the goats concerning the final judgment Jesus would have taught that the Son of man identifies himself with the righteous: "The King will answer them, 'Truly, I say to you, as you did it to one of the least of these my brethren, you did it to me'" (Matt 25:40). At 1 Cor 15:42–44 Paul proclaims that ultimately all those deemed worthy, both human and non-human creatures, will receive a spiritual body permeated with God's presence in the new creation. In Romans he speaks about the need for a renewal of the brethren's mind (Rom 12:2), so that not only their bodies but the entire creation may be imbued with the Spirit. In Colossians the belief that Jesus Christ has a cosmic significance is prominent. As at 1 Cor 8:6, so at Col 1:16 Paul declares that God creates through Christ, that "all things were created through him and for him." In Colossians is again proclaimed the belief that Christ introduced a renewal of all creation, to be accomplished with the cooperation of the faithful, and that through Christ, God was reconciling the faithful and the cosmos to himself (Col 1:9–29). Taking the imagery further, the letter to the Ephesians is suggestive of a cosmic personification in Christ (Eph 1:22–23). Yet, there is not to be lost sight of the idea of "a holy temple in the Lord" (Eph 2:21–22) that is of cosmic dimensions, which is significant because it guards from too anthropomorphic an imagination. It is important to recognize as well the context wherein all this teaching is placed. In his early letters 1 Thessalonians, Galatians, and 1 Corinthians, Paul expected that Christ's coming was imminent and that there would be a radical and immediate transformation (e.g., 1 Cor 15:51–52) of the entire creation (15:28), so that the old world would be folded up and the new unfolded. In his subsequent letters, from 2 Corinthians and Romans onwards, as Christ's second coming was found to be delayed, even though it was still expected (e.g., Col 3:4), preaching was adapted and a more continuous transformation was being envisaged. The present cosmos is thus not to be demolished, but to be interiorly renewed and to be purged from all that

Personal Existence in Christ and in the Spirit

is evil. Accordingly, in the church fathers, and in Maximus in particular, creation and re-creation are perceived as the two sides of a single continuous event wherein creatures attain the fullness of their being in God.

Maximus has taken up the presented scriptural ideas from a post-Chalcedonian perspective wherein God is believed in as a tri-personal community of love, wherein Christ is discerned as having two complete natures in hypostatic union, namely a human and a divine nature coming together into one person, and wherein the natural and personal levels are clearly distinguished. Paul M. Blowers and Robert Louis Wilken describe Maximus' achievement as "a panoramic commentary on the first chapter of Ephesians and on Colossians 1:15–23, the Apostle Paul's reflection on the mystery of Christ as the mystery of the world. Though filtered through a mature trinitarian theology and Christology . . . we see in Maximus's achievement the echoes of Irenaeus's principle of cosmic *recapitulation* (ἀνακεφαλαίωσις), and a critical rehabilitation of Origen's masterful insight into the divine penetration and permeation of all things (1 Cor 15:28)."[1] For discerning continuity and development in cosmological thought from Paul to Maximus, the perception offered by Russell Bradner Norris, Jr. in his article "Logos Christology as Cosmological Paradigm" (1996) is helpful. Norris points out that Maximus offers a sophisticated explanation for the Christian claim that "the Christ of the Gospel" is the redeemer of the cosmos.[2]

Maximus holds with traditional Christian belief that it is not an abstraction that has an ultimate and universal significance, in which created realities partake, but that on the contrary, as Norris describes, the particular person Jesus Christ is the key to the metaphysical structure of reality. Norris interprets that in Maximus' Christology Jesus has universal redemptive significance, not as embodying general characteristics on the natural level (of οὐσία) wherein many others partake, but on the personal level (of ὑπόστασις), as the central focal point of a configurational pattern in reference to which others can find their place in the pattern.[3] This perception seems to be a consistent development of Paul's participation language (e.g., as found at 1 Cor 10:16–17; 12:12–27, and Rom 12:4–13).

Yet, Maximus upholds with Irenaeus, Athanasius, Chalcedon, and all orthodoxy in tension with this that Jesus Christ is the Son and Word

---

1. Blowers and Wilken, *Cosmic Mystery*, 20–21.
2. Norris, Jr., "Logos Christology," 193–94.
3. Ibid., 195–98; Yeago, "Jesus," 163ff., esp. 183.

Cosmic Prayer and Guided Transformation

of God. This Word includes a word (*logos*) for every created entity. It is the role of creatures to try to fulfill this word, or principle, or reason, for themselves. As such, they are being deified (while retaining creaturehood) and enter into the divine union and communion through, with, and in Jesus Christ. This as well is continuous with Paul's conviction that God the Father creates through his Son, Jesus Christ; that Jesus' life, desire, cross, and reign (e.g., 1 Cor 15:24–25; Phil 2:1–8) enable through the disciples' prayer, love, and kenosis, as well as through their sharing in the fellowship of Jesus Christ and through their life in accordance with the (specific gifts from the) Spirit, together with creation's travail and expectation, a cosmic renewal to take place wherein Christ-followers are participant as they are united among each other, with the wider creation, and with God. From our discussion in chapter 2 of the *logoi* in Maximus it can be concluded that if we strive with our will (θέλημα) to live in accordance with the *logoi*, and if we let ourselves be guided by the Spirit, as Jesus has enabled us, then our own and other creaturely "voices" enter into unison with the voice of Jesus, who manifests the Word that is spoken for all existence.

The fact that creatures can pursue the life-giving modes of existence and thus aim to live in accordance with the God-given *logoi* is only possible because the created order is enfolded in God's love (John 3:16). We are reminded of the Spirit of God moving over the face of the waters, preparing the event of universal creation and permeating it with God's presence. The love of God is a cosmic force with which creatures need to become attuned so as to reach the God whom John identified as the God who is love (1 John 4:8). This divine love was manifested in Jesus and taught by Him.

LOVE AS THE UNIFYING FORCE

The union within the Trinity takes place in a dynamic of love. Maximus perceived that this dynamic of love in God aims to include the universe. It is as a result of this prior dynamic of love and because of God's goodness that the Son became incarnate in creation, in Scripture, in Jesus, and in other people's humanity. For, as was quoted in chapter 2 in our study of Maximus' doctrine of the *logoi*, "For always and in all, the Word of God, and God, wants the mystery of His embodiment to be accomplished."

Personal Existence in Christ and in the Spirit

The dynamic of love found its full realization and was made manifest between God the Father and Jesus, who, while being truly God, was a human being among us. In particular, the dynamic of love coming down from God enabled with the cooperation of the created entities, foremost of Mary and Joseph, and then of Jesus, the realization of the union of the divine nature and human nature within Jesus, who thus existed as a single person who was Christ the Lord. Specifically, this union in Jesus Christ was by the Council of Chalcedon taught to be a union into a single person (or *prosōpon*) and hypostasis (that is, subsistence). Chalcedon provided in its declaration known as the *Chalcedonian Definition of the Faith* explanation as to the orthodox manner of interpreting this union: "one and the same Christ, Son, Lord, Only-begotten, to be acknowledged in two natures, without confusion (ἀσυγχύτως), without change (ἀτρέπτως), without division (ἀδιαιρέτως), without separation (ἀχωρίστως); the distinction of natures being in no way abolished because of the union, but rather the characteristic property of each nature being preserved, and concurring into one Person and one subsistence, not as if Christ were parted or divided into two persons, but one and the same Son and only-begotten God, Word, Lord, Jesus Christ."[4] It is a union that is real and complete, so that it is impossible to draw a dividing line with on the one side the divine and on the other the created, even though both the divine and the created remain intact and distinct. This kind of union wherein is constituted a single hypostasis is called a hypostatic union. Chalcedon itself refrained from using this term. But the term was used by Cyril of Alexandria (bishop from 412 to 444) as language about Christ. The term was also employed by, among others, Maximus and has become widely used in theological discourse. It is this union in Jesus Christ that is at the heart of the mystery within Christ.

The outreach of divine love towards the created entities wants to include those people who aim to live in accordance with their human nature and the created entities that contribute positively to the various ensembles. As Maximus envisaged, God's love wants to bring them into a hypostatic union within Christ, though this obviously not in Jesus of Nazareth's particular humanity, but as part of the configurational pattern to which Norris referred. It is in this way that we may read Paul's testimony in Galatians. "It is no longer I who live, but Christ who lives in me; and the life I now live in the flesh I live by faith in the Son of God,

---

4. Greek text at Bindley and Green, *Oecumenical Documents*, 193; trans. Stevenson, *Creeds, Councils and Controversies*, 353.

Cosmic Prayer and Guided Transformation

who loved me and gave himself for me" (Gal 2:20). The creatures that attain this union in Christ are also in a union with the Spirit. One cannot be had without the other. Just as no line can be drawn between the two natures in Jesus, so no line can be drawn between the divine persons, even though they are truly distinctive persons. As Paul expresses in the same letter, "God has sent the Spirit of his Son into our hearts, crying 'Abba! Father!'" (Gal 4:6). Hence, for Paul, to be in Christ is to be born according to the Spirit (4:29), it is to walk by the Spirit (5:16) and to live by the Spirit (5:25).

Life in the Spirit and in Christ cannot take place in isolation. Maximus teaches with John 3:5 in mind that those "who are mystically reborn out of Christ's Spirit"[5] allow God to associate with them other creatures on their path towards unification in God.[6] For other creatures as well have various possible modes of existence.[7] All beings with their hypostatic particularities are created within a universe of various interdependent creatures. Hence, the modes of human beings' existence cannot be unrelated to that of other beings but are interdependent. The rational beings (both human and angelic) have a particular responsibility to cooperate with the Spirit so as to direct their modes of existence towards God and so that in accord with God's providence all created beings are led towards their deification within God.

In *Mystagogy*, a work on the church and on the symbolism of the various elements of the liturgy, Maximus elaborates on the creaturely dynamic towards God. Maximus explains, "In his providence he binds all things to one another and to himself—both the intelligible (τά νοητά) and the sensible beings (τά αἰσθητά)—and while as their cause, beginning and end, he directs all beings round about himself (περὶ ἑαυτὸν)—beings that according to their nature are separate from one another—he makes them harmonious with each other by the singular force of natural attraction towards him (κατὰ μίαν πρὸς αὐτόν σχέσεως δύναμιν), since he is their origin."[8] As envisaged in this extract, the various beings are despite their differences and despite all that separates them being bound to one another and to God. This suggests that it is the dynamic of love coming from God that is at work in creatures in an all-pervasive manner.

---

5. *Thal.* 61; CCSG 22:91:129–30.
6. *Thal.* 2; PG 90:272AB or CCSG 7:51:7–22.
7. Ibid. and *Amb.* 42; PG 91:1344A.
8. *Myst.* 1; PG 91:664D.

Personal Existence in Christ and in the Spirit

Maximus continues by speaking of a force that leads all beings to a convergence within God's divine simplicity. He does, however, in this extract not explicitly identify this force with the universal dynamic of love. It is later in the same work that it is affirmed that love takes on a central importance for the realization of the union between intelligible and sensible beings in the process towards the union with God. Maximus speaks of "the principle (or *logos*) of the unifying force (τῆς ἑνοποιοῦ δυνάμεως ὁ λόγος) . . . the kinship in love (τῆς φιλικῆς συγγενείας) mysteriously inspired in them in quest of union (καθ' ἕνωσιν)."[9] This kinship in love "constitutes the totality unmixed (ἄφυρτα) and undivided (ἀδιαίρετα) both within themselves and among each other."[10] Maximus envisages that in this way God's presence and his singular force that is in all things, can lead all towards him according to the *logoi* and *tropoi* (that is, the divinely inspired modes of existence) that are ultimately encompassed within one *logos*, one *tropos*.[11]

For a confirmation and complementation of the issues discussed in this section and in this chapter I can recommend the splendid chapter by Janet P. Williams, which she has contributed in *The First Christian Theologians* (2004), edited by G. R. Evans. She writes: "All aspects of our nature are taken up and healed in Christ. Maximus allies to this the ancient understanding that love is the force which brings diverse realities together into one, whether at the interpersonal or the astronomical level: since God is Creator, and God is Love, then it is the mark of the divine love to integrate fractured and broken reality, healing division and bringing all things together."[12] It is thereby to be observed that Maximus was very much involved with the Christological controversies of his time, and his entire vision is Christ-centered. As noted in the course of this chapter and in the earlier chapter 2, this should be complemented with an emphasis on the role of the Spirit and on the union with the Spirit, leading us into a union with God the Father.

---

9. *Myst.* 7; PG 91:685AB.
10. Ibid.; PG 91:685B.
11. Ibid. and *Amb.* 41; PG 91:1308B.
12. Williams, "Pseudo-Dionysius and Maximus," 194.

KENOSIS AND DEATH

The thought with which we began the previous section is that God aims to include the created entities in the dynamic of love within him. It is for this reason that the Son became incarnate in Jesus. The Incarnation exemplified God's loving outreach towards his creation. As Maximus says in *Letter* 44 and in so many places, "The most mysterious of all mysteries: God himself became truly a human being out of love."[13] It is the gift of God himself for us. God's love shows that in love there is no holding back; it is the giving of one's self.

The outreach of God in love required a kenosis of the Son, whereby he needed to willingly forsake his divine dignity and glory to take on our human nature with all its inherent weaknesses, apart from sin.[14] In Jesus Christ this self-emptying out of love was taken to its ultimate completion when he freely gave himself over to be tried and crucified in fulfillment of the Scriptures, and when as such he died in innocence for the sake of those belonging to him.[15]

The inclusion of people and of creation within a hypostatic union within God, such as explained in the foregoing pages, takes place within this outreach of divine love towards us. But for its realization there is required a kenosis of the people belonging to God and of creation that empties them of all that does not befit the divine will.[16] Hence, notwithstanding the unifying natural disposition (ἡ ἑνοποιὸς σχέσις) of all things that Maximus envisages at *Mystagogy* chapter 7,[17] the transformation involved requires a kenosis in accord with the love that unites creatures to each other rather than to themselves. It is a kenosis that allows the created to overcome the mortality of the flesh and to be entirely lifted up towards the spiritual realm. This insight was taken up by Pope Benedict XVI in a Wednesday general audience at the Vatican on June 25, 2008 as he introduced Maximus to the crowds:

> St Maximus demonstrates that man does not find his unity, the integration of himself or his totality within himself but by surpassing himself, by coming out of himself. Thus, also in Christ, by coming out of himself, man finds himself in God, in the Son

---

13. *Ep.* 44; PG 91:644B.
14. *Amb.* 60; PG 91:1385C and *Op. th. pol.* 7; PG 91:77C.
15. *Ep.* 44; PG 91:644A.
16. *Exp. or. dom. prooem.*; PG 90:877A–C or CCSG 23:33:107—34:127.
17. *Myst.* 7; PG 91:685B; similarly *Myst.* 1; PG 91:665A.

of God. It is not necessary to amputate man to explain the Incarnation; all that is required is to understand the dynamism of the human being who is fulfilled only by coming out of himself; it is in God alone that we find ourselves, our totality and our completeness. . . . The height of freedom is the "yes," in conformity with God's will. It is only in the "yes" that man truly becomes himself; only in the great openness of the "yes," in the unification of his will with the divine, that man becomes immensely open, becomes "divine." . . . . . . God entrusted to man, created in his image and likeness, the mission of unifying the cosmos. . . . He showed us how to unify the cosmos in the communion of Christ. . . . . . . Christ indicates that the cosmos must become a liturgy, the glory of God, and that worship is the beginning of true transformation, of the true renewal of the world.[18]

The salvific process wherein the created is lifted up towards the spiritual realm requires from the faithful a kenosis concerning the "flesh." This kenosis is a dissociation of what is ultimately not required in the constitution of human nature.[19] It is a path that we are called to set out upon during our earthly life and that finds its continuation at the moment of death when the flesh is left behind altogether, while body and soul are beyond death transformed towards and into God. In this manner our hypostasis is perfected.

The flesh is made up of material elements that make the form of the body during earthly life sense perceptible and that allow for interaction with other created realities in the present dispensation. It is also spoken of as representative of the misused passions that are being directed upon pleasure and self-gratification. For, whereas a virtuous life directs the desires upon God, a life of vices is focused upon the sensations that derive from the body while it is bonded with matter.

What are left behind at a human's death and what dissolve in the grave or in the sea or are cremated are the material elements that are needed for earthly life and that are associated to an individual during his or her earthly existence. These material elements will thus after a human being's death continue their own journey within the earth as a whole according to their own *logoi* and their own movement. Turning once more to Maximus, it appears that he was well aware that the material constituents are only temporarily associated with a human or animate being, and

---

18. (Ratzinger) Benedict XVI, "St Maximus," para. 2, 5, 6.
19. *Myst.* 7; PG 91:685D–8A.

Cosmic Prayer and Guided Transformation

that thereafter they may be associated with another being. This perception of Maximus can be found in *Ambigua* 42. "The body clearly comes from the underlying matter (ὕλη) of another body at conception."[20] According to Vladimir Lossky, this perception of Maximus would have been continuous with that of Gregory of Nyssa.[21]

Clearly, a kenosis concerning the flesh should within a Christian tradition that is faithful to its foundation in Christ not imply a negative attitude or a disparaging of flesh and matter as such. The Gospels show that Jesus healed people entirely, body and soul; at the Last Supper he introduced the New Covenant in his body and blood, which he identified with the broken bread and the cup of wine that he shared out among his disciples; and later, John could write in the prologue to his Gospel, "The Word became flesh" (John 1:14). When we turn to Paul, we find that he does not have much positive to say about the flesh (σάρξ). Some texts in Galatians and Romans indicate an outright negative attitude towards the flesh and the world as it is (e.g., Gal 1:3–4; 3:3; 5:16–24; Rom 7:18–8:8). Yet, a careful reading of these same texts and the surrounding verses may show that it is not necessarily the flesh as such that is targeted by Paul. In these texts Paul associates the flesh with sin and opposition to God, and it is the latter that he targets. In Galatians there would also have played the association of flesh with circumcision (Gal 6:12–13), which for the converted gentiles would devalue the salvation in Christ by faith that Paul preaches. Despite, therefore, the negative light in which the flesh is presented, it can be noted that in Galatians, for example, Paul testifies, "The life I now live in the flesh I live by faith in the Son of God" (Gal 2:20). Hence, though he appears to have held at the time that he wrote Galatians that it is less than ideal to be in the flesh, he acknowledges that it does not exclude to be already in Christ. In Romans, after having extensively spoken about the "sinful flesh" (Rom 8:3) and about the fact that those in the flesh cannot please God (8:8), he says, "But you are not in the flesh, you are in the Spirit" (8:9). Yet, he is addressing people of flesh and blood. Given that Paul held in his earlier letters that the world he knew would soon come to end when Christ would appear, an element of dualism is not entirely absent (e.g., 1 Cor 15:50). But as he adapted towards envisioning a more continuous transformation, the dualism needed to give way to an appreciation of inclusiveness. The verses of Romans here

20. *Amb.* 42; PG 91:1324C.
21. Lossky, *Mystical Theology*, 103.

quoted reveal traces of his still ongoing struggle in adapting his outlook, even though he has come to perceive that it is the present world that will be delivered and will come to share in the glory of God (Rom 8:19–23). Support of the reading of Paul presented here is found in Edward Adams' study of Paul's cosmological language in *Constructing the World* (2004).[22] Turning to Maximus at the end of the patristic era, careful reading shows that he did not despise any created material elements themselves, but again rather the misuse of our natural drives.

When Maximus speaks of "the passing character of material things,"[23] he means that when all the created realities, which according to their *logoi* and hypostases run their earthly course, have advanced into the spiritual realm, all tangibility associated with material based sensitivity will disappear. For all created existence that tried to realize existence in accord with its own nature will be taken up in a perfect spiritual existence. As we discerned, the non-rational beings attain this transformed spiritual existence through association with human and angelic beings. It involves that in the realization of their existence all created entities are taken up in an ever more intricate web of relationships. It therefore also means that the much-localized material elements are taken up in this process, in this dynamic of life, which transforms all existence in such a way that it can only be found in these relationships and in the union that is developed. Refusing to enter into relationship, that is, refusing the path of salvation, leads to an absolute isolation, to perdition. This perdition is signified by the decomposing body, by the disintegration of its material elements. The disintegration of these elements is not their eternal perdition, but rather a warning for human beings that are depending on them for their earthly existence.

Hence, the ascetic element involved in kenosis, and Paul's and Maximus' talk about the flesh and the material or worldly matters, need not bring us to adopt a dualistic scheme that involves a negative perception of creation. As Paul testified to the Corinthians: physical death, which he held to have been introduced as a result of the fall, was overcome by Christ, so that through death the faithful and all creatures would be set free from corruptibility and attain immortality (1 Cor 15:51–57). In continuity with Paul's perception of the cosmic dynamic is that of Maximus. For Maximus believes that by exercise of the virtues the own body and

---

22. Adams, *Constructing the World*, 182, 192, 231.
23. *Myst.* 15; PG 91:693C.

soul and all that is created can be taken up in transformation towards divine unity.

In continuity of a virtuous life and of a contemplation that aims to discern the *logoi* (which Maximus believes to be secretly revealed by all God's works within the physical order),[24] at death, the faithful, as microcosms (a term coined in recent times that is inspired by the Cappadocian fathers; see for example in chapter 6 as regards Gregory of Nazianzen), can give themselves (their souls) entirely over to God whereby they bring all their (bodily) macrocosmic relationships; and complementarily, inseparably, they (their bodies) can be taken up in the dynamic of the macrocosm towards God, which shall have become informed by their soul's dynamic towards God.[25] As such, the disintegration of the flesh and assimilation with the earth can be seen to be in expectation of the cosmic unification attained in God.

This chapter so far has approached from various angles the contingent order's participation in the mystery in God; the veil has been partially lifted by considering participation in the *logoi*, the dynamic of love that can lead the created into the divine communion, and the transformation that is realized through kenosis and death. The forthcoming final section focuses upon the resulting process of unification itself; that is, the choreography, as it were, of the movements whereby God and the created enter into a hypostatic union. At the end of the forthcoming section we will once more consider in the company of Maximus the union itself that is being actualized.

PERICHORESIS AND UNION

In chapter 1 it was noted that the concept *perichoresis* is a key concept of the new theology and that it is there applied to both the intra-trinitarian communion and to the creaturely participation therein. The concept conveys, as was said, the notion of a mutual permeation. With reference to G. L. Prestige (1889–1955), Thunberg brings to our attention that the term *perichoresis* (περιχώρησις) appears to have been a personal contribution of Maximus to Christology for understanding the hypostatic union between the divine and the created/human natures within Christ.[26]

---

24. *Thal.* 13; PG 90:296A or CCSG 7:95:9–12.
25. *Myst.* 7; PG 91:685C; see also Nellas, *Deification in Christ*, 64–66.
26. Prestige, *God in Patristic Thought*, 291, 293; Thunberg, *Microcosm and*

Personal Existence in Christ and in the Spirit

The literal meaning of the verb περιχωρεῖν can be rendered as "to go round," "to come round to (something)" or "to encircle," or also as "to rotate" or "to return to the same point by a circular movement." Hence, the noun (ἡ) περιχώρησις, εως was used by the ancient Greek philosopher Anaxagoras (c.500–428 BC) as meaning "a rotation." Maximus employed the term so as to convey the notion of "a reciprocal (or mutual) pervasion (or permeation)" or "a mutual and periodical turning around (one another)." An English equivalent of the word, and this by medium of the Latin translation, is "circumincession."[27]

Prestige, and more recently Thunberg, point out that Maximus would have come to this term in continuity with Gregory Nazianzen's *Epistle* 101, where the verb is used in its participle form περιχωρουσῶν with regard to the two natures within Christ.[28] The text is found quoted among the *scholia* (that is, commentaries) on *Epistle* 4 of Pseudo-Dionysius and attributed to Maximus (though many of the *scholia* are ascribed to John of Scythopolis, who lived during the first half of the sixth century).[29] However, Thunberg takes a different course from Prestige when he argues that Maximus would have been interested in the idea that *perichoresis* could indicate the activity that is effective for the formation of the union, rather than as a description of mutually shared effects by the unified natures within the one hypostasis, and that this notion of an active *perichoresis* he discerned in Gregory's *Epistle*: as Gregory held, the permeating into one another (περιχωρουσῶν εἰς ἀλλήλας) is for (on

---

Mediator, 23.

27. Alexandre, *Dictionnaire Grec-Français*; Liddell and Scott, *Greek-English Lexicon*; *Oxford English Dictionary*, at "circumincession"; Prestige, *God in Patristic Thought*, 291–94; LaCugna, *God for Us*, 270–72; Thunberg, *Microcosm and Mediator*, 23–29; Thunberg, "'Circumincession,'" 365–68.

28. Nazianzen *Ep.* 101; PG 37:181BC; trans. Stevenson and Frend, *Creeds, Councils and Controversies*, 90.

29. Maximus *Scholia in Corpus Areopagiticum* (*In Ep. Dionys.*); PG 4:533C; Prestige, *God in Patristic Thought*, 292; Balthasar, *Cosmic Liturgy*, 372; Thunberg, *Microcosm and Mediator*, 26 n. 29. Von Balthasar explains that John of Scythopolis tends to call Gregory of Nyssa, "the Theologian," whereas Maximus usually calls Gregory of Nazianzen "the Theologian," as it is the case in this passage. Maximus also comments upon *Ep.* 4 of Pseudo-Dionysius concerning the expression "theandric energy" (PG 3:1072C) at *Amb.* 5 and *Op. th. pol.* 7. It can further be pointed out that Maximus quotes the next sentence of Gregory's *Ep.* 101 (PG 37:181C) at *Op. th. pol.* 15 and that he quotes from this letter (PG 37:184A) the same idea in its positive wording at *Amb.* 42; PG 91:1336A.

Cosmic Prayer and Guided Transformation

account of) the union, or adhesion (τῷ λόγῳ τῆς συμφυΐας).[30] Moreover, Thunberg argues that within the divine-human relationship *perichoresis* is meant to express reciprocity; that is, it is descriptive of a relationship wherein both sides are actively engaged and that results in a unified common activity within the union that is effected.[31]

As von Balthasar describes,[32] it is because of his polemic against the various emerging forms of Monophysitism (the doctrine that Jesus only had a divine nature and that his humanity was absorbed into his divinity) that Maximus needed to develop his understanding of the union between the divine and the human in Christ. The term *perichoresis* relies on the insights of Chalcedon and the four adverbs (without confusion, change, division, or separation) with which it defended the orthodox faith. Accordingly, the mutual ontological presence as understood by Maximus draws both natures into a union and yet preserves their own characteristics, it preserves the distinction; in the union perfection is reached while also the difference between both natures is entirely manifested.[33] This is the only possible union wherein love can take root and grow. Against the background of the said polemic, Maximus developed his perception of the cosmic reality, aided of course by other factors that constituted his intellectual background. Given that he believed that the mystery in Christ is of a cosmic significance, the idea of *perichoresis* was significant for the development of his cosmic ontological understanding. This is illustrated in, for example, the following extract from *Ambigua* 7, which contains an implicit reference to the promise contained in 1 Cor 15:28: "God's activity (ἐνέργεια) alone will be totally permeating (περιχωρήσαντος) the whole being of all those who are his in a manner that is worthy and suited to them."[34] Another example is found at *Ambigua* 41, where it is envisaged that "the human person unites the created nature with the uncreated through love . . . showing them to be one and the same through the possession of grace, the whole [creation] wholly interpenetrated

---

30. Thunberg, *Microcosm and Mediator*, 26; supportive of this perception is Larchet, *La divinisation*, 335; cf. Prestige, "περιχωρέω," 244, 246–48; Prestige, *God in Patristic Thought*, 292–93.

31. Thunberg, *Microcosm and Mediator*, 29–30; Larchet, *La divinisation*, 336–38; cf. Prestige, *God in Patristic Thought*, 294.

32. Balthasar, *Cosmic Liturgy*, 63–64.

33. *Amb.* 5; PG 91:1053B (this text relates the ideas of hypostatic union and of *perichoresis* as here described).

34. *Amb.* 7; PG 91:1076C.

(περιχωρήσας) by God, and become completely whatever God is, save at the level of being."[35] Janet P. Williams fully confirms in her contributing chapter in *The First Christian Theologians* from which was quoted earlier in the present chapter that Maximus applies the concept *perichoresis* in various spheres of reality; and that "even further: perichoresis comes to flavour the whole cosmic drama."[36]

Interesting is the following text from *Quaestiones ad Thalassium* 59 where *perichoresis* is seen once more in the context of the process of deification. It can be observed that it is not unequivocally clear in this text who it is that performs the *perichoresis*. The *perichoresis* here considered is that between God and the faithful. Both the divine and the human subject appear actively involved in the process, since it is a true revelation of the divine in proportion to faith. The reason I draw attention to this text, despite the fact that it does not refer to the wider creation, is that *perichoresis* functions here in such manner that it allows us to discern an aspect of literally turning around: namely, as a return towards the origin, or first cause; yet, with this qualification that the result is not a mere return to a starting point. By means of *perichoresis* there is brought about a new reality for the creature, as it attains its fulfillment in the unification with God. This is similarly the case in the mutual *perichoresis* of Christ's two natures, which brings about the new reality of the hypostatic union, of the one divine incarnate person. Furthermore, in this text Maximus speaks of an ever moving rest, which he explicitly relates to *perichoresis*:

> The salvation of souls is properly the end of faith. The end of faith is the true revelation of him who was being believed in. The true revelation of him who was being believed in is the ineffable circumincession (ἡ ἄρρητος περιχώρησις) of him who has been believed in, in proportion to the faith within each. The circumincession of him who has been believed in constitutes the return towards the origin as the end of those that have believed. The return towards the proper origin as the end of those that have believed is the fulfillment of desire. The fulfillment of desire is the ever-moving rest (ἡ ἀεικίνητος στάσις) of they that are desiring around the desired (περὶ τὸ ἐφετὸν).[37]

It is envisaged that the creaturely rest is dynamic as an eternal revolution. This is a perception that accords with the belief that the rest of the created

35. *Amb.* 41; PG 91:1308B; trans. Louth, *Maximus the Confessor*, 158.
36. Williams, "Pseudo-Dionysius and Maximus," 197.
37. *Thal.* 59; PG 90:608CD or CCSG 22:53:122–31.

Cosmic Prayer and Guided Transformation

order in God is a participation in the living and personal communion within him. It is the attainment of a fullness of life; and life is not static but, as we considered at the end of chapter 3, is an enduring dynamism wherein a labile equilibrium is maintained, which allows for a diversity that is unified.

Life and its dynamic are envisaged as becoming an ultimate characteristic of all existence, which is eternal life in all its fullness as shared with and within God himself. Maximus expresses it in *Ambigua 7*, from which we have already quoted a number of times: "[God] giving them life is bestowing eternal and ineffable life; it is a life altogether free from all that one recognizes as the constitutive properties of the present age; a life that is maintained beyond the decay. Eternal life is not the breathing of air, neither is it maintained by streams of blood that flow from the liver, but it is the fullness of God being participated in by all."[38]

This intended goal is reached when by way of a process of transformation all divisions that exist have been overcome. For, as Maximus envisages, if people set out according to the virtuous modes of living opened up by Christ, all creation becomes ever more associated, closer to them, and this until "Christ is everything and in all (τὰ πάντα καὶ ἐν πᾶσι Χριστός)."[39] Then the entire transformed creation will be at one, personal, within the resurrected Christ, the Son of God, and within God. At that point, the hypostatic union in Christ will have come to encompass all existence: "Thus he divinely recapitulates the universe in himself, showing that the whole creation exists as one, like another human being, completed by the gathering together of its parts one with another in itself, and inclined towards itself by the whole of its existence, in accordance with the one, simple, unspecified and undifferentiated idea of production from nothing, in accordance with which the whole of creation admits of one and the same undiscriminated *logos*, as having not been before it is."[40] The created reality that in the present dispensation consists of an entire spectrum of creatures is thus destined to evermore partake in a communion with God that is nothing less than intensely personal. Informed

---

38. *Amb.* 7; PG 91:1088BC.

39. *Char.* 2:30; PG 90:993B.

40. *Amb.* 41; PG 91:1312AB; trans. (altered) Louth, *Maximus the Confessor*, 160 (Alteration: I have translated ἀπροσδιόριστον . . . καὶ ἀδιάφορον as "unspecified and undifferentiated" instead of "undifferentiated and indifferent"). See also *Amb.* 31; PG 91:1281A and Stanilaoe, "Commentaires," 480; *Thal.* 60; PG 90:621AB and Andia, "Transfiguration," 318–19.

by the cosmological vision of Maximus and by the various contemporary resources mentioned in this book, it can be suggested that the single *logos* that informs the whole of God's creative initiative and that shall be expressed by the created entities that attain fullness of life in God is a *logos* that sets up wisdom within the created order, a *logos* that binds all together in various levels of organization and according to various *holons*; it is a *logos* that instills a desire for fullness of being as well-being and eternal well-being in accordance with the particular natures; it is a *logos* that thereby instills a longing for loving communion with and within the Holy Trinity; and it is a *logos* that enables the capacity to pray in hope and love. Those that come to express this *logos* by their lives shall not only be united within Christ but in the Spirit as well.

Those that attain such communion with the God who is love shall be in the light. For, as expressed at 1 John 1:5–7, "God is light and in him is no darkness at all. . . . [I]f we walk in the light, as he is in the light, we have fellowship with one another." Finally, so as to end this chapter on a trinitarian note, let us observe that John writes further down in this letter: "If what you heard from the beginning abides in you, then you will abide in the Son and in the Father. And this is what he has promised us, eternal life. . . . And by this we know that he abides in us, by the Spirit which he has given us" (2:24–25; 3:24).

9

Conclusion

THE CREATOR-CREATURE RELATIONSHIP

THE SYNTHESIS PRESENTED IN this section enshrines the outline of a well-informed contemporary Christian cosmological vision. This synthesis gathers in various elements of the discussion that has been entertained in the foregoing chapters. It brings together insights both old and new, insights from Scripture, from patristic writers, from contemporary theologians; insights from ancient Greek and Hellenic philosophers, from various more recent writers and polymaths; insights from contemporary human and natural sciences; insights from church councils and from writers on spirituality.

Peoples of various epochs and various places have in the Western world before the Enlightenment—and up to the present in non-Western cultures—envisaged reality with and through a cosmological vision that enshrined their knowledge and beliefs, until eventually it proved deficient in the light of new insights, experiences, and events. The synthesis proposed here likewise enshrines a perception that if considered valuable to begin with can be brought to touch upon various elements of contemporary intellectual pursuits and experiences and thereby be refined or adapted. The synthesis runs as follows:

Conclusion

There is a loving and compassionate personal God, whom mainstream Christianity (as professed in the Creed of Nicaea of A.D. 325 and in the Niceno-Constantinopolitan Creed of A.D. 381) believes to be not a solitary monad, but a communion of three persons who are substantially one (*homoousios*) by their mutual engagement in a dynamic interweaving of subsistent relationships. This God is at the origin of the entire created reality and of the particular beings therein: without God and his creative initiative nothing would exist. This, however, does not mean that God needs to be the primary cause of the emergence, and hence existence, of each and every contingent entity that exists at some time, but rather that God upholds those that happen to come into existence by bestowing on them their every capacity and potentiality from the moment of their inception onwards. To put it crudely, many creatures, including human beings, that are around at some point, are here considered to exist as a consequence of several indeterminate factors and/or the wills, either noble and natural, and/or voluptuous and sinful, of those of previous generations that engendered them, and possibly, in continuity of Scripture, of influences of holy and/or demonic spiritual forces upon these factors and ancestors. Moreover, it is not satisfactory to alternatively hold on to a deterministic divine creativity at the species-level or even at the level of the various macroscopic ensembles. For in the evolving ecosystems individual beings are born from one another and kinds are "born" from one another; just as also the solar system, comprising Sun and Earth, has come about by the stardust of earlier stars and general physical laws. Yet, it is God who enables the emergence of created entities out of non-being by informing the physical and biological processes, and by informing every entity that is being brought about in the infinitesimal, astronomical, and biological spheres with a form (elementary or composite) or a soul, including intelligence, that is correlated with the network of relationships wherefrom and wherein the entity emerges (as is envisaged by dialectical evolutionary biology and by the idea of intelligent design). Moreover, since God loves and the divine persons are lovable, the informed ensembles, species, and entities are not static but dynamic, so that a continuous transformation towards the emergence of love can take place (as is suggested at, for example, Eph 1:5–10). Thereby, God guides and stirs the various contingent entities that change and are within time, as well as those that are immaterial and eternal, towards love and towards those characteristics that constitute the fully personal, so that they exist not merely for themselves but become oriented towards the well-being of others.

Those coming into being within the ensembles to which they belong answer God's beneficial workings by their participation in the cosmic prayer in accordance with their received nature and in various degrees of perfection. Or, alternatively, they (e.g., demons, tsetse flies, and disease-causing bacilli) distort God's workings and as a deforming disease need to be overcome and expelled in the transformation through cosmic prayer and love. The guided transformation through and towards love involves a unification whereby the various partial or initial creaturely expressions of the cosmic prayer attributable to the ensembles that behave intelligently lead into a harmonious expression of cosmic prayer carried by a representative group of creatures, namely human beings; this besides the expression of cosmic prayer by the invisible spiritual beings who exist in close conjunction with the ensembles within the visible realm and who are cooperative in the process of harmonization.

The process indicated here, which by God's freely bestowed gift involves the creation and salvation of each and everything, is thus co-determined by these latter reacting to/answering the summons for the life beyond the temporal, the self-sufficient, and the selfish. This existential dynamic includes the ensembles, their elementary constituents of the physical realm, their compounded macro-material entities, basic organic living forms and more complex beings with self-awareness, then also human beings, and spiritual beings. The various ontological levels at which these entities are being identified co-exist in a network of interactions, which includes the well-known ecological circles and which constitutes the ensembles. As the created order has been forming and transforming so as to include all emergent ontological levels and all beings therein, it has been invited to let itself be guided into the interpersonal (circular) divine communion of love, wherein it is actualized. Elementary constituents contribute towards corporeality, whereas holy spiritual beings mediate information and, thereby, orientation, so that human beings have emerged that are capable of the personal.

The end or goal of everything that is taken up in the existential dynamic, the answer to the sum total of cosmic prayer, is enabled through and in the Spirit (e.g., 1 Thess 1:6; Rom 7:6; 8:26; Phil 1:19), as well as by the life and prayer, by the baptism, the eucharistic meal of the new covenant, the symbolic actions and teachings, and by the cross and resurrection of the Incarnate Son of God, Jesus Christ (e.g., Gal 3:13–14,

Conclusion

23–29; 6:14–15; 1 Cor 1:17–18; 10:16; 15:22–28; Rom 5:8–11), who is as the central focal point of a configurational pattern. This goal consists in a perfect harmonious existence with and within God, a nothing excluding existence that itself (at the same time) is the perfect gift of the created beings themselves for God, so that cosmic prayer and its fulfillment coincide; the telos or ultimate end of all things that are turned towards God is an act of existence that perfects their former (contribution to) cosmic prayer, and hence, ultimately, their entire existence is taken up in the praying itself.

Accordingly, significant for the salvation of the faithful, for all people who address God, for those who are touched by the love of God, and for the wider creation, is the cooperation of the faithful, their participation in Christ's baptism and eucharistic covenant in his body and blood (e.g., 1 Cor 6:2–20; 10:15–17; 11:23–26; 15:20–29; Rom 8:19–28; Phil 2:15; 3:17–21). By the participation of all that exists and that is not evil in the cosmic prayer, by the prayers and admirable life of various peoples, and through the association of the faithful with the Christ event, all created existence is by God graciously taken up in a dynamic of self-transcendence, so that new existence is attained.

Creaturely existence is in transformation towards a corporeal and personal mode of existence wherein each is invited to contribute according to the given nature. During this process of becoming, the created reality comes into being within the interpersonal divine communion and yet remains contingent.

THE CHALLENGE OF CHRISTIAN FAITH

It is in the biblical revelation that God as Creator and the world with all therein as his creation are both seen as real, instead of as a delusive appearance, without one or the other being absorbed into either God or creation. In the biblical tradition, both came to be seen as in enduring relationship whereby the highly elevated God is not distant or absent, but is at the origin of all creaturely existence and life, and he came to be perceived as well aware of all whereabouts within the created realm. Expressive of such perception are: that God is believed in as personal; the theme of justice; reflection upon wisdom; and awareness of his continuing creative activity, which we explored at the beginning of chapter 3.

Cosmic Prayer and Guided Transformation

Against this biblical background, as von Balthasar explained, "the insight began to dawn, at the beginning of the Christian era, that transcendence and immanence in fact only complement one another."[1] In the New Testament the involvement of God in the world by his Spirit, creative speech, and wisdom, came to be focused upon Jesus Christ, the Word that appeared as human, and upon his close relationship with God. In the subsequent centuries, as Christological doctrine developed, the understanding that crystallized and that was formulated at the sixth Ecumenical Council, Constantinople III, held in 680–681, was in continuity of Chalcedon and of the Christological doctrine of Maximus. It professed that Jesus is both fully human and fully divine, which was understood as including the possession of a human and a divine will, both being in perfect harmony, so that the humanity of Jesus was in perfect obedience to the divinity and so that he was identified as being a divine person who willed with a single will. A central significance for understanding the union in Christ was thereby taken on by the concept of the hypostatic union between the Word and the humanity of Jesus, which we discussed in chapter 8. Hence, as with the earlier challenge of recognizing both God and creation, the challenge of Christian faith consists in recognizing both the humanity and the divinity of Jesus, both as distinct and real, and as coming together into the one divine person Jesus Christ.

The challenge of Christian faith is the informed recognition also of different realities coming together into a hypostatic union in various instances within the created realm. It challenges us to recognize that various created entities are constituted by both body and soul, by which they are taken up in a network of existence that connects to both the surrounding contingent entities and to God. It challenges us to recognize that the Hebrew and Christian Scriptures are both human writings and Word of God. It challenges us to recognize that there are both a process of natural evolution that is taking place within the realm of space and time, and a direct divine informing; that there are both a physical and a metaphysical realm. It challenges us to recognize that there are not only sensible entities but also intelligible entities, that is, spiritual beings, and that together they constitute a single cosmos.

In continuity of Scripture and Christian tradition, the account given in the foregoing chapters has not denied or disregarded the existence of spiritual beings. Including the intelligible beings in a contemporary

---

1. Balthasar, *Cosmic Liturgy*, 82.

cosmology is a challenge. In this work (in chapters 3 and 6) they have been presented as focal personal beings within the spiritual realm who accompany the ensembles made up of a combination of various contingent entities, and who provide orientation for the transforming dynamic. They have also been presented as alternatively exerting a negative and destructive influence within the creative process and as thus opposing the dynamic towards life, love, and eternal well-being in God. It would be a mistake to deny that creaturely existence takes place in a great variety of forms and to opt for developing a contemporary Christian cosmology that is entirely centered upon the process of a natural evolution within the physical realm, or alternatively to hold on to a cosmology that denies the knowledge provided by the natural sciences and that is out of touch with the world as it is. A Christian cosmology that aims to account realistically for the manifoldness of manifestations of events and entities in the physical realm, including all that is marvelous, beautiful, and good, and all that is despicable, ugly, and evil, such a cosmology would be very handicapped if it were to disregard from the outset the existence of entire categories of entities, or alternatively, if it were to deny the very contingency of creaturely existence.

With Maximus it is envisaged in this and the foregoing chapters that the transformed creation at its destiny will be undivided, as one, personal, within the resurrected Christ, within the Spirit, and will have been taken up in the divine communion of love. The miracle is believed to be taking place as each of the faithful, supported by the wider creation, emerges in a process from becoming to being, while progressing upon a spiritual path from conversion to worship and love, and while appropriating *logoi* that lead into God. This realization of being is for the faithful further believed to take place through a process of kenosis, whereby they and the wider creation enter with God into *perichoresis* and into union. In the union the creaturely order is taken up into God, yet, as for Jesus Christ, is not absorbed or annihilated by the divinity. Maximus envisages in Neoplatonic language creative rays that go out from the divine threefold center, while in the meantime these divine rays, carrying the existence of various creatures, gather into the center, which is not located at any circumscribed place. As such, there is no permanent duality, neither a quaternity, but an eternal Trinity, even while the particularity of the various creatures is retained as deified. This is the Christian equivalent perception of the Hindu expression "*advaita*" (non-duality).

Cosmic Prayer and Guided Transformation

Christian faith thus resists a reducing to a one dimensionality, but instills recognition of the existence of those that are different, yet without confusion, change, division, or separation. Such faith can be perceived as closely related to the realities of life and love. For as we discussed in respectively chapters 3 and 8, life resists the reduction to an undifferentiated oneness, whereas love only exists where there is fully recognized the distinction between the self and the other.

In view of the cosmological vision here outlined, the challenge of Christian faith does not so much consist in acceptance that God is not determining the events that happen, but rather, in view of all the dreadful events constantly taking place and in view of the numerous challenges that life can and does bring, that God is involved at all with the lives of his creatures. Coming back to what I said at the beginning of this section, the challenge of faith is an upholding of the belief that there is a God who loves his creatures, takes care of them, and does not abandon them into the chaos. It is *the* challenge of faith as is shown throughout the Bible. The Psalmist, for example, gives expression to the anxiety:

> Has his steadfast love for ever ceased?
> Are his promises at an end for all time?
> Has God forgotten to be gracious?
> Has he in anger shut up his compassion?
> And I say, "It is my grief
> that the right hand of the Most High has changed"
> (Ps 77:8–10).

Overall, our situation is, as Paul expresses it, "For now we see in a mirror dimly, but then face to face" (1 Cor 13:12). But at the same place, Paul is adamant, "Love never ends" (13:8). Again, at 2 Cor 5:7 he writes, "We walk by faith, not by sight."

ENGAGEMENT UPON THE THREEFOLD SPIRITUAL PATH

From early Christian writers until the present day a prominent place has been given in Christian tradition to the threefold spiritual path. Its three steps have been named differently and emphasis in its understanding has varied. A significant proponent of this path was Maximus, and it will be useful to introduce the way he understood it, for it will allow a situating of intellectual pursuit and the role of faith for attainment of the fullness

Conclusion

of life in God. Maximus calls the first stage the practical life (πρακτική) and it involves primarily an overcoming of the passions. It also implies an acquisition of the virtues, which are to express the double commandment to love God and one's neighbor. The second stage is attributed different names by Maximus in his writings: sometimes, following Evagrius, he calls it *gnōsis* (γνῶσις), but more often, natural contemplation (φυσικὴ θεωρία), or still other names to denote the same activity. It involves a contemplation that is related to the created world. In particular, it is a trying to discern the *logoi* of things.[2] The object of this contemplative activity is for Maximus, the Bible, the Liturgy, the writings of the fathers, the declarations of the councils, and God's creatures.[3] Maximus was, moreover, well acquainted with the ideas of Neoplatonism, the main philosophy of his day. This second step is for Maximus not subsequent but complementary to the first. Thereby, as Thunberg brings to our attention, "the mind advances to a simple knowledge (γνῶσις) which is according to the primal Logos—in order, however, later to be united with God *above* all notion."[4] To indicate the third stage Maximus prefers to adopt the Dionysian terminology, mystical contemplation of God (μυστικὴ θεολογία), and sometimes other similar expressions. Thunberg observes that it is "entirely the gift of grace, the gift of divine love" and that as such it is not to be seen as in continuity with the earlier two stages;[5] yet, its reception requires a soul's preparation. It denotes a state of union with God.

The faithful enter and progress upon this path by their willingness and desire to fulfill their natural existence and to contribute to God's glory; they thus progress by their cooperation with God's gifts. As they enter upon the third step of this path, they will have become entirely open to God's grace, which draws them evermore towards him. It is a way upon which all beings journey in interdependence. For the faithful, love, as the unifying force, has to be practiced throughout their journey upon this path.

Intellectual pursuit (step two) by itself will not bring the faithful to the fulfillment of their being in God. It is essential that it is accompanied by a prayerfulness (step one) wherein they entrust themselves into God's hands.

---

2. Thunberg, *Microcosm and Mediator*, 333–43.
3. Nichols, *Byzantine Gospel*, 29.
4. Thunberg, *Microcosm and Mediator*, 351.
5. Ibid., 355; Larchet, *Saint Maxime le Confesseur*, 183.

Cosmic Prayer and Guided Transformation

THE SPIRITUAL APPROACH TO CRISIS

The world-population is increasing rapidly. In the meantime climactic conditions are becoming less favorable as happened (as a natural phenomenon) in medieval Europe, so that staple crops are bound to fail (unless one believes that through genetic engineering plants will become indifferent to weather conditions). In the eventuality that there occurs the spread of disease as happened with the plague, large parts of humanity may perish through starvation, polluted water, and disease. Or alternatively, as scarcity sets in, through violent competition surrounding what will be available.

In the meantime also, large-scale desertification takes place worldwide in semi-desert areas and around the Equator through, amongst other things, deforestation.

Moreover, the earth-system has been able to maintain for the last 350 million years a stable atmospheric combination of oxygen and other gases. Gaia, our living planet, also has been exercising a regulating function of the temperature for the last 3.5 billion years that has allowed higher life forms to develop, including humans. If, however, people keep destroying the forests and polluting the oceans so that all plankton dies off (as is happening), then it becomes likely that the earth would need to reset the balance of the atmospheric gases to a new equilibrium. The release of enormous amounts of greenhouse gases (carbon dioxide and methane) into the atmosphere while the natural systems dealing with them have been largely diminished and indeed are made to release their enormous stores of these same gases (forests, peat bogs, wetlands, permafrost surfaces, and undersea methane hydrates), make it likely that the earth is very rapidly warming up and eventually may settle for an elevated temperature for the foreseeable future (probably for several millions of year). The melting of ice stored at the Arctic and in Antarctica will lead to higher sea levels that will prove an enormous challenge to the populations that live in cities and areas likely to be submerged. Whereas with a much depleted ozone layer harmful radiation is increasing. The earth will thus to a large extent shake off the higher, more vulnerable species and especially humanity, whereby it is especially the poor who already are suffering most. It is, of course, not the earth but humanity itself that is causing this suffering for our and other species.

This is to be expected if people do not fulfill the function for the universe that they are destined to play, namely to give voice to the cosmic prayer. I have considered above that human beings emerged at that phase in natural evolution where individual creatures reached sufficient complexity so as to exercise the cosmic prayer not only within an ensemble of beings, but by themselves. If a species is not true to its own nature and purpose in the totality then it will go, for it becomes a mere burden to itself and others. It no longer maintains and influences in its advance the ecological system upon which it depends for survival: "For, such is nature, punishing as much those who are set to corrupt it, as those who aim to live contrary to nature, who do not acquire the whole power of nature naturally, and cause its soundness to deteriorate, and are therefore fit to be punished, since they thoughtlessly and mindlessly provide themselves with a deficiency of being through their inclination towards non-being."[6]

God creates us so as to enter into a personal relationship and to become part of the divine communion together with various other created realities. If, however, we fail to pray, to worship, to mediate the beauty of God's creation, to love, to become gentle and humble, to walk and work with the greatest sensitivity—"intelligently," as Maximus would say—whereto then do we continue to exist? We would be mere parasites on the face of the earth, within God's creation. By adopting a spiritual approach and by recognizing that all reality has a spiritual dimension, human beings become attuned to their own existence, and come to live not in isolation but in association with the wider creation. Such people gain a sensitivity that allows them to be wise stewards for all existence and for all future generations.

The spiritual approach is essential for tackling every crisis situation. For it is by adopting the divinely inspired modes of being that human life comes to resonate with the divine energies and with the power of love that leads to well-being and to eternal well-being.

I end with the last stanza of the morning hymn of *The Divine Office*'s Psalter that is sung on Wednesdays of week 1:

> *We praise you, Father, with your Son*
> *And Spirit blest,*
> *In whom creation lives and moves,*
> *And finds its rest.*

---

6. *Amb.* 10; PG 91:1164CD.

Bibliography

TEXTS AND TRANSLATIONS OF ANCIENT WRITERS

Augustine

The complete works of Augustine are available in PL 32–45. Online: http://www.sant-agostino.it/latino/index.htm.
Confessiones. PL 32:659–868.
De civitate dei. PL 41:13–804.
De Genesi ad litteram. PL 34:245–466.
De libero arbitrio. PL 32:1221–1310.
De sermone Domini in Monte. PL 34:1229–1308.
De Trinitate. PL 42:820–1098.
De vera religione. PL 34:121–72.
Sermones 125. PL 38:688–98.

Benjamin, Anna S., and L. H. Hackstaff, translators. *Saint Augustine: On Free Choice of the Will.* The Library of Liberal Arts 150. Indianapolis: Bobbs-Merrill, 1964.
Bettenson, Henri, translator. *St Augustine: City of God.* Penguin Classics. Harmondsworth, UK: Penguin, 1984.
Burleigh, John H. S., translator. *Augustine: Earlier Writings.* LCC 6. London: SCM, 1953.
Findlay, William, translator. "St Augustine. Our Lord's Sermon on the Mount." Revised by D. S. Schaff. In NPNF 1st series, vol. 6, edited by Philip Schaff, 1–63.
Hill, Edmund, translator. *Saint Augustine: The Trinity.* The Works of Saint Augustine: A translation for the 21st century, Part 1, vol. 5. Hyde Park, NY: New City, 1991.
———. *Saint Augustine: On Genesis.* The Works of Saint Augustine: A translation for the 21st century, Part 1, vol. 13. Hyde Park, NY: New City, 2002.
Members of the English Church, translators. *Sermons on Selected Lessons of the New Testament by S. Augustine.* Library of Fathers of the Holy Catholic Church, anterior to the division of the East and West. Oxford: Parker / London: Rivington, 1845. (Sermon 125 is found at vol. 2:527–40.)
Pine-Coffin, R. S., translator. *Saint Augustine: Confessions.* Penguin Classics. London: Penguin, 1961.

Bibliography

Basil

Epistula 236. PG 32:876–85.
Liber de Spiritu Sancto. PG 32:67–218. SC 17bis, 2nd ed., edited by Benoît Pruche, 1968.

Jackson, Blomfield, translator. *Basil: Letters and Select Works.* NPNF 2nd series, vol. 8. 1895. Reprint. Grand Rapids: Eerdmans, 1978. Online: http://www.newadvent.org/fathers/3202.htm and http://www.newadvent.org/fathers/3203.htm.

Benedict

Horner, Timothy, et al., translators. *RB 1980: The Rule of St. Benedict. In Latin and English with Notes.* Edited by Timothy Fry et al. Collegeville, MN: Liturgical, 1981.

Boethius

De consolatione Philosophiae. PL 63:547–870. CCSL 94, edited by L. Bieler, 1957.
De persona et duabus naturis contra Eutychen et Nestorium. PL 64:1337–54.

Stewart, H. F., et al., translators. *Boethius: The Theological Tractates and The Consolation of Philosophy.* Latin text and translation. 2nd ed. LCL 74. Cambridge, MA: Harvard University Press, 1973.
Wippel, John F., translator. "Boethius: On the Consolation of Philosophy 5." In *Medieval Philosophy: From St. Augustine to Nicholas of Cusa*, edited by John F. Wippel and Alan B. Wolter, 84–96. Readings in the History of Philosophy. New York: Free, 1969.

Clement of Alexandria

Stromateis. Books 1–4 at PG 8:685–1381; books 5–8 at PG 9:9–601.

Hort, F. J. A., and J. B. Mayor, translators. *Clement of Alexandria: Miscellanies Book VII.* Greek text and translation. London: Macmillan, 1902.

Diadochus of Photiki

Capita centum de perfectione spirituale. SC 5bis. 2nd ed. revised with additions. Edition and translation into French by Édouard des Places. 1966. Reprint with corrections, 1997.

Palmer, G. E. H., et al., translators. "St Diadochus of Photiki: On Spiritual Knowledge and Discrimination: One Hundred Texts." In *The Philokalia* 1:254–296.

Bibliography

Ecumenical Council of Chalcedon (451)

Definition of the Faith. In *The Oecumenical Documents of the Faith*, edited by T. Herbert Bindley, revised by F. W. Green, 191-93 and 232-35. London: Methuen, 1950.

Evagrius Pontikus

De oratione. PG 79:1165-1200.

Palmer, G. E. H., et al., translators. "Evagrios the Solitary: On Prayer: One Hundred and Fifty-Three Texts." In *The Philokalia* 1:55-71.
Casiday, A. M. *Evagrius Ponticus.* The Early Church Fathers. New York: Routledge, 2006.

Gregory of Nazianzen

Epistula 101. PG 37:176A-93B.
Hymn to God - Ὦ πάντων ἐπέκεινα.
Oratio 38 - *In Theophania* (*On the Nativity*). PG 36:312-33.

Chatfield, Allen W., translator. *Songs and Hymns of Earliest Greek Christian Poets, Bishops and Others translated into English verse.* London: Rivingtons, 1876. Online: http://www.ccel.org/ccel/chatfield/greeksongs.txt.
Christ, W., and M. Paranikas. *Anthologia graeca carminum christianorum.* Leipzig: Teubner, 1871.

Gregory of Nyssa

De hominis opificio. PG 44:125-256. SC 6, introduction and translation into French by Jean Laplace, notes by Jean Daniélou, 1943.
On the Difference between Ousia *and* Hypostasis (preserved as *Ep.* 38 of Basil). PG 32:326-40.

Wiles, Maurice, and Mark Santer, translators. "Gregory of Nyssa: On the Difference between *Ousia* and *Hypostasis*." In *Documents in Early Christian Thought*, edited by Maurice Wiles and Mark Santer, 31-35. Cambridge: Cambridge University Press, 1975.
Wilson, H. A., translator. "Gregory of Nyssa: On the Making of Man." In NPNF 2nd series, vol. 5. Online: http://www.ccel.org/ccel/schaff/npnf205.x.ii.ii.i.html or http://www.ecmarsh.com/fathers/npnf2/NPNF2-05/index.htm.

Irenaeus

Adversus haereses. PG 7:437-1224.

Bibliography

Roberts, Alexander, and William Rambaut, translators. "Irenaeus: Against Heresies." In ANCL 5 and 9 or in ANF 1. Online: http://www.newadvent.org/fathers/0103.htm.

John of Damascus

De fide orthodoxa. PG 94:790–1228.

Justin Martyr

Apologia secunda pro Christianis. PG 6:441–69.

Maximus the Confessor

The majority of Maximus' texts are provided in PG 90–91. Online: http://www.myriobiblos.gr/texts/greek/maximos/index.htm.
Ambiguorum liber. PG 91:1032–1417.
Capita de charitate. PG 90:960–1080.
Epistulae. (45 letters) PG 91:364–649.
Expositio orationis dominicae. PG 90:872–909. CCSG 23, edited by Peter Van Deun, 1991.
Mystagogia. PG 91:657–717.
Opuscula theologica et polemica. PG 91:9–285.
Quaestiones ad Thalassium. PG 90:244–785. CCSG 7 and 22, both volumes edited by Carl Laga and Carlos Steel, 1980 and 1990 respectively.
Scholia in Corpus Areopagiticum. PG 4:15–432, 527–76. (Authorship: Maximus and John of Scythopolis.)

Berthold, George C., translator. *Maximus Confessor: Selected Writings.* The Classics of Western Spirituality. Mahwah, NJ: Paulist, 1985. (This volume contains translations of, among others, *Char.*; *Exp. or. dom.*; *Myst.*)
Blowers, Paul M., and Robert Louis Wilken, translators. *On the Cosmic Mystery of Jesus Christ: Selected Writings from St Maximus the Confessor.* Popular Patristics Series. Crestwood, NY: St. Vladimir's Seminary Press, 2003. (This volume contains translations of *Amb.* 7, 8, 42; *Thal.* 1, 2, 6, 17, 21, 22, 42, 60, 61, 64; *Op. th. pol.* 6.)
Larchet, Jean-Claude (introd.) and Emmanuel Ponsoye, translator. *Saint Maxime le Confesseur: Lettres.* Sagesses chrétiennes. Paris: Cerf, 1998.
———. *Saint Maxime le Confesseur: Opuscules théologiques et polémiques.* Sagesses chrétiennes. Paris: Cerf, 1998.
———. *Saint Maxime le Confesseur: Questions à Thalassios.* Collection l'Arbre de Jessé. Suresnes: l'Ancre, 1992.
Larchet, Jean-Claude (introd.), Emmanuel Ponsoye (trans.), and Dimitri Staniloae (commentary). *Saint Maxime le Confesseur: Ambigua.* Collection l'Arbre de Jessé. Suresnes: l'Ancre, 1994.

Louth, Andrew. *Maximus the Confessor.* The Early Church Fathers. London: Routledge, 1996. (This volume contains translations of *Amb.* 1, 5, 10, 41, 71; *Ep.* 2; *Op. th. pol.* 3, 7.)

Palmer, G. E. H., et al., translators. "St. Maximos the Confessor." In *The Philokalia* 2:48–305. (This volume contains translations of, among others, *Char.*; *Exp. or. dom.*)

Sherwood, Polycarp. *St. Maximus the Confessor: The Ascetic Life. The Four Centuries on Charity.* Ancient Christian Writers 21. Ramsey, NJ: Newman, 1955.

Nemesius of Emesa

De natura hominis. PG 40:503–818.

Telfer, William, translator. *Cyril of Jerusalem and Nemesius of Emesa.* LCC 4. London: SCM, 1955.

Origen

De principiis. PG 11:116–414. Online: http://www.john-uebersax.com/plato/origen2.htm and follow the internal link to PG 11. SC 252.

Butterworth, G. W., translator. *Origen on First Principles.* London: SPCK, 1936.

Crombie, Frederick, translator. In ANF 4:239–382. Online: http://www.ccel.org/ccel/schaff/anf04.vi.v.i.html or http://www.newadvent.org/fathers/0412.htm.

Plato

Archer-Hind, R. D., translator. *The Timaeus of Plato.* Greek text and translation. London: Macmillan, 1888.

Davis, Henry, translator. *Plato's Republic.* 1901. Reprint. Universal Classics. Paris: Amiel, 1970.

Fowler, Harold North, translator. *Plato: Euthyphro. Apology. Crito. Phaedo. Phaedrus.* LCL. Greek text and translation. Cambridge: Harvard University Press, 1914.

Lee, H. D. P., translator. *Plato: Timaeus.* Penguin Classics. Harmondsworth, UK: Penguin, 1965.

Shorey, Paul, translator. *Plato: The Republic.* LCL. 2 vols. Greek text and translation. London: Heinemann, 1963.

Pseudo-Dionysius

De caelesti hierarchia. PG 3:119–369. SC 58, edited by Günter Heil, 1958.
De divinis nominibus. PG 3:585–996.
Epistolae. PG 3:1065–1122.

Bibliography

Luibheid, Colm, translator. *Pseudo-Dionysius: The Complete Works*. The Classics of Western Spirituality. Mahwah, NJ: Paulist, 1987.

Qumran Community

Vermes, Geza. *The Complete Dead Sea Scrolls in English*. 2nd ed. London: Penguin, 2004.

Tertullian

Adversus Praxean. PL 2:175–220.
De oratione. PL 1:1245–1304.

The various works of Tertullian and the various books that present his texts indicated here following are entirely available online: http://www.tertullian.org/works.htm.
Evans, Ernest, translator. *Tertullian's Tract on the Prayer*. Latin text and translation. London: SPCK, 1953.
———. *Tertullian's Treatise Against Praxeas*. Latin text and translation. London: SPCK, 1948.
Holmes, Peter, translator. "Against Praxeas." In *The Writings of Tertullian*, vol. 2, ANCL 15:333–406.
Souter, Alexander, translator. *Tertullian's Treatises concerning Prayer, concerning Baptism*. Translations of Christian Literature, series 2, Latin texts. New York: Macmillan, 1919.
Thelwall, S., translator. "About Prayer." In *The Writings of Quintus Sept. Flor. Tertullianus*, vol. 1, ANCL 9:178–204.

Thomas Aquinas

The complete works: *Opera omnia*. Turin: Casa Marietti, 1950–65. Online: http://www.corpusthomisticum.org/iopera.html.
The complete works: Latin texts and translation. Online: http://www.josephkenny.joyeurs.com/CDtexts/index2.htm.
Saint Thomas Aquinas: Summa contra gentiles. 5 vols. Translated by Anton C. Pegis et al. 1955–1957. Reprint. Notre Dame, IN: University of Notre Dame Press, 1975.
St Thomas Aquinas: Summa theologiae. Blackfriars edition. General edition: T. Gilby. Latin text and translation. New York: McGraw-Hill, 1963–75.
Fathers of the English Dominican Province, translators. *St Thomas Aquinas: Summa theologiae*. Benziger Bros edition (1947). Online: http://www.ccel.org/ccel/aquinas/summa.html.

MODERN WRITERS

Abhishiktananda. *Prayer*. London: SPCK, 1967.

———. *Saccidananda: A Christian Approach to Advaitic Experience*. English edition revised by the author and translated from the French with the help of his friends. Delhi: I.S.P.C.K., 1974.

Adams, Edward. *Constructing the World: A Study in Paul's Cosmological Language*. Studies of the New Testament and Its World. Edinburgh: T. & T. Clark, 2000.

Alexandre, C. *Dictionnaire Grec-Français*. 11th ed. Paris: Hachette, 1855.

Allchin, A. M. "The Theology of Nature in the Eastern Fathers and among Anglican Theologians." In *Man and Nature*, edited by Hugh Montefiore, 143–54, 203–4. London: Collins, 1975.

Anatolios, Khaled. *Athanasius: The Coherence of His Thought*. London: Routledge, 1998.

Andia, Ysabel de. "Transfiguration et théologie négative chez Maxime le Confesseur et Denys l'Aréopagite." In *Denys l'Aréopagite et sa postérité en Orient et en Occident*, actes du Colloque International, Paris, 21–24 septembre 1994, edited by Ysabel de Andia, 293–328. Collection des Études Augustiniennes, Série Antiquité 151. Paris: Institut d'Études Augustiniennes, 1997.

Andrews, Donald Hatch. *The Symphony of Life*. Lee's Summit, MO: Unity, 1966.

Apostolic Delegation, London. *Pierre Teilhard de Chardin: A Warning of the Supreme Sacred Congregation of the Holy Office of the 30th June, 1962, together with a translation of an article from the "Osservatore Romano" of 30th June, 1962.*

Arbesmann, R. "Prayer." In *NCE* 11:588–91.

Artigas, Mariano. *The Mind of the Universe: Understanding Science and Religion*. Philadelphia: Templeton Foundation, 2000.

Atkins, Margaret. "I Think Therefore I Love: On Being a Human Kind of Animal." *The Way* 41 (2001) 191–200.

Attenborough, David. *Life on Earth: A Natural History*. 2nd ed. London: Collins and the BBC, 1979.

Bahn, Paul G. (with photography by Jean Vertut). *Journey through the Ice Age*. Berkeley: University of California Press, 1997.

Balthasar, Hans Urs von. *Cosmic Liturgy: The Universe according to Maximus the Confessor*. 3rd ed. Translated by Brian E. Daly. San Francisco: Ignatius, 2003.

———. *The Theology of Henri de Lubac: An Overview*. Translated by Joseph Fessio and Michael M. Waldstein. San Francisco: Ignatius, 1991.

Barrow, John D. *The World within the World*. Oxford: Oxford University Press, 1990.

Barrow, John D., and Frank J. Tipler. *The Anthropic Cosmological Principle*. Oxford: Oxford University Press, 1986.

Bartholomew I, Archbishop of Constantinople and Ecumenical Patriarch of the Orthodox Christians. "Speeches of his all holiness ecumenical patriarch Bartholomew at the environmental symposium, Saint Barbara Greek Orthodox Church, Santa Barbara, California, 8 November 1997." Online: http://www.ec-patr.eu/docdisplay.php?lang=en&id=461&tla=en.

———. Bartolomew's various addresses on ecological issues are provided by the official website of the Ecumenical Patriarchate at http://www.ec-patr.eu/docdisplay.php?lang=en&cat=15.

Behe, Michael J. "Evidence for Design at the Foundation of Life." In *Science and Evidence for Design in the Universe*, by Michael J. Behe et al., 113–29. The Proceedings of the Wethersfield Institute 9. San Francisco: Ignatius, 2000.

Behr, John. "The Rational Animal: A Rereading of Gregory of Nyssa's *De hominis opificio*." *Journal of Early Christian Studies* 7 (1999) 219–47.

Bibliography

Berry, Thomas. "Christianity's Role in the Earth Project." In *Christianity and Ecology: Seeking the Well-Being of Earth and Humans*, edited by Dieter T. Hessel and Rosemary Radford Ruether, 127–34. Religions of the World and Ecology. Cambridge: Harvard University Center for the Study of World Religions, 2000.

———. *The Dream of the Earth*. Sierra Club Nature and Natural Philosophy Library. San Francisco: Sierra Club, 1988.

———. *The Great Work: Our Way Into the Future*. New York: Bell Tower, 1999.

Blowers, Paul M. "The Analogy of Scripture and Cosmos in Maximus the Confessor." In *Studia Patristica* 27, papers presented at the Eleventh International Conference held in Oxford 1991, edited by Elizabeth A. Livingstone, 145–49. Leuven: Peeters, 1993.

Blowers, Paul M., and Robert Louis Wilken. *On the Cosmic Mystery of Jesus Christ: Selected Writings from St. Maximus the Confessor*. Popular Patristics Series. Crestwood, NY: St. Vladimir's Seminary Press, 2003.

Bohm, David. *Wholeness and the Implicate Order*. London: Routledge, 1980.

Bonner, Gerald. "Predestination and Freewill: Augustine's Letter 2." In *Studia Patristica* 43, papers presented at the Fourteenth International Conference on Patristic Studies held in Oxford 2003, edited by F. Young et al., 15–18. Leuven: Peeters, 2006.

Brague, Rémi. *The Wisdom of the World: The Human Experience of the Universe in Western Thought*. Translated by Teresa Lavender Fagan. Chicago: University of Chicago Press, 2003.

Breuil, Henri, and Raymond Lantier. *Les hommes de la pierre ancienne (Paléolithique et Mésolithique)*. Bibliothèque Scientifique. Paris: Payot, 1951.

Bright, Michael. *Intelligence in Animals*. London: Reader's Digest, 1994.

Broglie, Louis de. *Matter and Light: The New Physics*. Translated by W. M. Johnston. New York: Norton, 1939. Online: http://www.archive.org/details/matterandlightth000924mbp.

Brother Ramon. *Franciscan Spirituality: Following St Francis Today*. London: SPCK, 1994.

Caldwell, Douglas E. "Post-Modern Ecology—Is the Environment the Organism?" *Environmental Microbiology* 1 (1999) 279–81.

Capra, Fritjof. *The Web of Life: A New Synthesis of Mind and Matter*. London: HarperCollins, 1996.

Catechism of the Catholic Church. Translated from Latin. London: Chapman, 1994.

Chadwick, Henry. "Augustine." In *The Cambridge History of Early Christian Literature*, edited by Frances Young et al., 328–41. Cambridge: Cambridge University Press, 2004.

Chardin, Pierre Teilhard de. "The Christic." 1955. In *The Heart of Matter*, translated by René Hague, 80–102. London: Collins, 1978.

———. "The Convergence of the Universe." 1951. In *Activation of Energy*, translated by René Hague, 283–96. London: Collins, 1970.

———. *The Phenomenon of Man*. 1940. 2nd English ed. Translation edited by Bernard Wall. Various contributing translators. London: Collins, 1965.

———. "The Place of Technology in a General Biology of Mankind." 1947. In *Activation of Energy*, translated by René Hague, 155–63. London: Collins, 1970.

———. "Postscript: The Essence of *The Phenomenon of Man*." 1948. In *The Phenomenon of Man*, 2nd English ed., translation edited by Bernard Wall, 300–310. London: Collins, 1965.

———. "The Transformation and Continuation in Man of the Mechanism of Evolution." 1951. In *Activation of Energy*, translated by René Hague, 299–309. London: Collins, 1970.

Chopra, Deepak. *Quantum Healing: Exploring the Frontiers of Mind/Body Medicine*. New York: Bantam, 1989.

Clark, Brett, and Richard York. "Dialectical Nature: Reflections in Honor of the Twentieth Anniversary of Levins and Lewontin's *The Dialectical Biologist*." *Monthly Review* 57 (May 2005) 13–22. Online: http://www.monthlyreview.org/0505clarkyork.htm.

Clarke, Chris. *Living in Connection: Theory and Practice of the New World View*. Warminster, UK: Creation Spirituality, 2002.

Clarke, T. E. "Incommunicability." In *NCE* 7:379–40.

Clegg, Arthur G., and P. Catherine Clegg. *Man against Disease*. London: Heinemann Educational, 1973.

Clottes, Jean. "Art of the Light and Art of the Depths." In *Beyond Art: Pleistocene Image and Symbol*, edited by Margaret W. Conkey et al., 203–16. Memoirs of the California Academy of Sciences 23. San Francisco: California Academy of Sciences, 1997.

Clottes, Jean, and David Lewis-Williams. *The Shamans of Prehistory: Trance and Magic in the Painted Caves*. Translated by Sophie Hawkes. New York: Abrams, 1998.

Corey, M. A. *God and the New Cosmology: The Anthropic Design Argument*. Lanham, MD: Rowman & Littlefield, 1993.

Cornford, Francis MacDonald. *Plato's Cosmology: The Timaeus of Plato Translated with a Running Commentary*. International Library of Psychology, Philosophy, and Scientific Method. London: Routledge & Kegan Paul, 1937.

Coyle, J. Kevin. "What Was 'Prayer' for Early Christians?." In *Prayer and Spirituality in the Early Church*, vol. 2, edited by Pauline Allen et al., 25–41. Everton Park, Queensland: Centre for Early Christian Studies, 1999.

Crick, Francis. *Life Itself: Its Origin and Nature*. New York: Simon & Schuster, 1981.

Crooker, Peter P. "Blue Phases." In *Chirality in Liquid Crystals*, edited by Heinz-Siegfried Kitzerow and Christian Bahr, 186–222. Partially Ordered Systems. New York: Springer, 2001.

Crouzel, Henri. *Origen*. Translated by A. S. Worrall. Edinburgh: T. & T. Clark, 1989.

Dalmais, Irénée-H. "L'innovation des natures d'après S. Maxime le Confesseur (à propos d' Ambiguum 42)." In *Studia Patristica* 15, papers presented at the Seventh International Conference held in Oxford 1975, edited by Elizabeth A. Livingstone, 285–90. Leuven: Peeters, 1984.

Dar, Arnon, et al. "Life Extinctions by Cosmic Ray Jets." *Physical Review Letters* 80 (1998) 5813–16. Online: http://www.cita.utoronto.ca/~shaviv/preprints/PRL05813.pdf.

Darwin, Charles. *The Complete Works of Charles Darwin Online*. University of Cambridge, 2002–7. Online: http://darwin-online.org.uk.

———. *The Descent of Man and Selection in Relation to Sex*. 2nd ed. 1874. Reprint. London: The Folio Society, 1990.

———. *The Origin of Species: By Means of Natural Selection*. 1st ed. London: Murray, 1859.

Bibliography

———. *The Origin of Species: By Means of Natural Selection.* 6th ed. London: Murray, 1872.
Davies, Paul. *About Time: Einstein's Unfinished Revolution.* London: Penguin, 1995.
———. *God and the New Physics.* London: Dent, 1983.
———. *The Mind of God: Science and the Search for Ultimate Meaning.* 1992. Reprint. London: Penguin, 1993.
Dawkins, Marian Stamp. *Through Our Eyes Only?: The Search for Animal Consciousness.* Oxford: Freeman, 1993.
Dawkins, Richard. *River out of Eden: A Darwinian View of Life.* Science Masters. London: Weidenfeld & Nicolson, 1995.
Déchanet, Jean-Marie. *Christian Yoga.* Translated by Roland Hindmarsh. London: Burns & Oates, 1960.
———. "Introduction." In *William of Saint Thierry. Exposition on the Song of Songs,* translated by Columba Hart, vii–xlviii. Saint Joseph's Abbey, Spencer, MA: Cistercian, 1968.
Deissler, Alfons. "The Theology of Psalm 104." In *Standing before God: Studies on Prayer in Scriptures and in Tradition with Essays,* in Honor of John M. Oesterreicher, translated by Nora Quigley; edited by Asher Finkel and Lawrence Frizzell, 31–40. New York: KTAV, 1981.
Dembski, William A. "The Third Mode of Explanation: Detecting Evidence of Intelligent Design in the Sciences." In *Science and Evidence for Design in the Universe,* by Michael J. Behe et al., 17–51. The Proceedings of the Wethersfield Institute 9. San Francisco: Ignatius, 2000.
Dillard, Annie. *Pilgrim at Tinker Creek.* London: Pan, 1976.
The Divine Office: The Liturgy of the Hours according to the Roman Rite. 3 vols. London: Collins, 1974.
Dossey, Larry. *Healing Words: The Power of Prayer and the Practice of Medicine.* San Francisco: HarperCollins, 1993.
Drees, Willem B. "Gaps for God?" In *Chaos and Complexity: Scientific Perspectives on Divine Action,* edited by Robert John Russell et al., 223–37. Vatican City State: Vatican Observatory, 1995.
Dyson, Freeman. *Infinite in all Directions.* Gifford Lectures given at Aberdeen University, 1985. London: Penguin, 1989.
Eddington, Arthur S. *New Pathways in Science.* Messenger Lectures 1934. Cambridge: University Press, 1935.
Edwards, Denis. "The Discovery of Chaos and the Retrieval of the Trinity." In *Chaos and Complexity: Scientific Perspectives on Divine Action,* edited by Robert John Russell et al., 157–75. Vatican City State: Vatican Observatory Publications, 1995.
———. *The God of Evolution: A Trinitarian Theology.* Mahwah, NJ: Paulist, 1999.
Einstein, Albert. *Relativity: The Special and the General Theory. A Popular Exposition.* 5th ed. Translated by Robert W. Lawson. London: Methuen, 1921.
Eliade, Mircea. *The Sacred and the Profane: The Nature of Religion.* Translated by Willard R. Trask. Harper Torchbooks. New York: Harper & Row, 1961.
Elisabeth of the Trinity. "Prayer to the Trinity." Online: http://www.catholic-forum.com/saints/ste46001.htm.
Elizondo, Miguel. "Jesus and Prayer." *The Way* 44.3 (July 2005) 9–20.
Elphinstone, Andrew. *Freedom, Suffering and Love.* London: SCM, 1976.

Espagnat, Bernard d'. "The Quantum Theory and Reality." *Scientific American* 241 (1979) 128–40.
Facchini, Fiorenzo. "Man, Origin and Nature." In *Interdisciplinary Encyclopedia of Religion and Science*, edited by G. Tanzella-Nitti, P. Larrey, and A. Strumia; translated by Barbara Zanotti and Eva Bruno. No pages. Online: http://www.disf.org/en/Voci/121.asp.
Fergusson, David A. S. *The Cosmos and the Creator: An Introduction to the Theology of Creation*. London: SPCK, 1998.
Feynman, Richard P. *The Character of Physical Law*. London: Penguin, 1992.
Fiddes, Paul S. *The Creative Suffering of God*. Oxford: Clarendon, 1988.
———. *Participating in God: A Pastoral Doctrine of the Trinity*. London: Darton, Longman & Todd, 2000.
Finbar, I. L. *Organic Chemistry. Volume 1: The Fundamental Principles*. 5th ed. London: Longmans, 1967.
Fosdick, H. E. *The Meaning of Prayer*. 29th ed. 1954. Reprint. Fontana Series 378R. Glasgow: Collins, 1960.
Fox, Andrew. "Being Human: Some Post-Darwinian Theological Reflections." *Epworth Review* 36 (2009) 32–45.
Frizzell, Lawrence. "A Hymn of Creation in Daniel." In *Standing before God: Studies on Prayer in Scriptures and in Tradition with Essays*, in Honor of John M. Oesterreicher, edited by Asher Finkel and Lawrence Frizzell, 41–52. New York: KTAV, 1981.
Funkenstein, Amos. *Theology and the Scientific Imagination from the Middle Ages to the Seventeenth Century*. Princeton, NJ: Princeton University Press, 1986.
Gapanov-Grekhov, A. V., and M. I. Rabinovich. "Nonlinear Physics. Stochasticity and Structures." In *Physics of the 20th Century: History and Outlook*, translated by Alexander Repyev, edited by Ye. P. Velikhov et al., 230–92. Moscow: Mir, 1987.
Getcha, Job. "La transfiguration du monde." *Irénikon* 80 (2007) 23–35.
Gibson, Kathleen R. "Animal Minds, Human Minds." In *Tools, Language and Cognition in Human Evolution*, edited by Kathleen R. Gibson and Tim Ingold, 1–13. Cambridge: Cambridge University Press, 1993.
Gill, Sam D. "Prayer." 1987. In *Encyclopedia of Religion*, vol. 11, 2nd ed., edited by Lindsay Jones, 7367–72. Detroit: Gale, 2005.
Gilson, Étienne. *The Christian Philosophy of St. Thomas Aquinas*. 1948. Translated by L. K. Shook. 1956. Reprint. New York: Octagon, 1983.
———. *History of Christian Philosophy in the Middle Ages*. London: Sheed & Ward, 1955.
Gorbenko, Alexander. "Prayer Restores Dead Cells Back to Life." *De Numine* 41 (Autumn 2006) 15–16.
Gore, Charles. *Belief in God*. London: Murray, 1921.
Gottfried, Robert S. *The Black Death: Natural and Human Disaster in Medieval Europe*. London: Macmillan, 1983.
Gould, Stephen Jay. *Ever Since Darwin: Reflections in Natural History*. Harmondsworth, UK: Penguin, 1977.
Govaerts, Robert. "A Dying Blackbird and Participation in Cosmic Prayer." *De Numine* 48 (Spring 2010) 5–8. Online: http://www.alisterhardysociety.org; and select the internal link Publications.

Bibliography

———. "Prayer and the Healing of Nature." *The Way* 49.4 (October 2010) 103–15. Online: http://www.theway.org.uk/Back/494Govaerts.pdf

———. "A Transcendental that Calls for Recognition: The Longing for Loving Communion with and within God." *The Downside Review* 455 (April 2011) 22–48.

Grant, Edward. *Physical Science in the Middle Ages*. The Cambridge History of Science Series. Cambridge: Cambridge University Press, 1977.

Greene, Brian. *The Fabric of the Cosmos: Space, Time and the Texture of Reality*. London: Penguin, 2007.

Greenfield, Susan. *Brain Story: Unlocking our Inner World of Emotions, Memories, Ideas and Desires*. London: BBC Worldwide, 2000.

Griffin, Donald R. *Animal Minds: Beyond Cognition to Consciousness*. 2nd ed. Chicago: University of Chicago Press, 2001.

Griffiths, Bede. *Christ in India: Essays towards a Hindu-Christian dialogue*. New York: Scribner's Sons, 1966.

———. *The Golden String*. London: Harvill, 1954.

———. *The Marriage of East and West*. London: Collins, 1982.

———. *A New Vision of Reality: Western Science, Eastern Mysticism and Christian Faith*. Edited by Felicity Edwards. Springfield, IL: Templegate, 1990.

———. *Return to the Centre*. London: Collins, 1976.

———. *The Universal Christ: Daily Readings with Bede Griffiths*. Edited by Peter Spink. London: Darton, Longman & Todd, 1990.

Grillmeier, Aloys. *Christ in Christian Tradition. Vol. 1: From the Apostolic Age to Chalcedon (451)*. 2nd ed. Translated by John Bowden. Atlanta: John Knox, 1975.

Gunton, Colin E. *Christ and Creation*. The Didsbury Lectures. Carlisle, UK: Paternoster, 1992.

———. *The One, the Three and the Many: God, Creation and the Culture of Modernity*. The Bampton Lectures 1992. Cambridge: Cambridge University Press, 1993.

Haken, Hermann. *Advanced Synergetics: Instability Hierarchies of Self-Organizing Systems and Devices*. 2nd ed. Berlin: Springer, 1987.

———. *Synergetics, An Introduction*. 3rd ed. Berlin: Springer, 1983.

Hanby, Michael. *Augustine and Modernity*. Radical Orthodoxy. London: Routledge, 2003.

Harding, Stephen. *Animate Earth: Science, Intuition and Gaia*. Foxhole, UK: Green, 2006.

Hardy, Alister. "Another View of Evolution." In *Biology and Personality: Frontier Problems in Science, Philosophy and Religion*, edited by I. T. Ramsey, 74–82. Oxford: Blackwell, 1965.

———. *The Divine Flame: An Essay Towards a Natural History of Religion*. The second of two series of Gifford Lectures delivered in the University of Aberdeen, 1964–65. London: Collins, 1966.

Harman, Willis W., and Elisabet Sahtouris. *Biology Revisioned*. Berkeley, CA: North Atlantic, 1998.

Harris, Marvin "Why We Became Religious, and The Evolution of the Spirit World." In *Magic, Witchcraft, and Religion: An Anthropological Study of the Supernatural*, 4th ed., edited by Arthur C. Lehmann and James E. Myers, 6–9. Mountain View, CA: Mayfield, 1997.

Harrison, Victoria S. "On Defining the Religious Person." *Theology* 110 (2007) 243–50.

Bibliography

Haught, John F. *God after Darwin: A Theology of Evolution.* Boulder, CO: Westview, 2000.
Hawking, Stephen. *Black Holes and Baby Universes and Other Essays.* London: Bantam, 1993.
Hawkins, Bradley K. *Buddhism.* Religions of the World. London: Routledge, 1999.
Healy, K. J. "Prayer (Theology of)." In *NCE* 11:593.
Heiler, Friedrich. *Prayer: A Study in the History and Psychology of Religion.* Translated by Samuel McComb. New York: Oxford University Press, 1932.
Heisenberg, Werner. *The Physicist's Conception of Nature.* Translated by Arnold J. Pomerans. London: Hutchinson, 1958.
Holford, Patrick. *Improve Your Digestion.* London: Piatkus, 1999.
Hoyle, Fred. *The Intelligent Universe: A New View of Creation and Evolution.* Edited by David Burnie. London: Joseph, 1983.
Jacob, Benno. *The First Book of the Bible: Genesis.* Abridged, edited, and translated by Ernest I. Jacob and Walter Jacob. New York: KTAV, 1974.
Jeans, James. *The Mysterious Universe.* 2nd ed. London: Penguin, 1931.
John Paul II, Pope. "Created World Exists for New Life in Christ." Homily at the Liturgy of the Word in Zamość, Poland, 12 June 1999. *L'Osservatore Romano* no. 25–23 June 1999, 11–15. Online: http://www.vatican.va/holy_father/john_paul_ii/homilies/1999/documents/hf_jp-ii_hom_19990612_zamosc_en.html.
———. *Crossing the Threshold of Hope.* Edited by Vittorio Messori. Translated by Jenny McPhee and Martha McPhee. London: Cape, 1994.
———. *Dominum et vivificantem.* Encyclical letter, 1986. Title of the translated encyclical: "On the Holy Spirit in the Life of the Church and the World." Online: http://www.vatican.va/holy_father/john_paul_ii/encyclicals/documents/hf_jp-ii_enc_18051986_dominum-et-vivificantem_en.html.
———. "God Made Man the Steward of Creation." *General Audience*, Wednesday 17 January 2001. Online: http://www.vatican.va/holy_father/john_paul_ii/audiences/2001/documents/hf_jp-ii_aud_20010117_en.html.
———. *Orientale lumen.* Apostolic letter, 1995. Title of the translated letter: "Light of the East." Online: http://www.vatican.va/holy_father/john_paul_ii/apost_letters/documents/hf_jp-ii_apl_02051995_orientale-lumen_en.html.
Johnson, Aubrey R. *The One and the Many in the Israelite Conception of God.* 2nd ed. Cardiff: University of Wales Press, 1961.
———. *The Vitality of the Individual in the Thought of Ancient Israel.* 2nd ed. Cardiff: University of Wales Press, 1964.
Johnston, William. *Silent Music: The Science of Meditation.* London: Collins, 1974.
Kant, Immanuel. *Critique of the Power of Judgment.* Edited by Paul Guyer. Translated by Paul Guyer and Eric Matthews. Cambridge: Cambridge University Press, 2000.
Kattan, Assaad Elias. *Verleiblichung und Synergie: Grundzüge der Bibelhermeneutik bei Maximus Confessor.* Supplements to Vigiliae Christianae 63. Leiden: Brill, 2003.
Kauffman, Stuart. *Investigations.* New York: Oxford University Press, 2000.
———. *Origins of Order: Self-Organization and Selection in Evolution.* New York: Oxford University Press, 1993.
Keel, Othmar. *The Symbolism of the Biblical World: Ancient Near Eastern Iconography and the Book of Psalms.* Translated by Timothy J. Hallett. New York: Seabury, 1978.
Kessler, Martin, and Karel Deurloo. *A Commentary on Genesis: The Book of Beginnings.* New York: Paulist, 2004.

Bibliography

Koestler, Arthur. *The Ghost in the Machine*. 1967. Reprint. London: Pan, 1970.

Kristensen, W. Brede. "Prayer." In *Experience of the Sacred: Readings in the Phenomenology of Religion*, edited by Sumner B. Twiss and Walter H. Conser, Jr., 168–76. Hanover, NH: University Press of New England, 1992.

LaCugna, Catherine Mowry. *God for Us: The Trinity and Christian Life*. New York: HarperCollins, 1991.

La Liturgie des Heures, 4: Temps ordinaire, semaines 22–34. Paris: Cerf, 1980.

Lampmann, Jane. "A Frontier of Medical Research: Prayer." *The Christian Science Monitor*, 25 March 1998. 16. Online: http://www.csmonitor.com/1998/0325/032598.us.us.1.html.

Landsberg, G. *Cours élémentaire de physique. Vol. 3: Vibrations et ondes, optique, physique atomique et nucléaire*. Translated by Vassili Koliméev. Moscow: Mir, 1988.

Larchet, Jean-Claude. *La divinisation de l'homme selon Maxime le Confesseur*. Cogitatio Fidei 194. Paris: Cerf, 1996.

———. *Saint Maxime le Confesseur (580–662)*. Initiations aux Pères de L'Église. Paris: Cerf, 2003.

Laszlo, Ervin. *The Creative Cosmos: A Unified Science of Matter, Life and Mind*. Edinburgh: Floris, 1993.

———. *Science and the Akashic Field: An Integral Theory of Everything*. 2nd ed. Rochester, VT: Inner Traditions, 2007.

———. *Science and the Reenchantment of the Cosmos: The Rise of the Integral Vision of Reality*. Rochester, VT: Inner Traditions, 2006.

Leakey, Richard E. *The Making of Mankind*. London: Abacus, 1982.

Lee, Phylis C. "Cognitive and Behavioural Complexity in Non-human Primates." In *Interpreting Archaeology: Finding meaning in the past*, edited by Ian Hodder, 68–75. New York: Routledge, 1995.

Leech, Kenneth. *True Prayer: An Introduction to Christian Spirituality*. London: Sheldon, 1980.

Leroi-Gourhan, André. *The Dawn of European Art: An Introduction to Palaeolithic Cave Painting*. Translated by Sara Champion. The Imprint of Man Series. Cambridge: Cambridge University Press, 1982.

———. *Les religions de la préhistoire: Paléolithique*. 1964. Reprint. Quadrige 44. Paris: Presses Universitaires de France, 1995.

Leroi-Gourhan, Arlette. "The Flowers Found with Shanidar IV, a Neanderthal Burial in Iraq." *Science* 190 (1975) 562–64.

Levins, Richard, and Richard Lewontin. *The Dialectical Biologist*. Cambridge: Harvard University Press, 1985.

Levy, Gertrude Rachel. *The Gate of Horn: A Study of the Religious Conceptions of the Stone Age, and their Influence upon European Thought*. London: Faber & Faber, 1948.

Lewontin, Richard. *The Triple Helix: Gene, Organism, and Environment*. Cambridge: Harvard University Press, 2000.

Liddell, Henry George, and Robert Scott. *A Greek-English Lexicon*. 9th ed. Revised by Henry Stuart Jones and Roderick McKenzie. Oxford: Clarendon, 1968.

Lorenz, Konrad Z. *King Solomon's Ring: New Light on Animal Ways*. Translated by Marjorie Kerr Wilson. 1952. Reprint. London: Reprint Society, 1953.

Bibliography

Lossky, Vladimir. *The Mystical Theology of the Eastern Church.* Translated by members of the Fellowship of St. Alban and St. Sergius. 1957. Reprint, Crestwood, NY: St. Vladimir's Seminary Press, 1976.
Louf, André. "Prayer and Ecology." *The Way* 45.4 (October 2006) 119–36.
Louth, Andrew. *Maximus the Confessor.* The Early Church Fathers. London: Routledge, 1996.
———. *Wisdom of the Byzantine Church: Evagrios of Pontos and Maximus the Confessor.* 1997 Paine Lectures in Religion, University of Missouri, Columbia. Edited by Jill Raitt. Columbia: University of Missouri, 1998.
Lovelock, James. *The Ages of Gaia: A Biography of Our Living Earth.* Commonwealth Fund Book Program. Oxford: Oxford University Press, 1988.
Lubac, Henri de. *Catholicism: Christ and the Common Destiny of Man.* Translated by Lancelot C. Sheppard and Sr. Elizabeth Englund. 1950. Reprint, with foreword by Joseph Cardinal Ratzinger. San Francisco: Ignatius, 1988.
Lumsden, W. H. R. "Protozoa." In *Mackie & McCartney Medical Microbiology. Vol. 1: Microbial Infections,* 13th ed., edited by J. P. Duguid et al., 563–88. Edinburgh: Churchill Livingstone, 1978.
McElroy, Michael B. "Atmosphere." In *The New Encyclopedia Britannica,* 15th ed., edited by Philip W. Goetz et al., Macropaedia vol. 14, 305–28. Chicago: Encyclopaedia Britannica, 1974.
McFague, Sallie. *The Body of God: An Ecological Theology.* London: SCM, 1993.
McGrew, William C. "The Intelligent Use of Tools: Twenty Propositions." In *Tools, Language and Cognition in Human Evolution,* edited by Kathleen R. Gibson and Tim Ingold, 151–70. Cambridge: Cambridge University Press, 1993.
MacNutt, Francis. *Healing.* Notre Dame, IN: Ave Maria, 1974.
Main, John. *Word into Silence.* London: Darton, Longman & Todd, 1980.
Mania, Dietrich, and Ursula Mania. "The Natural and Socio-Cultural Environment of *Homo Erectus* at Bilzingsleben, Germany." In *The Hominid Individual in Context: Archaeological Investigations of Lower and Middle Palaeolithic Landscapes, Locales and Artefacts,* edited by Clive Gamble and Martin Porr, 98–114. London: Routledge, 2005.
Marett, R. R. *Faith, Hope and Charity in Primitive Religion.* Oxford: Clarendon, 1932.
Margulis, Lynn. *The Symbiotic Planet: A New Look at Evolution.* Science Masters. London: Weidenfeld & Nicolson, 1998.
Margulis, Lynn, and Dorion Sagan. *Acquiring Genomes: A Theory of the Origins of Species.* New York: Basic, 2002.
Maringer, Johannes. "Adorants in Prehistoric Art: Prehistoric Attitudes and Gestures of Prayer." *Numen* 26 (1979) 215–30.
Marshack, Alexander. "Early Hominid Symbol and Evolution of the Human Capacity." In *The Emergence of Modern Humans: An Archaeological Perspective,* edited by Paul Mellars, 457–98. Edinburgh: Edinburgh University Press, 1990.
———. "Exploring the Mind of Ice Age Man." *National Geographic* 147 (January 1975) 64–89.
———. "On Paleolithic Ochre and the Early Uses of Color and Symbol." *Current Anthropology* 22 (1981) 188–91.
———. "Paleolithic Image Making and Symbolizing in Europe and the Middle East: A Comparative Review." In *Beyond Art: Pleistocene Image and Symbol* (Memoirs

Bibliography

of the California Academy of Sciences 23), edited by Margaret W. Conkey et al., 53-91. San Francisco: California Academy of Sciences, 1997.

———. *The Roots of Civilization: The Cognitive Beginnings of Man's First Art, Symbol and Notation.* Revised and Expanded. Mount Kisco, NY: Moyer Bell, 1991.

———. "Some Implications of the Paleolithic Symbolic Evidence for the Origin of Language." *Current Anthropology* 17 (1976) 274-82.

Masson, Jeffrey Moussaieff, and Susan McCarthy. *When Elephants Weep: The Emotional Lives of Animals.* London: Cape, 1994.

Matsoukas, Nikos A. *La vie en Dieu selon Maxime le Confesseur: cosmologie, anthropologie, sociologie.* Translated by Maurice-Jean Monsaingeon. Grez-Doiceau, Belgium: Axios, 1994.

Maturana, Humberto R., and Francisco J. Varela. *Autopoiesis and Cognition: The Realization of the Living.* Boston Studies in the Philosophy of Science 42. Dordrecht, Holland: Reidel, 1980.

Merton, Thomas. *The Silent Life.* New York: Farrar, Straus & Cudahy, 1957.

Meyendorff, John. "Remarks on Eastern Patristic Thought in John Scottus Eriugena." In *Eriugena: East and West*, papers of the Eighth International Colloquium of the Society for the Promotion of Eriugenian Studies, Chicago and Notre Dame, 18-20 October 1991, edited by Bernard McGinn and Willemien Otten, 51-68. Notre Dame Conferences in Medieval Studies 5. Notre Dame, IN: University of Notre Dame Press, 1994.

Meyer, Stephen C. "Evidence for Design in Physics and Biology: From the Origin of the Universe to the Origin of Life." In *Science and Evidence for Design in the Universe*, by Michael J. Behe et al., 53-111. The Proceedings of the Wethersfield Institute 9. San Francisco: Ignatius, 2000.

Milbank, John, et al. *Radical Orthodoxy: A New Theology.* London: Routledge, 1999.

Moltmann, Jürgen. *The Crucified God: The Cross of Christ as the Foundation and Criticism of Christian Theology.* Translated by R. A. Wilson and John Bowden. London: SCM, 1974.

———. *God in Creation: An Ecological Doctrine of Creation.* The Gifford Lectures 1984-85. Translated by Margaret Kohl. London: SCM, 1985.

———. "Reflections on Chaos and God's Interaction with the World from a Trinitarian Perspective." In *Chaos and Complexity: Scientific Perspectives on Divine Action*, edited by Robert John Russell et al., 205-10. Vatican City State: Vatican Observatory Publications, 1995.

———. *The Spirit of Life: A Universal Affirmation.* Translated by Margaret Kohl. London: SCM, 1992.

———. *The Trinity and the Kingdom of God: The Doctrine of God.* Translated by Margaret Kohl. London: SCM, 1981.

———. *The Way of Jesus Christ: Christology in Messianic Dimensions.* Translated by Margaret Kohl. London: SCM, 1990.

Morowitz, Harold J. *The Emergence of Everything: How the World became Complex.* Oxford: Oxford University Press, 2002.

Mother Teresa. *Jesus, the Word to be Spoken: Prayers and Meditations for Every Day of the Year.* Compiled by Brother Angelo Devananda. London: Fount, 1987.

Muir, John. *A Thousand-Mile Walk to the Gulf.* Edited by William Frederic Badè. 1916. Reprint, with foreword by Peter Jenkins. New York: Houghton Mifflin, 1998.

Bibliography

Murphy, Nancey C. "Does Prayer Make a Difference?" In *Cosmos as Creation: Theology and Science in Consonance*, edited by Ted Peters, 235–45. Nashville, TN: Abingdon, 1989.

Murray, Robert. *The Cosmic Covenant: Biblical Themes of Justice, Peace and the Integrity of Creation*. Heythrop Monographs 7. London: Sheed & Ward, 1992.

Nasr, Seyyed Hossein. *The Encounter of Man and Nature: The Spiritual Crisis of Modern Man*. London: Allen & Unwin, 1968.

Nellas, Panayiotis. *Deification in Christ: Orthodox Perspectives on the Nature of the Human Person*. Translated by Norman Russell. Contemporary Greek Theologians 5. Crestwood, NY: St. Vladimir's Seminary Press, 1987.

Nestle-Aland. *Novum Testamentum Graece*. 26th ed. Stuttgart: Deutsche Bibelgesellschaft, 1979.

Nichols, Aidan. *Byzantine Gospel: Maximus the Confessor in Modern Scholarship*. Edinburgh: T. & T. Clark, 1993.

Norris, Richard A., Jr. *God and World in Early Christian Theology: A Study in Justin Martyr, Irenaeus, Tertullian and Origen*. Studies in Patristic Thought. London: Black, 1966.

Norris, Russell Bradner Jr. "Logos Christology as Cosmological Paradigm." *Pro Ecclesia* 5 (1996) 183–201.

Oliver, Simon. *Philosophy, God and Motion*. Routledge Radical Orthodox Series. London: Routledge, 2005.

O'Mahony, Gerald. *Praying St Mark's Gospel*. London: Chapman, 1990.

Ó Murchú, Diarmuid. *Religion in Exile: A Spiritual Vision for the Homeward Bound*. Dublin: Gateway, 2000.

Papanikolaou, Aristotle. "Divine Energies or Divine Personhood: Vladimir Lossky and John Zizioulas on Conceiving the Transcendent and Immanent God." *Modern Theology* 19 (2003) 357–85.

———. "Is John Zizioulas an Existentialist in Disguise? A Response to Lucian Turcescu." *Modern Theology* 20 (2004) 601–7.

———. Review of *God for Us*, by Catherine Mowry LaCugna. *The Journal of Religion* 73 (1993) 437–38.

Patella, Michael. *The Lord of the Cosmos: Mithras, Paul and The Gospel of Mark*. London: T. & T. Clark, 2006.

Peacocke, Arthur. "Chance and Law in Irreversible Thermodynamics, Theoretical Biology, and Theology." In *Chaos and Complexity: Scientific Perspectives on Divine Action*, edited by Robert John Russell et al., 123–43. Vatican City State: Vatican Observatory Publications, 1995.

———. "God's Interaction with the World." In *Chaos and Complexity: Scientific Perspectives on Divine Action*, edited by Robert John Russell et al., 263–87. Vatican City State: Vatican Observatory Publications, 1995.

———. *Theology for a Scientific Age*. Enlarged ed. London: SCM, 1993.

Pecker, Jean Claude. *Understanding the Heavens: Thirty Centuries of Astronomical Ideas from Ancient Thinking to Modern Cosmology*. Edited by Susan Kaufman. Berlin: Springer, 2001.

Pendergast, Richard J. "Evil, Original Sin, and Evolution." *Heythrop Journal* 50 (2009) 833–45.

Perdue, Leo G. *Wisdom and Creation: The Theology of Wisdom Literature*. Nashville, TN: Abingdon, 1994.

Bibliography

Phillips, D. Z. *The Concept of Prayer*. 1965. Reprint, Oxford: Blackwell, 1981.

Pius XII, Pope. *Humani generis*. Encyclical letter, 1950. Title of the translated encyclical: *False Trends in Modern Teaching*. 2nd ed. Translated by Ronald A. Knox. London: Catholic Truth Society, 1959.

Polkinghorne, John. "The Laws of Nature and the Laws of Physics." In *Quantum Cosmology and the Laws of Nature: Scientific Perspectives on Divine Action*, edited by Robert John Russell et al., 437–48. Vatican City State: Vatican Observatory Publications, 1993.

———. "The Metaphysics of Divine Action." In *Chaos and Complexity: Scientific Perspectives on Divine Action*, edited by Robert John Russell et al., 146–56. Vatican City State: Vatican Observatory Publications, 1995.

Prestige, G. L. *God in Patristic Thought*. London: Heinemann, 1936.

———. "περιχωρέω and περιχώρησις in the Fathers." *The Journal of Theological Studies* 29 (1928) 242–52.

Price, R. M. "'Hellenization' and Logos Doctrine in Justin Martyr." *Vigiliae Christianae* 42 (1988) 18–23.

Prigogine, Ilya, and Isabelle Stengers. *Order out of Chaos*. New York: Bantam, 1984.

Quincey, Christian de. "The 'Metaverse Story': Where Science Meets Spirit." In *Science and the Reenchantment of the Cosmos: The Rise of the Integral Vision of Reality*, by Ervin Laszlo, 109–20. Rochester, VT: Inner Traditions, 2006.

Rad, Gerhard von. *Genesis: A Commentary*. Translated by John H. Marks. The Old Testament Library. London: SCM, 1961.

Rahner, Karl. "Christology within an Evolutionary World." In *Theological Investigations*, vol. 5, translated by Karl-H. Kruger, 157–92. Baltimore: Helicon, 1966.

Raj, Udit (Ram Raj). *Essence of Buddhism*. New Delhi: All India Confederation of SC/ST Organizations and Lord Buddha Club, 2001.

Randles, W. G. L. *The Unmaking of the Medieval Christian Cosmos 1500–1760: From Solid Heavens to Boundless Æther*. Aldershot, UK: Ashgate, 1999.

Rappaport, Roy A. *Ritual and Religion in the Making of Humanity*. Cambridge Studies in Social and Cultural Anthropology 110. Cambridge: Cambridge University Press, 1999.

Ratzinger, (Cardinal) Joseph. "Foreword." In *Catholicism: Christ and the Common Destiny of Man*, by Henri de Lubac, translated by Lancelot C. Sheppard and Sr. Elizabeth Englund, 11–12. San Francisco: Ignatius, 1988.

———. *"In the Beginning . . ." : A Catholic Understanding of the Story of Creation and the Fall*. Translated by Boniface Ramsey. Ressourcement Series. Edinburgh: T. & T. Clark, 1995.

———. "Retrieving the Tradition: Concerning the Notion of Person in Theology." Translated by Michael Waldstein. *Communio* 17 (1990) 439–54.

(Ratzinger), Pope Benedict XVI. "St Maximus the Confessor." *General Audience*, Wednesday 25 June 2008. Online: http://www.vatican.va/holy_father/benedict_xvi/audiences/2008/documents/hf_ben-xvi_aud_20080625_en.html.

Rees, Martin. *Just Six Numbers: The Deep Forces that Shape the Universe*. Science Masters. London: Phoenix, 2000.

———. *Our Cosmic Habitat*. London: Phoenix, 2003.

Ridley, Matt. *Genome: The Autobiography of a Species in 23 Chapters*. London: Fourth Estate, 1999.

Rolston III, Holmes. *Science and Religion: A Critical Survey*. 1987. Reprint. Philadelphia: Templeton Foundation, 2006.
Romero, (Archbishop) Oscar. "The Church of Salvation." *Homily for the Third Sunday of Advent*, 11 December 1977. Online: http://www.romerotrust.org.uk/index.php?nuc=homilies&func=view&item=66.
Ruether, Rosemary Radford. *Gaia and God: An Ecofeminist Theology of Earth Healing*. London: SCM, 1993.
A Russian Pilgrim. *The Way of a Pilgrim*. Translated by R. M. French. 1930. Reprint, together with *The Pilgrim Continues His Way*, translated by R. M. French. London: SPCK, 1941.
Scheindlin, Raymond P. *The Book of Job*. New York: Norton, 1999.
Schmemann, Alexander. *The World as Sacrament*. London: Darton, Longman & Todd, 1965.
Schmidt, W. H. "*dābhar*." In *The Theological Dictionary of the Old Testament*, edited by G. Johannes Botterweck and Helmer Ringgren, translated by John T. Willis and Geoffrey W. Bromiley, vol. 3, 84–125. Grand Rapids: Eerdmans, 1978.
Schrödinger, Erwin. *What is Life? with Mind and Matter and Autobiographical Sketches*. Cambridge: Cambridge University Press, 1992.
Schroeder, C. Paul. "Suffering towards Personhood: John Zizioulas and Fyodor Dostoevsky in Conversation on Freedom and the Human Person." *St Vladimir's Theological Quarterly* 45 (2001) 243–64.
Schroeder, Gerald L. *The Science of God: The Convergence of Scientific and Biblical Wisdom*. New York: Broadway, 1997.
Seybold, Kevin S. *Explorations in Neuroscience, Psychology, and Religion*. Ashgate Science and Religion Series. Aldershot, UK: Ashgate, 2007.
Sheldrake, Rupert. *A New Science of Life: The Hypothesis of Formative Causation*. 2nd ed. London: Grafton, 1985.
Shivanandan, Mary. *Crossing the Threshold of Love: A New Vision of Marriage in the Light of John Paul II's Anthropology*. Edinburgh: T. & T. Clark, 1999.
Simmons, Geoffrey. *What Darwin Didn't Know*. Eugene, OR: Harvest House, 2004.
Smart, Ninian. *The World's Religions*. 2nd ed. Cambridge: Cambridge University Press, 1998.
Sonnerwirth, Alex C., et al. "Indigenous Bacteria; Oral Microbiology." In *Microbiology*, 3rd ed., edited by Bernard D. Davis et al., 808–16. Hagerstown, MD: Harper & Row, 1980.
Southgate, Christopher. *The Groaning of Creation: God, Evolution, and the Problem of Evil*. Louisville, KY: Westminster John Knox, 2008.
Staniloae, Dumitru. "Commentaires." Translated by Aurel Grigoras from Rumanian. In *Saint Maxime le Confesseur. Ambigua*, by Jean-Claude Larchet et al., 373–540. Collection l'Arbre de Jessé. Suresnes: l'Ancre, 1994.
Stevenson, J. (editor) and W.H.C. Frend (rev. editor). *Creeds, Councils and Controversies: Documents Illustrating the History of the Church, AD 337-461*. London: SPCK, 1989.
———. *A New Eusebius: Documents Illustrating the History of the Church to AD 337*. London: SPCK, 1987.
Stringer, Chris, and Peter Andrews. *The Complete World of Human Evolution*. London: Thames & Hudson, 2005.

Bibliography

Strycker, E. De. *Beknopte Geschiedenis van de Antieke Filosofie*. Kapellen, Belgium: DNB & Pelckmans, 1987.

Swimme, Brian, and Thomas Berry. *The Universe Story: From the Primordial Flaring Forth to the Ecozoic Era—A Celebration of the Unfolding of the Cosmos*. New York: HarperSanFrancisco, 1992.

Tattersall, Ian. *Becoming Human: Evolution and Human Uniqueness*. New York: Oxford University Press, 1998.

Theillier, Patrick. "*Talking about Miracles*." Translation by First Edition Translations Limited, Cambridge UK. Chawton, UK: Redemptorist, 2003.

Thunberg, Lars. "'Circumincession' once more: Trinitarian and Christological Implications in an Age of Religious Pluralism." In *Studia Patristica* 29, papers presented at the Twelfth International Conference on Patristic Studies held in Oxford 1995, edited by Elizabeth A. Livingstone, 364–72. Leuven: Peeters, 1997.

———. *Microcosm and Mediator: The Theological Anthropology of Maximus the Confessor*. 2nd ed. La Salle, IL: Open Court, 1995.

Tinbergen, N. *Social Behaviour in Animals with Special Reference to Vertebrates*. 2nd ed. London: Chapman & Hall, 1964.

Tollefsen, Torstein. *The Christocentric Cosmology of St Maximus the Confessor*. Oxford Early Christian Studies. New York: Oxford University Press, 2008.

Toolan, David S. "Praying in a Post-Einsteinian Universe." *Crosscurrents* 46 (1996) 437–70.

Torrance, T. F. *The Christian Doctrine of God, One Being Three Persons*. Edinburgh: T. & T. Clark, 1996.

———. *Divine and Contingent Order*. 1981. Reprint, with a preface to the reprint edition. Edinburgh: T. & T. Clark, 1998.

———. "The Soul and Person, in Theological Perspective." In *Religion, Reason and the Self: Essays in Honour of Hywell D. Lewis*, edited by Stewart R. Sutherland and T. A. Roberts, 103–18. Cardiff: University of Wales Press, 1989.

———. *The Trinitarian Faith*. Edinburgh: T. & T. Clark, 1988.

———. *Trinitarian Perspectives: Toward Doctrinal Agreement*. Edinburgh: T. & T. Clark, 1994.

Toulmin, Stephen, and June Goodfield. *The Architecture of Matter*. Harmondsworth, UK: Penguin, 1965.

Trakatellis, Demetrius C. *The Pre-Existence of Christ in the Writings of Justin Martyr*. Harvard Dissertations in Religion 6. Missoula, MT: Scholars, 1976.

Turcescu, Lucian. "'Person' versus 'Individual,' and Other Modern Misreadings of Gregory of Nyssa." *Modern Theology* 18 (2002) 527–39.

Tylor, Edward Burnett. *Primitive Culture: Researches into the Development of Mythology, Philosophy, Religion, Language, Art and Custom*. 2nd ed. London: Murray, 1873.

Ulanov, Ann, and Barry Ulanov. *Primary Speech: A Psychology of Prayer*. Atlanta: John Knox, 1982.

Van Peursen, C. A. *Body, Soul, Spirit: A Survey of the Body-Mind Problem*. Translated by Hubert H. Hoskins. London: Oxford University Press, 1966.

Vatican II. *Gaudium et spes*. Title of the translated document: "Pastoral Constitution on the Church in the Modern World." In *The Documents of Vatican II*, general editor W. M. Abbott, translation editor J. Gallagher, 199–308. New York: Guild Press, America Press, and Association Press, 1966.

———. *Lumen gentium*. Title of the translated document: "Dogmatic Constitution on the Church." In *The Documents of Vatican II*, general editor W. M. Abbott, translation editor J. Gallagher, 14–101. New York: Guild Press, America Press, and Association Press, 1966.
Vaughan, Henry. "The Morning Watch." *The Ark* 207 (Winter 2007). Online: http://www.all-creatures.org/ca/ark-207-the.html.
Velecky, Ceslaus. "Appendix 7: Divine Persons." In *St Thomas Aquinas. Summa theologiae*, Blackfriars ed., vol. 6, edited by T. Gilby et al., 145–48. London: Eyre & Spottiswoode, 1963–75.
Waal Malefijt, Annemarie de. *Religion and Culture: An Introduction to Anthropology of Religion*. New York: Macmillan, 1968.
(Ware), Bishop Kallistos of Diokleia. "The Origins of the Jesus Prayer: Diadochus, Gaza, Sinai." In *The Study of Spirituality*, edited by Cheslyn Jones et al., 175–84. 1986. Reprint, with corrections. London: SPCK, 1992.
———. "Through the Creation to the Creator." *Ecotheology* 2 (1997) 8–30.
Watson, Lyall. *Lifetide: A Biology of the Unconscious*. London: Hodder & Stoughton, 1979.
———. *The Romeo Error: A Matter of Life and Death*. London: Hodder & Stoughton, 1974.
Waxman, Denny. "Secret of the Fountain of Youth." No pages. Online: http://www.surrenderworks.com/library/imports/fountainofyouth.html.
Whitehead, Alfred North. *Science and the Modern World*. Lowell Lectures, 1925. Cambridge: Cambridge University Press, 1926.
Wilber, Ken. *A Brief History of Everything*. Dublin: Gill & Macmillan, 1996.
Wildiers, Max. *Kosmologie in de Westerse cultuur: Historisch-kritisch essay*. Kapellen, Belgium: DNB & Pelckmans, 1989.
Willard, Barbara. *Field and Forest*. Harmondsworth, UK: Kestrel, 1975.
Williams, Janet P. "Pseudo-Dionysius and Maximus the Confessor." In *The First Christian Theologians: An Introduction to Theology in the Early Church*, edited by G. R. Evans, 186–200. The Great Theologians. Malden, MA: Blackwell, 2004.
Williams, Rowan. "Origen." In *The First Christian Theologians: An Introduction to Theology in the Early Church*, edited by G. R. Evans, 132–42. The Great Theologians. Malden, MA: Blackwell, 2004.
Wolinsky, Emanuel. "Mycobacteria." In *Microbiology*, 3rd ed., edited by Bernard D. Davis et al., 723–42. Hagerstown, MD: Harper & Row, 1980.
Yeago, David S. "Jesus of Nazareth and Cosmic Redemption: The Relevance of St. Maximus the Confessor." *Modern Theology* 12 (1996) 163–93.
Zaleski, Philip, and Carol Zaleski. *Prayer: A History*. New York: Houghton Mifflin, 2005.
Ziesler, John. *Paul's Letter to the Romans*. TPI New Testament Commentaries. Philadelphia: Trinity Press, 1989.
Zizioulas, John D. *Being as Communion: Studies in Personhood and the Church*. 1985. Reprint. London: Darton, Longman & Todd, 2004.
(Zizioulas), Metropolitan John of Pergamon. *Communion and Otherness: Further Studies in Personhood and the Church*. Edited by Paul McPartlan. London: T. & T. Clark, 2006.

General Index

act of (*or* event of) universal creation, 31, 52, 126, 160–61, 168
Acts of the Apostles, 27, 86, 118
Adams, Edward, 175
"*advaita*" (non-duality), 187
Andrews, Donald Hatch, 69–70, 119–20, 138
angels, 8, 32, 34, 44, 47, 48, 53–57, 64, 73, 81, 102, 116, 122, 124, 125, 141–42, 156
   See also spiritual beings.
animals, 36–37, 51–52, 56, 60, 64, 74, 77, 90, 94–98, 112, 129, 132, 134, 151
   See also beasts, wild.
anthropocentrism, 67, 146
anthropology, 90
Aquinas, Thomas. *See* Thomas Aquinas.
Aristotle, 36–37, 58, 62, 63–64, 75, 80, 87, 99
Artigas, Mariano, 72
Athanasius, 89, 167
Atkins, Margaret, 93
atmosphere, 21, 136, 140, 190
Attenborough, David, 29
Augustine, Saint, 2, 2n3, 5, 12, 13, 14n68, 60, 86–87, 99, 143, 144, 154
Augustinio-Thomistic approach, 7–8, 13
Australopithecines, 90, 90n25
autopoiesis, 146

bacteria; bacilli

bacterial flagellum, 155
   complexity of behavior of, 72–73
   in outer space, 149
   pathogenic, 48, 139, 157, 184
   in symbiotic relationships, 139, 155
Balthasar, Hans Urs von, 4–5, 11, 145, 177n29, 178, 186
Barth, Karl, 8, 10, 11, 104
Bartholomew I, Patriarch, 133, 144
Basil, Saint, 22, 88–89, 127
beasts, wild, 98, 123–24, 125
beauty (the beautiful), 3, 30, 112
   divine, 72
   of creation, 128, 130–31, 156, 191
Behe, Michael C., 155
Benedicite, the (hymn of all creation), 124, 128, 138
Benedict, Saint, 114
   Benedictine monks, 119, 120–21
Berry, Thomas, 15, 145–46
big bang, 80, 150
Black Death, 66
blood flukes, 157
blood sucking bugs, 157
Blowers, Paul M., 44, 167
body
   in Aristotle, 62, 99
   contingency of, 159
   in the Judaeo-Christian tradition, 62, 125, 138, 152, 174
   in Maximus, 62, 174, 175–76
   mind and, 72–73
   in Paul, 166
   in Plato, 58–60, 62, 99

215

General Index

involvement of, in prayer, 114, 118–21, 141–42
from a scientific perception, 138–39, 155
and soul, 47, 62, 114, 125, 152, 173–74, 186
See also Christ: body of.
Boethius, 63, 87
Bohm, David, 78–79
Brague, Rémi, 1, 67
Brahe, Tycho, 75
Breuil, Abbé Henri, 96
Buddhism, 108–9, 115n34

Cappadocian fathers, 12, 88–89, 176
See also Basil; Gregory of Nazianzen; Gregory of Nyssa.
Catechism of the Catholic Church
on prayer, 111–12, 114, 116
support for cosmic prayer in the, 131–32
causes, creative, 2, 40–42
cave art. *See* Upper Paleolithic cave art.
Chalcedon, Council of, 88, 89, 167, 169, 178, 186
chance events, 16, 148, 155–57
See also indeterminacy.
chaos, 3, 22–25, 28, 56, 82, 188
Chopra, Deepak, 73
Christ
body of, 106, 166
cosmic personification in, 85, 103–7, 166–67, 169, 179–81
event, 62, 106, 125, 146, 184–85
the Incarnate Son/Word, 22, 39, 48
in, and in the Spirit, 34, 85, 170, 181, 187
See also Jesus Christ.
church,
cosmic, 13, 133
early, 56
Eastern, 115, 129
local, and worldwide, 117
Roman Catholic Church, 115, 152
the, 106, 121, 130–31, 170
circumincession. *See* perichoresis.
Clement of Alexandria, 40, 113
climate change, xi, 65, 190

Colossians, Letter to the, 13, 166–67
communion
creation-inclusive personal, within God, 28, 81, 90, 103, 106, 135, 150, 155, 180–81, 184–85, 187, 191
human, 105
intra-divine (*or* trinitarian), 6, 9, 10, 12, 13, 17, 25, 26–27, 34, 48, 57, 176, 183
of saints, 116
community
ecological, 149, 151
of prayer, 10, 106
See also God: as *perichoretic* community.
Confucianism, 109
consciousness, xiii, 49, 73, 78, 83, 86, 97, 148–49, 150
Constantinople, third Council of, 186
contemplation, 52, 118, 134, 142, 145, 176, 189
contingency, 7–8, 23–27, 28, 30, 35, 42, 49, 52, 115, 150, 158–60, 162, 176, 183, 185, 187
cooperation, 2, 26, 31, 61, 75, 80, 99, 125, 136, 143, 155, 166, 169, 185, 189
Copernican worldview, 65, 67
Copernicus, 66, 67
Corey, M. A., 120n48
Corinthians
First Letter to the, 34, 40, 85, 98, 116, 126, 142, 166–68, 174–75, 178, 185, 188
Second Letter to the, 85, 126, 166, 188
Cornford, Francis M., 58–59
cosmic covenant, 123–24, 126
cosmic liturgy, 133, 144–46, 173
cosmic prayer, 17, 107, 122–47, 153, 155, 158, 159, 184–85, 191
definition of, 134–35
cosmic renewal, 34, 166, 168, 173
cosmogenesis, 14
Cosmological Principle, the, 80
cosmology
ancient Hebrew, 50–57, 65

216

General Index

ancient Western, 36, 58–63, 64
emergent (*or* contemporary) Christian, 14–18, 50, 53, 181–85, 187
of Maximus the Confessor, 151, 167–68, 178
medieval, 14, 63–67, 84
possibility of, 1, 67
cosmos, ix, 1, 3, 5, 14, 18, 28, 50, 60, 64–65, 67, 71, 72, 73, 84, 116, 132, 133, 143, 165–67, 173, 186
course of events, 15, 31, 42, 156
creation; *or* created reality; *or* created order
as evolutionary, 11
as fallen, 9
universal, 15–17, 27, 48, 50, 135, 143–44
wider, xii–xiii, 7, 17, 19, 34, 48, 92, 94, 118, 123–25, 129, 160, 161, 179, 185, 187, 191
creation out of nothing (*ex nihilo*), 3, 20, 26, 40
creationism, 143
creative process, 30, 85, 103, 187
as exclusive "top-down," 14n68
as reciprocal (*or* as a two-way dynamic), 2–3, 11, 13–14, 46, 143
Creator. *See* God: Creator.
creatures, gruesome, 156
Crick, Francis, 148, 149
crisis, 190–91
Cro-Magnons, 95–98
cross, xiii, 118–19, 125, 168, 184

dābār (word), 31, 71
Daniel, Book of, 21, 56–57, 98, 124, 142
Darwin, Charles, 66, 111, 148, 153, 155
Dawkins, Marian Stamp, 74
Dawkins, Richard, 148
death, xiii, 38, 66, 90, 101, 109, 117, 156, 172–73, 175–76
beyond, 94
violent, 156
Déchanet, Jean-Marie, 119, 120, 138
deism, 67, 142, 153
Dembski, William A., 155

demons, 48, 56, 184
See also powers: spiritual.
Descartes, René, 66, 75–76
destiny of created reality, xiii, 14–15, 17, 25, 28, 34, 49, 51, 75, 81, 85, 126, 144, 165, 187
devil, the, 65, 98, 142
Diadochus of Photiki, 114
dialectic
in the creative process, 85, 101, 143, 160–61
definition, 143
See also creative process: as reciprocal; relationship: dialectical Creator-creature.
dialectic evolutionary biology, 154, 183
divine dance, 10, 12, 104–5
divine informing, 16, 62, 71, 72, 99, 136–37, 183, 186
Divine Office (according to the Roman rite), 127, 128
The Divine Office (according to the Roman rite), 191
divine plan, xiii, 15–16, 47, 153–58
divinization, 105
dualism, 68, 73, 118
anti-material, 13, 174–75
dynamic; dynamism, 5–6, 14, 25, 73, 83, 115, 117, 118, 122, 129, 134, 137, 140–42, 144, 146, 149, 152, 158, 168–69, 170–72, 173, 175–76, 180, 184–85, 187
See also creative process; God: dynamic in.

earth, 13, 42, 51–53, 56, 60–62, 64–65, 67, 74, 114, 124, 129, 136–38, 149, 183, 190–91
air, water, fire, and, 38, 128
early, 19–25, 27, 28–29, 82, 136, 155
Gaia, our living, 12–13, 83n96, 138, 140, 190
new, 12
as a nurturing mother, 30
upon the, as it is, 14, 51, 156
as a whole, 83, 140, 173
ecofeminist theologians, 12–14

217

General Index

ecological circle (*or* community; *or* network); ecosystem, 30, 57, 69, 73, 77, 83, 92, 137, 140, 149, 151, 156, 183-84, 191
Eddington, Arthur S., 1, 67-70, 79, 149
Edwards, Denis, 6, 10-11
Einstein, Albert, 76
Einstein-Podolsky-Rosen thought experiment, 77-78
Einsteinian space-time, 162-63
Eliade, Mircea, 145
Enlightenment, ix, 1, 67, 84, 182
ensemble, 57, 78, 141-42, 150-52, 154, 161, 169, 183-84
  and cosmic prayer, 92-93, 127, 134-38, 143, 184, 191
  ecological, 91-92, 137, 151
environmental crisis. *See* crisis.
Ephesians, Letter to the, 160, 166-67, 183
erosion, xi
essence (*ousia*), 41, 43, 44-45, 70n49, 89
  See also fifth essence; God: essential being of.
ether, 38, 68, 75-76, 80
ether-like field, 150
Eucharist, 34, 106, 119, 123, 133, 166, 184-85
Evagrius, 74, 113-14, 189
evil, 7-8, 15, 16, 17, 34, 51, 167, 185, 187
  See also powers, spiritual.
evolution, natural, 9, 77, 152, 153-54, 157, 191
  evolutionary process, 4, 8-9, 13, 91, 151, 186-87
  spiritual dimension of, 17
  theory of, 1-3, 14, 70, 77, 153
Ezekiel, Book of, 32, 54, 55-56

Facchini, Fiorenzo, 90-91, 93
faith, ix-x, 4-5, 15-16, 22, 27, 30, 33, 48, 62-63, 64, 71, 84, 117, 121, 146, 154, 158, 159, 169, 174, 178, 179, 188
  all, traditions, 121, 133

challenge of Christian, 185-88
Faraday, Michael, 76
Fiddes, Paul S., 6, 10, 11, 12, 104-5, 144, 162
fifth essence, 75
force fields (various physical fields), 21, 69, 76, 80
Fosdick, Harry Emerson, 108-11
Francis of Assisi, 128
freedom
  of Christ, 105
  of the created order, 7, 9, 16, 23, 25, 35, 56, 88, 103, 130, 137, 154-55
  of God, 8
  height of, 173
  song of, 131
Frizzell, Laurence, 124
Funkenstein, Amos, 76, 81n89

Gaia. *See* earth: Gaia, our living.
Galatians, Letter to the, 85, 166, 169-70, 174, 184-85
Galileï, Galileo, 66
general evolutionary theory (GET), 70, 77
Genesis, 19-32, 49, 50, 52-55, 93, 112, 120, 123, 125, 126, 133, 152, 154
genetic aberrations, 157
Gilson, Étienne, 4, 39
goal
  common, of soul and body, 62
  of creation, 4, 8, 9, 105, 180, 184-85
  of human beings, 100
God
  as being affected, 3, 16, 162
  as communion in love, 10, 167, 184, 187
  creative activity of, 7, 8, 10, 26, 28, 35, 43, 50, 55, 156, 161-62, 185
  the Creator, xii, 2, 2n4, 4, 17, 28, 30, 38, 51, 97, 101, 120, 128, 131, 133, 138, 146, 151, 153, 161, 163, 171, 182, 185
  dynamic in, 4, 8, 26, 146, 168, 183
  essential being (*ousia*) of, 28, 89, 161

218

General Index

the Father, 9, 26, 33, 39-40, 55, 57, 61, 81, 105, 114, 116-17, 126, 129, 158, 163, 168, 169, 170-71
Father, Son, and Spirit, 8, 10, 20, 34, 40, 86-87, 89, 103, 181, 191
of heaven and earth, xii, 19, 123
immanence of, within creation, 7, 11-12, 54, 61-63, 186
interactive engagement of, with creation, 4, 143, 162-63, 178-79
kingdom (*or* reign) of, 12, 130
life of, 11, 104
outreach of, 17, 26, 49, 52-53, 61, 97, 120, 154, 169, 172
as *perichoretic* community, 8, 10-11, 104
as personal, 3, 6, 8, 16, 28, 36, 62-63, 84, 85, 90, 100, 103, 109, 115, 135, 142-43, 150-51, 164, 183, 185
self-disclosure of, 11, 16
mode of suffering of, 6-10, 13, 16, 103
transcendence of, 11-12, 16, 41, 61-65, 99, 135, 146, 162-64, 186
will of, 2, 32-33, 39, 42-43, 47, 56, 114, 142, 143, 159, 173
Word of, 7, 19, 22, 24-26, 27, 28, 31, 34, 35, 43-44, 46, 48, 49, 61-62, 71, 116, 134, 137, 140, 147, 152, 161, 167-68, 169, 174, 186
See also Christ; communion: intra-divine; Holy Spirit; Holy Trinity; Son, divine.
"God of the gaps," 71
Gould, Stephen Jay, 154
grace, divine, 2, 4, 33-34, 61, 100, 115, 129-130, 134, 144, 160, 178, 185, 188, 189
grand unified theory (GUT), 70, 77
Grant, Edward, 64, 76
Greene, Brian, 70, 78, 120
Gregory of Nazianzen, 88, 126-28, 176, 177
Gregory of Nyssa, 1-2, 72, 89n18, 105, 107, 113, 174
Gregory Palamas, 161
Griffin, Donald R., 74, 90

Grillmeier, Aloys, 89
guided transformation. *See* transformation: guided.
Gunton, Colin E., 6, 9-10

Harding, Stephen, 74
harmonization, 18, 48, 60, 61, 71, 81-83, 98, 99, 117, 135, 152, 170, 184
harmony, 1, 3, 47, 61, 64, 73, 74, 114, 123, 125, 133, 156, 186
Haught, John F., 3-4
heaven(s), 12, 33, 38, 44, 53, 55-57, 114, 118, 124, 133
court of, 54, 57
non-astronomic spheres, 64
worship of, 125
Hebrews, Letter to the, 33, 57, 142, 159
Heiler, Friedrich, 111, 112
hell, in medieval cosmology, 65
Heraclitus, 35-36, 37
Hildegard of Bingen, 14
holon, 79-80, 81, 84, 92, 116, 136, 181
Holy Spirit
in Christ and in the, 17, 34, 85, 165-81, 187
in the life of Jesus, 33, 61-62, 125
presence/action in creation of, 7, 9, 10, 11, 20, 22-26, 28, 30-31, 47, 49, 51-52, 57, 71, 81, 104, 106, 120, 126, 134, 137, 140, 152, 161, 184, 186
and virtuous living, 92, 100, 102-3, 104, 116, 132, 140
and wisdom, 27, 40, 52, 186
See also God: Father, Son, and Spirit.
Holy Trinity, 6-7, 12, 16, 26, 42, 55, 57, 86-87, 103, 134, 162, 168, 181, 187
See also communion: intra-divine.
hominids, 90, 90n24, 91, 95, 137
hominines, 90, 90n26, 93
Homo erectus, 91n30, 94
hookworms, 157
Hoyle, Fred, 149
human kind; *or* humanity; *or* human being, 9, 15
definition, 99-100
emergence of, 90-99, 111, 137

219

General Index

as God's image, 16, 29, 67, 72, 87, 94, 105, 107, 133, 173
priesthood for all creation of, 10, 62, 106, 133, 145
relation to creation of, ix, xii–xiii, 10, 13, 15, 19–20, 29, 47, 51–52, 61, 63–64, 67, 77, 81, 116, 118, 123–24, 134, 138–40, 152, 170, 173, 190–91
what is, 9, 17, 86, 90–95, 99–100, 111, 127, 137, 138–41, 151, 159
See also Jesus: humanity of; purpose: human.
Humani generis, Encyclical, 152
hymn, xii, 114, 116, 124, 127–28, 131, 132, 191
"hymning circulations," x
of silence, 128
See also Benedicite.
hypostasis, 45, 88, 89, 102, 105–6, 169, 173
hypostatic union, 106, 167, 169, 172, 176, 180, 186

Incarnation, the, 9, 15, 39, 61–62, 172–73
Scotist view of, 9
See also Christ: the Incarnate Son/Word; Jesus Christ, the Incarnate Son/Word.
indeterminacy (unpredictability), 16, 23, 24–25, 71, 155–57, 183
See also chance events; freedom.
intelligence (*also* noetic feature), 28, 57, 60, 63, 78, 80–81, 83, 90–91, 101–2, 137, 140, 143, 150, 152, 155, 183
participation in, 72–75, 92, 107
See also mind.
intelligent design, 143, 154–56, 158, 183
See also divine plan.
intelligible beings. See spiritual beings.
intention; intentionality
divine, 9, 14n68, 42, 47, 56, 135, 162
human, 9, 90–91, 114, 117, 151
of Jesus, 34
intercession, 10, 113, 147

interdependence, 77, 126, 133, 142, 154, 189
Irenaeus, Saint, 27, 40, 167
Isaiah, Book of, 20, 26, 32, 39, 51, 55, 98, 122–24, 125, 130–31, 133, 160, 163

Jacob, Benno, 20
James, William, 108, 111
Jeans, James, 69, 70, 70n49, 71
Jeremiah, Book of, 27, 31, 120, 123–24
Jesus; Jesus Christ
and cosmic prayer, 125–26, 129, 168, 184–85
cosmic significance of, 165–68
humanity of, 15, 48, 61–62, 116, 169, 186
the Incarnate Son/Word, 16, 22, 33–34, 39, 44, 48, 158, 165, 168, 172, 184
mystery in, 20–22, 33, 44, 61, 89, 166–67, 169, 186
passion of, 7, 103, 172
prayer of, 33, 113, 117, 18, 184
redemption and salvation through, 48, 125–26, 129, 142, 165–68, 184–85
revelation in and by, 13, 16–17, 33–34, 61, 86, 100, 125, 158, 168
signs and miracles of, 33–34, 125, 158, 174
teaching of, 33, 57–58, 110, 117, 123, 129, 163, 166
two natures in, 61, 167, 169–70, 176–79
Job, Book of, 24, 50–54
John (the Evangelist), 20, 26, 168, 174, 181
Gospel of, 20, 22, 26, 33, 34, 39, 57, 61, 98, 105, 163, 166, 168, 170, 174
First Letter of, 16, 34, 135, 168, 181
John Damascene, 6, 10, 113–14
John Paul II, Pope, 103, 131–33, 144, 146
joy; joyfulness, 48, 83, 92, 93, 99, 100, 102, 110, 120, 131, 152
Justin Martyr, 38–39, 40

General Index

Kant, Immanuel, 66, 153
Kattan, Assaad Elias, 35–38, 40, 43
kenosis
  of Christians, 168, 172–76, 187
  of God, 6, 8, 11, 16, 172
  of Jesus, 172
Kepler, Johannes, 66, 75–76
Kings
  First Book of the, 54
  Second Book of the, 159
Koestler, Arthur, 79–80, 81, 92, 136, 150
Kristensen, W. Brede, 116, 117

LaCugna, Catherine Mowry, 12, 87, 104
Lamarck, Jean-Baptiste de, 66
la nouvelle théologie, 4–6
Larchet, Jean-Claude, 43n35, 89, 178n30
Leech, Kenneth, 100, 110, 116
Leroi-Gourhan, Arlette, 94
Levins, Richard, 154
Levy, Gertrude Rachel, 96
Lewontin, Richard, 140, 154
life, phenomenon of, 79, 82–83, 101, 152
  See also origin: of life; web of creation and/or life.
lifestyle
  contemplative, xii
  humble, 118–21
liturgy, x, xii, 125, 132, 144, 170, 189
  See also cosmic liturgy.
logos (sg.); *logoi* (pl.)
  and contemporary cosmology, 11, 71, 135, 163, 173, 180–81
  discernment of the, 176, 189
  doctrine of the, 35–49, 171, 180
  participation in the, 165, 168, 187
  and *tropoi*, 47–48, 135, 171
  See also God: Word of.
Logos Christology, 5, 34, 39–41, 48, 61, 167–69, 186
longing, 5, 112, 126, 151, 181
  cosmic prayer as, 17, 134
  prayer as a, 17, 110, 115

Lossky, Vladimir, 174
Louf, André, 129
love, ix, 6, 10, 13, 16–17, 25, 47, 83–84, 93, 99, 100–102, 103–4, 129–30, 135, 137, 141, 148, 151, 152, 160, 162–63, 168–71, 172, 178, 181, 183–84, 188, 189, 191
  See also God: as communion in love.
Lubac, Henri de, 4–5
Luke, Gospel of, 33–34, 57, 61, 118, 119, 123, 125, 142, 166
Luther, Martin, 66
Lutheran, 112

McFague, Sallie, 12, 13–14, 146
many-universes hypothesis, 149–150
Margulis, Lynn, 139, 157
Maringer, Johannes, 97
Mark, Gospel of, 33, 34, 57, 86, 114, 118, 119, 125, 142, 158, 163, 165, 166
Marshack, Alexander, 96–97
Mary, Holy, 39, 61, 116
Mary and Joseph, 61, 169
Matsoukas, Nikos A., 151
Matthew, Gospel of, 33, 34, 57, 61, 110, 114, 118, 123, 125, 142, 166
Maximus the Confessor, 5–6, 57, 60, 62, 85, 88–89, 103, 105–6, 133, 145, 152, 155, 167–74, 180, 186–87
  logos doctrine in, 35, 42, 43–49, 71, 163, 165
  perichoresis in, 176–79
  spiritual path in, 188–89
  See also body: in Maximus; cosmology: of Maximus.
Maxwell, James Clerk, 76
meaning. *See* purpose.
metaphysical realm, 23, 25, 30, 53–57, 68, 71, 73, 118, 186
  See also spiritual beings; spiritual powers; wisdom.
Meyendorff, John, 105
microorganisms, 48, 136, 139
  See also bacteria.
Milky Way, 136, 141
mind

General Index

in Aristotle, 62
of created entities, 25
divine, 28, 62, 115
(effects of), within the natural realm, 4, 73-74, 78-79, 83, 92
human, 37, 72, 105, 114, 117, 119, 127-28, 166, 189
in Plato, 58-59, 62
in Stoicism, 37, 62
See also intelligence.
modernism, 5, 143
Moltmann, Jürgen, 6-7, 8, 11, 76, 103-4, 120, 138, 145, 161-62
Morowitz, Harold J., 72
morphogenetic fields, 80
Mother Teresa of Calcutta, 118, 121
Muir, John, 120
multiverse. See many-universes hypothesis.
Murray, Robert, 123

narrative. *See* story.
natural evolution. *See* evolution, natural.
nature
 corporeal, 75
 divine, 6, 61, 88
 human, 47, 93, 99, 112, 114, 127, 139, 172-73
 laws, 16, 23, 52, 71
 rational, 87-88
 spiritual, 68-69, 84
 as what is intrinsic to a certain existence, 4-5, 4n9, 8, 39, 43, 44, 47, 49, 68-69, 72, 89, 135, 151-52, 170, 175, 184, 191
 as a whole, 13, 37, 129, 130-31, 145, 148
 See also Jesus Christ: two natures in.
Neanderthals, 93-94
Nemesius of Emesa, 2
neo-Darwinists, 148, 154, 155
Neoplatonism, 39, 43, 187, 189
new biology, 80
new physics, 68-70, 69n45, 77-78
 See also relativity theory; quantum theory.
new theology, 4, 6-14, 15, 161-62, 176

Newton, Isaac, 66, 75-76, 80, 81n89
Newtonian laws, 75, 153
Nicaea, Creed of, 89, 183
Niceno-Constantinopolitan Creed, 183
Nicholas of Cusa, 66
Noah, 32, 112, 123
Norris, Russell Bradner, Jr., 167, 169

Oliver, Simon, 14n68, 76
Ó Murchú, Diarmuid, 133-34
ontological level, 45, 78-80, 84, 163, 184
organism, 69, 72-73, 80, 83, 149
 human being as, 86, 92, 139
 micro, 48, 72, 136, 139-40
 organismically organized entities, 77, 81
 as paradigm, 83
 symbiogenesis of, 157
Origen, 38, 39-41, 42, 47, 89, 167
origin
 of created reality and those therein, 15-16, 19, 25, 36, 49, 71, 75, 80-81, 83-84, 85, 115, 150, 170, 179, 183, 185
 of prayer, 116, 138
outreach towards God, 17, 72, 113, 117, 121, 140

paleoanthropology, 90
panspermia, theory of, 149
pantheism; pantheistic tendency, 12, 67, 142
Papanikolaou, Aristotle, 12, 89n22, 106
paradigm, 36, 38, 83
parasites, 48, 157, 191
Paul, Saint, 7, 17, 57, 85, 118, 126, 130, 132, 142, 165-68, 169-70, 174-75, 188
 See also Colossians; Corinthians; Ephesians; Romans.
Peacocke, Arthur R., 6, 8-9, 11, 91, 161-62
perfectedness; perfection, 9, 14, 103, 119, 130, 132, 139, 175, 178, 185, 186

degrees of, 37, 184
perfect paradigm, 36, 58–59
of prayer/cosmic prayer, 109, 135, 185
realm of divine, 163
perichoresis, ix, 5, 6–7, 8, 10–11, 12, 13, 17, 49n53, 104–5, 162, 176–79, 187
person, 6, 12, 16, 43, 46, 57, 61, 79, 84, 85–90, 100–107, 114, 115, 135, 140, 150–51, 167, 169–70, 179, 183
multifarious personified existence, 154
See also God: as personal.
personalization. *See* transformation: towards the personal.
Philippians, Letter to the, 168, 184, 185
Phillips, D. Z., 115
Philo of Alexandria, 35, 38
physical constants, 149, 155
Plato, 14n68, 36–37, 38, 42, 58–60, 62, 63, 64, 87, 99
poetry, ix–x, 50–51, 128–29, 131
See also hymn.
Polkinghorne, John, 74, 79
power
  delegated, 16, 132, 135, 191
  divine, of attraction, 4
  evil as, 8, 56
  of God, 9, 26, 30, 47, 49, 125, 131, 162
  of God's speech/ Word, 28, 31, 33, 34–35
  growth, of a seed, 163
  of love, 191
  natural, 2, 102
  in/of prayer/cosmic prayer, 114, 121, 131
  transcendent, 99
  See also spiritual powers; willpower.
praise (offered by human beings/wider creation), 7, 9, 51, 106, 113, 114, 119, 123, 126–28, 129, 130, 132–33, 138, 144–46, 147, 191
prayer
  Christian, 101, 113–15, 116–17, 118

cosmicality of, 9, 74, 107, 111–12, 117, 129, 130, 132, 134, 141, 145, 147
definition of, 115, 134
of the divine persons, 135
engagement in, 10, 115, 119, 121
great project of, 74, 107
and health, 121, 159
human, and life, xiii, 61, 114, 119, 120–21, 130, 141–42, 145, 168, 185
institutes founded upon, 121
liturgical, xii, 117, 147
naturalness of, 108–9
in the Paleolithic, 91–93, 96–97, 99–100
as a personal virtue, 99–103
possibility of, 8, 61, 72, 143–44, 160
what is, 74, 100, 110–11, 112, 113–14, 115, 117–18
See also body: involvement of, in prayer; cosmic prayer; Eucharist; intercession; Jesus: prayer of; liturgy; outreach towards God; power: in/of prayer; praise; worship.
Prestige, G. L., 176–77
principle(s)
  for divine creation, 2, 5, 9, 35–37, 40, 44, 168
  the Father as unbegotten, 26
  Pauli's exclusion, 72
  soul as, 63, 152
  teleological, 153
  See also Cosmological Principle; logos.
process thought, 3–4, 13
protoctists, 72
Proverbs, 27, 53
providence, divine, 2n3, 7, 47, 143, 158–60, 170
Psalms, 20, 31, 32, 50–54, 56, 57, 81, 98, 113, 114, 118–19, 122, 124, 125, 132, 154, 156, 159–60, 163, 188
Pseudo-Dionysius, 41–43, 152, 177n29, 189
Ptolemaic worldview, 67

General Index

Ptolemy, 64
purpose
  God's, for creation, 16, 30, 157–58
  human, xii, 15, 191
  human sense of, 9, 91, 150
  of universally created order, xiii, 7, 33, 51, 81, 130, 132
purposeful ensembles, 92–93
Pythagoras, 64
Pythagoreans, 59

quantum theory, 1, 7, 23, 68–69, 71, 76, 78, 149, 162
quantum-vacuum, 24, 156
Qumran community, 124

Rad, Gerhard von, 54–55
"Radical Orthodoxy" movement, 14n68
Randles, W. G. L., 76
Rappaport, Roy A., 92–93
Ratzinger, Joseph (Pope Benedict XVI), 4, 86, 87, 93, 104, 131, 141, 172–73
redemption, 9, 48, 119, 126, 167
relationship
  dialectical Creator-creature, 2–3, 6, 8, 12, 15–17, 46, 49, 51, 134, 143, 144, 147, 153, 159, 161–62
  Jesus-God, 33, 113, 186
  human-creation, xii, 92, 133
  human-God, xii, 92, 105, 112, 162, 178
  inter-human, xii
  network of, within God, 26, 88, 162, 183
  personal, with God, 9, 84, 160, 191
  prayerful, with God, 51, 115, 142
  subsistent, 88, 105, 183
  symbiotic, 133, 139
  web of, within the universe, 15, 80, 133, 175, 183
  with God, xiii, 7, 30, 51–52, 55, 81, 83, 92, 102, 122, 143
  with Jesus and with God, 5
  See also communion; God: interactive engagement of, with creation; web of creation and/or of life.

relativity theory, special and general, 1, 7
  See also Einstein, Albert; Einsteinian space-time.
respect, xii, 123
responsibility, 14, 16, 25, 47, 49, 135, 159, 170
ressourcement, 5
resurrection of Christ, 56, 106, 184
Revelation, Book of, 26, 98, 125, 133, 141–42
Rolston III, Holmes, 157
Romans, Letter to the, 17, 126, 130, 132, 142, 146, 166, 167, 174–75, 184–85
Romero, Archbishop Oscar, 130–31, 146
Ruether, Rosemary Radford, 12–13

salvation, x, xii, 12, 61–62, 74, 105, 116, 126, 130, 141, 160, 174, 175, 179, 184–85
  Augustine's perception of, 87
Scheindlin, Raymond P., 52
Schmemann, Alexander, 106, 145
Schrödinger, Erwin, 73, 78, 79, 83, 152
Schroeder, Gerald L., 95, 99
Scripture, 5, 6, 19, 28, 31, 44, 50–57, 86, 114, 122–25, 135, 141, 158, 159, 168, 172, 182–83, 186
  See also Acts; Genesis; and so forth.
self-transcendence, 11, 136–37
Sheldrake, Rupert, 80
Shovlin, Teddy, 115
silent concert, 119–20, 138
Simmons, Geoffrey, 155
sin, 9, 41, 47–48, 130, 133, 174
solar system, 77, 136, 141, 183
solar systems, 150
Son, divine, 22, 26, 27, 35, 39–40, 42, 43, 48, 106, 116, 125, 140, 147, 168–70, 172
  See also God: Father, Son, and Spirit; God: Word of; Incarnation.
song, 124, 131
Sophronius of Jerusalem, 89
soul
  in Aristotle, 62, 99

in a contemporary cosmology, 63, 73, 183
human, xii, 47, 139, 154
in the Judaeo-Christian tradition, 62–64, 119, 152
in Maximus, 57, 176, 179
in Plato, 58–60, 62
in Stoicism, 37–38
See also body: and soul.
Southgate, Christopher, 6, 11, 157
space and time
beyond the ambit of, 4, 24, 74, 162–63
at a locus in, 2, 69
not restricted by, 23
within the realm of, 186
See also Einsteinian space-time.
Spirit. *See* Holy Spirit.
spiritual approach, 191
spiritual beings (intelligible beings), 38, 42, 46, 48, 49, 57, 58, 65, 71, 73, 98–99, 107, 170–71
existence of, 53–57, 73, 74, 92, 186–87
service of, 35, 57, 74, 81, 83, 126, 135, 141–42, 143, 158, 184
See also angels; demons.
spiritual path. *See* Maximus: spiritual path in.
spiritual powers, 44, 55, 126, 142, 156, 183
Staniloae, Dumitru, 44
Stoicism, 37–38, 39, 62–63, 64, 76, 80
story
biblical, 32, 33, 54–56, 159–60, 163
a Christian cosmological, 19
cosmology as, 14–15
creation, 19–22, 27, 53–54
string theory, 70
subjectivity, xiii, 4, 27, 30, 54, 56, 89, 102
suffering, xiii, 13, 15, 51, 52, 98, 103, 126, 128, 130, 146, 159, 190
devoid of, 51
See also God: mode of suffering of.
Sun, 21, 41–42, 75, 136, 183
Canticle of Brother, 128
in the Enlightenment, 67

in the medieval cosmology, 64
in Plato, 60
survival, 83, 148, 153, 191
Swimme, Brian, 15, 145
symbiogenesis, 157
symbiosis. *See* relationship: symbiotic.

tapeworms, 157
Tattersall, Ian, 157
Teilhard de Chardin, Pierre, 2, 2n4, 3–4, 5
Tertullian, 40, 86, 119
theological approach, 4, 6, 11
See also Augustinio-Thomistic approach; *la nouvelle théologie*; new theology; "Radical Orthodoxy" movement; trinitarian theology.
Thessalonians
First Letter to the, 142, 166, 184
Second Letter to the, 160
Thomas Aquinas, 2, 2n3, 5, 8, 9, 12, 13, 14n68, 62, 63–64, 75, 88, 99, 142–43, 144, 152, 153
Thunberg, Lars, 44, 145, 176–78, 189
Timaeus, 36, 58–60, 63, 75n61
Tobit, Book of, 56, 124
Tollefsen, Torstein Theodor, 35, 38, 40, 44
Toolan, David S., 141
Torrance, Thomas F., 6, 7–8, 10, 88, 103, 104
transformation
guided, 7, 9, 10, 16, 30, 143, 148, 150–51, 153, 154, 160–61, 172, 183–84
towards the personal, in God, 9, 16, 81, 84, 135, 136, 150, 154, 180
universal, 9, 18, 81, 134–35, 145, 166, 174, 180, 184–85
See also cosmic renewal.
trinitarian theology, 6, 9, 12, 167
Trinity. *See* Holy Trinity.
tropoi, 47–48, 171
Tylor, Edward Burnett, 111

ugliness, 3, 187
union
of body and soul, 62, 125

225

General Index

cosmic, 147
divine-creaturely, 6, 17, 145, 166–72, 178, 187, 189
See also Christ: cosmic personification in; harmonization; hypostatic union.
universe
 age of, 21
 symphony of, 70, 71, 119–20, 141
 unity of, 69, 75–81, 83, 135
unpredictability. *See* indeterminacy.
Upper Paleolithic cave art, 95–98

Vatican II, 5, 131
 Gaudium et spes, xii, 138
 Lumen gentium, 130, 131
Vaughan, Henry, x, 128–29

Waal Malefijt, Annemarie de, 109
water, xii, 21, 68–69, 123, 128, 140, 190
 drop of, 120
 spring of, 163
waters, the, 20–26, 30, 51, 53, 132
Watson, James, 148

Watson, Lyall, 155–56
The Way of a Pilgrim, 129
web of creation and/or of life, xii, 13, 15, 84, 125, 156, 175
Whitehead, Alfred North, 3–4, 83
wholeness, ix, 163
Wildiers, Max, 65
Wilken, Robert Louis, 167
Williams, Janet P., 171, 179
willpower, 101–2, 151
wisdom, 27, 33, 40, 44–45, 52, 53, 57, 81, 100–101, 103, 112, 152, 154, 158, 163, 181, 186
Word of God. *See* God: Word of.
Wordsworth, William, 129
worship, 9, 32, 51, 83, 91, 97, 113, 122, 125, 127, 131–32, 143, 144–45, 151, 156, 160, 163, 173, 187, 191

Zaleski, Philip and Carol, 109n8, 112, 117, 144n44
Zizioulas, John D. (Metropolitan John of Pergamon), 10, 86–87, 88, 89, 89n22, 104, 105–6

www.ingramcontent.com/pod-product-compliance
Lightning Source LLC
Chambersburg PA
CBHW051638230426
43669CB00013B/2350